I CAN'T BELIEVE IT! 2

DK Delhi
Project editors Janashree Singha, Antara Moitra
Project art editor Shreya Anand
Editor Aadithyan Mohan **Art editor** Revati Anand
Senior DTP designer Vishal Bhatia
DTP designer Rakesh Sharma
Jacket designer Suhita Dharamjit
Jackets editorial coordinator Priyanka Sharma
Managing editor Kingshuk Ghoshal
Managing art editor Govind Mittal

DK London
Editor Vicky Richards
Senior art editor Spencer Holbrook
US Executive editor Lori Hand
Jacket designer Surabhi Wadhwa-Gandhi
Jacket editor Claire Gell
Jacket design development manager Sophia MTT
Producer, pre-production Siu Chan
Producer Jude Crozier
Managing editor Francesca Baines
Managing art editor Philip Letsu
Publisher Andrew Macintyre
Associate publishing director Liz Wheeler
Art director Karen Self
Design director Phil Ormerod
Publishing director Jonathan Metcalf

Content previously published in *It Can't Be True!* in 2013,
True Or False? in 2014, *Strange But True!* in 2015, and
It Can't Be True! 2 in 2016

First American Edition, 2018
Published in the United States by DK Publishing
345 Hudson Street, New York, New York 10014

CONTENTS

Strange but true!

It can't be true!

True or false?

STRANGE BUT TRUE!

Have you ever seen caves filled with giant crystals, or a lizard that looks like a leaf? Discover a whole world full of strange wonders that really do exist, from crazy creatures to spectacular settings, and even some far-out festivals.

The Blood Pond hot spring in Beppu, Japan, is so hot it gives off steam. Although the water temperature is a fiery 172°F (78°C), it is actually one of the cooler pools in the city.

The Elephant Foot glacier is on the edge of the vast Greenland ice sheet.

Jumbo glacier

Eye-popping from the air, the **Elephant Foot Glacier** in Greenland is the exact shape of a giant elephant's foot. Made from **compacted snow** over **hundreds of years**, this icy mass has **perfect proportions** and **stunning symmetry**.

The mountains on either side of the glacier stand thousands of feet high, which helps to convey the scale of this icy expanse.

Piedmont glaciers are fan shaped, and often almost completely symmetrical.

FAST FACTS

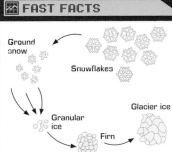

In cold regions, snow does not melt; it piles up in layers. The weight squeezes the snow beneath, forming grains of ice that gradually pack together until they become firn—a middle stage between snow and glacier ice. In a process that can take centuries, the air is squeezed out and the firn turns to dense glacier ice.

SILVER-TONGUED GLACIER

The Erebus Ice Tongue in Antarctica is a tongue-like projection extending from the Erebus glacier. Stretching for 7 miles (11 km), parts of the icy tongue have been known to splinter off into the sea, where they become icebergs.

Glaciers are masses of land-based ice that develop at the poles or in areas of high altitude. There are several different types, but all are made from layers of snow and move slowly under their own immense weight. Elephant Foot Glacier is a piedmont glacier, formed when the ice from a steep valley glacier spills over an open plain

On the hottest days temperatures in the Danakil Depression soar to more than 122°F (50°C).

Sulfur and mineral salt give Danakil its striking colors.

Explosive **heat**

Few people can stand the **heat** of the **Danakil Depression** in Ethiopia. Active **volcanoes** sizzle inside this desert basin, and sulfur springs emit **choking gases**. No wonder some have called it the **cruelest place** on Earth.

FAST FACTS

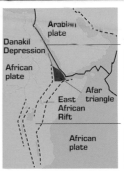

Danakil Depression

Arabian plate

African plate

East African Rift

Afar triangle

African plate

The Arabian plate is pulling away from the African plate.

The African plate is splitting into two along the East African Rift.

The Afar triangle is a vast low area created where Earth's tectonic plates are pulling apart. The huge forces in play as Earth's crust is stretched and thinned causes earthquakes and volcanic eruptions along the plate boundaries. The Danakil Depression, in the north of the triangle, owes its sulfur lakes and active volcanoes to these tectonic forces.

As well as fierce volcanoes and sulfur springs, the Danakil Depression in the Afar triangle is home to acid lakes and occasional earthquakes. It has little to no rainfall and searing temperatures day and night. For centuries local merchants have collected salt from the region's salt flats, and today the most intrepid tourists brave the dangers to marvel at the otherworldly landscape.

EARLIEST ANCESTORS

Fossilized remains of our earliest ancestors have been found in the Afar triangle, not far from the Danakil Depression. In 1974 a team working here found the bones of an early hominid. Dubbed "Lucy" (reconstruction pictured), she is thought to have lived a mind-boggling 3.2 million years ago.

It **rains** almost **every** **day** of the year on **Mount** **Roraima.**

Mount Roraima means "big blue-green" in Pemón, a reference to its stunning waterfalls and lush vegetation.

Island
in the sky

Imagine a paradise island floating above the clouds and **two billion years** in the making. Welcome to **Mount Roraima** in South America, one of the world's **oldest mountain formations**, with panoramic views across the borders of **Venezuela**, **Brazil**, and **Guyana**.

The cliff tops of this steep plateau stand 1,300 ft (400 m) tall, and the flat summit covers 12 sq miles (31 sq km).

📊 FAST FACTS

Rain and wind erode softer rocks.

Hard quartzite rock resists erosion.

Chunks of rock break away as the plateau is eroded.

Rainwater drains off the mountain.

Mount Roraima is what is known as a "tabletop" mountain because of its flat top. The flat summit was originally part of a huge sandstone plateau, which fragmented and eroded over millions of years, leaving the mountain towering over the surrounding lowlands.

This unusual mountain inspired Sir Arthur Conan Doyle's book about dinosaurs and humans, *The Lost World*.

TUMBLING TOADS

Mount Roraima is home to a diverse array of animals and plants. The strangest species living here are black pebble toads, said to predate the dinosaurs. Found in 1895, these tiny toads have limited mobility. Unable to swim or hop, they roll themselves into balls and bounce off rocks to escape attackers.

Mount Roraima is the highest peak in the dramatic Pakaraima mountains, considered some of the oldest geological formations ever known. Native Americans believe their gods inhabit these lush mountains, so they call the peaks *tepuis*, which translates in local Pemón as "houses of the gods."

Rainbow spring

One of the world's largest hot springs, **Grand Prismatic Spring** is located in Yellowstone National Park. Explorers gave the spring its name in 1871 after witnessing its incredible **prism of colors**. Measuring 370 ft (113 m) wide and 121 ft (37 m) deep, it releases 560 gallons (2,120 liters) of water a minute.

FIRES OF HELL

Beppu in Japan is home to eight fiery natural springs, known as "hells" (*jigoku*). The Blood Pond Hot Spring is the most famous because of its steaming red waters. This color comes from high levels of iron in the area.

The water at the center of the spring is a searing 180°F (82°C).

The kaleidoscope effect is caused by colorful bacteria, which thrive in these superhot springs. In the blue center is near-boiling water. This gradually cools across the spring's surface, and as the temperature changes, different types of bacteria are able to survive. The bacteria living in different parts of the spring are brightly colored, giving Grand Prismatic its characteristic rainbow rings.

The blue area at the spring's center is too hot to sustain most life-forms. The blue color is due to the clarity of the water.

FAST FACTS

The Grand Prismatic Spring is named for its colors, which match the spectrum of white light through a prism. When white light passes through a triangular block of glass (a prism), the light is split into different wavelengths—each a different color.

The prism bends the light.

Red has the longest wavelength.

White light enters the prism.

Violet has the shortest wavelength.

Ewe with a view

This lone lamb has broken away from the flock to make a gutsy stand on the **Kjeragbolten boulder** in Norway. The confident climber seems oblivious to the **3,228-ft (984-m) drop** below.

Kjeragbolten is the high point of a hiker's paradise on Kjerag mountain in southern Norway. This rock hasn't rolled since 50,000 BCE when it was wedged firmly in place during the last Ice Age. The spot has become the ultimate photo opportunity for tourists, while the area's mountain sheep aren't camera-shy, either.

Adrenaline junkies use the boulder for BASE jumping—leaping off, then opening a parachute.

FAST FACTS

The glacier moves downhill very slowly.

Ice

Rocks and stones in the ice erode downward, carving a U-shaped valley.

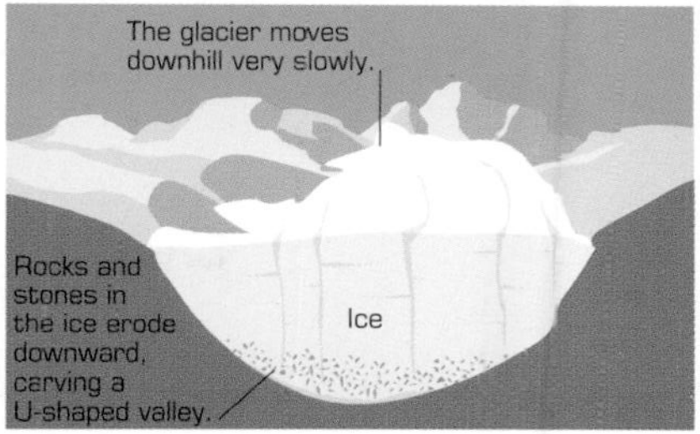

A fjord is a long, glacier-carved valley flooded by sea water after the glacier has retreated. With their high cliffs, fjords are often spectacularly beautiful.

The glacial deposit bridges a gap of 6 ft (2 m) over Lysefjord in the Kjerag mountain range.

AERIAL ADRENALINE

Extreme artist Eskil Ronningsbakken, shown here balancing over Trollstigen, Norway, amazes his fans with his aerial antics. He performed a handstand on a stack of chairs on Kjeragbolten, rode a unicycle on a cliff, and pushed a bicycle over a high-flying tightrope.

Deep freeze

Meaning **"glacier of rivers,"**
Vatnajökull is the **largest glacier** in
Europe, covering almost 10 percent
of Iceland. Underneath the ice is
a **frozen world** called the Crystal
Caves, a **hidden labyrinth** of
blue chambers and tunnels
that change with the seasons.

The ice is 3,300 ft
(1,000 m) deep at
its thickest point.

ADVANCING ICE

Stretching for 19 miles (30 km),
Perito Moreno in Argentina
is an unusual glacier because
it is advancing, rather than
shrinking. Heavy chunks of ice
break off regularly, dropping
into the shimmering waters
of Lake Argentino.

In the summer sunshine the surface of Vatnajökull's thick glacial ice melts, and the resulting water flows into holes and cracks on the surface. Underneath the glacier, rivers of this meltwater cut through the ancient glacier ice, leaving behind magnificent glacial caves. Each year the caves appear in different places—local guides scout their location and take tourists to those that are safe to visit.

FAST FACTS

Seven colors make up the white light that we see.

Only the blue light is reflected.

Dense glacier ice absorbs most of the colors.

Why is the ice blue? Thick, dense glacier ice doesn't contain air bubbles, which would reflect lots of light and make the ice appear white. Rather, the ice absorbs most of the colors that make up white light and reflects only the blue—which is what you see.

The **ice** comprising the **Vatnajökull** glacier is about **1,000** years old.

Cool caves

Hidden away deep inside **Earth's crust** is a magical **subterranean world** of caverns, such as these stunning examples.

Psychedelic salt mine
A former salt mine in Yekaterinburg, Russia, is now one of the world's most colorful caves. More than 650 ft (200 m) underground, its patterned rainbow walls are caused by the mineral carnallite swirling in layers through the rock.

Crystal caves
Only discovered in 2000, the Cave of the Crystals in Mexico is part of the Naica Mine and is home to the largest crystals in the world. Some of the giant selenite crystals it contains have grown to more than 33 ft (10 m) in length.

Marble marvels
Crashing waves have eroded and sculpted Patagonia's Marble Caves. One of the caves is called the Marble Cathedral, after its distinctive sweeping arches. Eye-catching reflections of the shimmering blue water dance across white marble ceilings.

Stone **forest**

Like an enchanted forest that's been turned to stone, **Grand Tsingy** in Madagascar is a somber scene of **spiky, tree-like rocks**. The world's largest stone forest was carved by **tropical rain** in a process that lasted millions of years.

Tsingy de Bemaraha covers a vast 230 sq miles (600 sq km).

The canyon walls are up to 328 m (100 ft) tall.

The razor-sharp, vertical stones of Grand Tsingy challenge even the most experienced rock climbers.

EXTREME LIVING

A surprising number of species call Tsingy de Bemaraha national park their home. More than 100 types of bird, at least 30 types of reptile, and 11 types of lemur, including the Decken's sifaka (above), live here. Many are found nowhere else in the world.

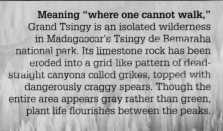

Meaning "where one cannot walk," Grand Tsingy is an isolated wilderness in Madagascar's Tsingy de Bemaraha national park. Its limestone rock has been eroded into a grid like pattern of dead-straight canyons called grikes, topped with dangerously craggy spears. Though the entire area appears gray rather than green, plant life flourishes between the peaks.

FAST FACTS

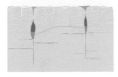

Groundwater flowing along fracture lines in the rock cut caves in the limestone of Grand Tsingy, while monsoon rains eroded the surface.

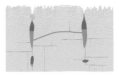

Over millions of years the water continued to erode the caves, causing them to expand and merge into deep, narrow underground caverns.

The cave ceilings then collapsed, exposing the network of towering canyons we see today, topped with sharp peaks carved by surface erosion.

Red **alert!**

Tanzania's Lake Natron has a **killer reputation**. Said to **turn local wildlife to stone**, its bright red waters certainly seem to **signal danger**. But in fact, the concentration of harmful chemicals in this **alkaline lake** supports a rich ecosystem.

THRIVING FLAMINGOS

Despite the dangers, about 2.5 million lesser flamingos nest on Lake Natron, making it one of the largest breeding grounds for this African species. They build their nests on small islands that form in the lake during the dry season, and feed on the plentiful algae inhabiting the waters.

Alkali salt deposits have formed a crisscross pattern on the lake.

The blood-red color is caused by microorganisms that thrive in the salty waters.

Algae thrive in the hot springs on the lake's shores, providing food for alkaline tilapia, a fish adapted to live in this extreme environment.

The water of Lake Natron reaches **scalding temperatures** of more than 104°F (40°C).

Fed by hot springs, Lake Natron's waters are warm and rich in minerals. These chemicals are so concentrated that the lake is highly alkaline—with a pH level of 10, it is the most caustic body of water in the world (capable of burning the eyes and skin of creatures that are not adapted to it). The lake takes its name from natron (hydrated sodium carbonate), which is left as a salt deposit when lake water evaporates.

This lake contains minerals that come from hot springs, the lake's volcanic bedrock, and the ash from a nearby volcano.

FAST FACTS

Just 12 miles (20 km) away from Lake Natron lies Ol Doinyo Lengai, the only active volcano in the world that erupts "cold" lava. Unlike normal, silicate-rich lava, the molten rock it spews forth contains calcium, carbon dioxide, and sodium. It erupts at about 932°F (500°C)—very hot, but half the temperature of normal lava— and emerges black, rather than red, cooling to stark white.

The volcano's summit looks snowcapped, but in fact is covered in ash.

Ol Doinyo Lengai is 9,711 ft (2,960 m) high, with a classic cone shape.

Food fight
festival

This crowd is restricted to 20,000 people—double the town's usual population. In the past, 50,000 people crammed into Buñol for the festival.

Tomatoes are weapons of war at the annual **La Tomatina**, the messiest day on Spain's festival calendar. This **celebratory fruit-fest** is now the world's biggest food fight. Armed with an endless supply of **squashed tomatoes**, thousands of participants **prepare for pelting**!

MELON MADNESS

The fruit of choice at the Chinchilla Festival in Australia is the watermelon. Taking center stage every other February, watermelons are celebrated in a number of activities, with melon skiing (above), melon tossing, and pip spitting all on the menu.

Participants are pulped with overripe tomatoes, transforming the crowd into a soupy red mess.

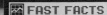
Tomato juice is acidic. It acts as a natural cleaning fluid on the streets of Buñol.

Since 1945 the town of Buñol has become a crimson tide of tomatoes on the last Wednesday of August, though no one knows why the event started. A water cannon fires and battle begins. Tomatoes are thrown in all directions for an hour before the lengthy cleanup operation gets underway.

Festival fun

Whether steeped in **ancient tradition** and **religious custom**, or just a good excuse to have fun, festivals are **special days**. They give communities the chance to congregate and **celebrate together**.

Songkran squirters
Thailand's traditional New Year gets underway with the Songkran water festival. Elephants spray water, children squirt pistols, and water-filled buckets drench passersby. This supersized water fight marks the wet season starting in April.

Big fish festival

Since 1934 the Argungu Fishing Festival has welcomed an influx of fishermen to the Matan Fada River in the Nigerian state of Kebbi. Brandishing nets and gourds, the person who catches the biggest fish within an hour wins money and a bus!

Remarkable radishes

The Night of the Radishes on December 23 sees Oaxaca City in Mexico grind to a halt. A radish-carving competition is held, with the fruits— or rather, vegetables—of participants' labor shown to an audience of thousands.

Snow sculptures

Since 1950 the world's biggest annual **celebration of snow** has caused flurries of excitement at **Sapporo** in Japan. More than **2.4 million visitors** descend on the city to wonder at the **snow sculptures** and toast the winner of the coolest competition around.

The **amount of snow** used at the Sapporo festival is more than **36,000 tons**.

SNOWY SANCTUARY

The Hôtel de Glace in Quebec, Canada, is a dream destination for snow bunnies. The hotel is crafted almost entirely from snow and ice, offering visitors an ice chapel for wedding ceremonies, an ice slide, and an ice bar.

Fairytale castles and giant figures are among the sculptures on display.

At the Sapporo Snow Festival, held every February, teams from around the world compete to develop the most imaginative and incredible snow sculptures. What began on a small scale, with school students displaying amateur efforts at the city's Odori Park, has grown to become one of the largest global events on the winter calendar, featuring hundreds of sculptures.

The largest snow sculptures can reach 50 ft (15 m) tall and 80 ft (24 m) wide.

FAST FACTS

Sculpting starts with trucks transporting snow to the site, where bulldozers pack it into a firm base.

A frame is packed with more snow to form a solid block. The wooden boards are removed and carving begins.

The frame is removed for the final details. Teams have just 20 hours from start to finish to create their art.

Plane spotter's **paradise**

The **jet blast** from the aircraft could **knock over or even kill a person** in its path.

One of the Caribbean's busiest airports, Princess Juliana International on Saint Martin island has unintentionally become a tourist attraction due to its low-flying aircraft. Saint Martin is the smallest island to be split between two nations. Holland and France share the idyllic isle, with Maho Beach on the Dutch side.

A ROUND ON THE RUNWAY

Kantarat's 18-hole golf course is tightly sandwiched between two runways of Thailand's Don Mueang Airport. Traffic signals help golf carts to cruise between holes safely.

Maho Beach is no peaceful paradise. Its blue skies are overshadowed by **low-flying jets**, while the crashing Caribbean surf is drowned out by **roaring engines**. With the runway just 20 ft (6 m) from the sand, thrill seekers and plane spotters can experience **extreme encounters** with aircraft every single day.

Sunbathers face powerful winds of 150 mph (240 kph) every time an aircraft comes in to land.

📊 FAST FACTS

With Princess Juliana's short runway of 7,152 ft (2,180 m), aircraft must fly at low altitude to land safely. As they make their descent, they pass just 30–60 ft (9–18 m) above the beach.

30–60 ft (9–18 m)

20 ft (6 m)

7,152 ft (2,180 m)

SEA · BEACH · STREET · RUNWAY

Leap of faith

Before bungee jumping, there was a scarier sport. A **daredevil diving ritual** called Naghol has been a tradition for centuries on **Pentecost Island** in the South Pacific. Local men risk life and limb to throw themselves from **dizzying heights** with only a **jungle vine** around their ankles.

Land diving was first performed from treetops, but now fragile towers have been constructed. Before the jump, men and women chant and dance until one man climbs the tower, where vines are attached to his ankles. The diver jumps headfirst, dropping to the ground at high speed. Locals believe that the braver the divers are, the more bountiful the yam harvest will be.

Land diving takes place after the wet season, so that the vines will be water-logged to maximize their elasticity and strength.

Land diving is a rite of passage for the island's young men.

FAST FACTS

One of the world's highest bungee jumps is the Macau Tower in China. Sending adrenaline junkies spiraling down from a 764-ft (233-m) platform on the tower's outer rim, there is a six-second freefall before the elastic bounces back. The top height for a Naghol diving tower is 130 ft (40 m)—you'd have to stack six end to end to match the Macau bungee.

Naghol diving towers

Macau Tower

The divers leap from platforms that may be more than 65 ft (20 m) off the ground.

LUCKY ESCAPE

The land diving ritual stems from a legend of an unhappy marriage, in which a woman was running through the jungle desperate to escape her pesky husband. She climbed a tree with him hot on her heels, tied a vine to her ankle, and jumped. She landed safely, but her husband did not secure himself and did not survive the jump.

Street View has also gone **underwater** to capture the Great Barrier Reef.

The Street View Trekker camera can also be worn as a backpack, allowing people to photograph hard-to-reach places.

Raffia and her guide trekked the desert at sunrise to capture the best lighting for their shots.

TIMING IS EVERYTHING

When the Street View car cameras have been in the right place at the right time, they have caught rainbows (above), lightning strikes, and butterflies landing on their lenses. But when the timing goes wrong, birds narrowly miss crashing into cameras, or their droppings seriously spoil the view!

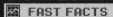 FAST FACTS

Street View covers over 5 million miles (8 million km) of road across more than 50 countries, and continues to add more images. In addition to cities and towns, the project has captured panoramas of iconic sites such as the pyramids of Giza and Everest Base Camp.

Green areas have yet to be added.

Blue areas of the map are covered by Street View.

Google Maps has been providing Google Street View online since 2007. The panoramic views it provides are made of still photographs, often captured by a car-mounted camera. But the Liwa Desert in the United Arab Emirates is not the average street view. These sprawling dunes needed a unique photographer, and an animal already adapted to desert life was the obvious choice.

Camel's **camera**

Traditionally called "ships of the desert," camels are now vessels for photographing the world. Ten-year-old Raffia captured the **Liwa Desert** on a **camera attached to her hump**, becoming the first creature to assist Google in its quest to **map our planet**.

Daredevil **climber**

Spider-Man **scaling skyscrapers** is the stuff of superhero stories. But one Frenchman has **brought comic strips to life** with a series of incredible climbs. His **amazing antics** have led to both awards and arrests around the world.

Alain Robert has spent so long as a **free climber,** he can no longer fully straighten his fingers.

Free solo climber Alain Robert is seen here on his way up the Abu Dhabi Investment Authority (ADIA) Building, United Arab Emirates, in 2007. The skyscraper is 607 ft (185 m) high.

FAST FACTS

Sydney Opera House, 1997

ADIA Building, 2007

Eiffel Tower, 1996

Empire State Building, 1994

Burj Khalifa, 2011

Robert has conquered some of the world's most iconic buildings. In 2011 he climbed the world's tallest—the 2,716-ft (828-m) Burj Khalifa in Dubai. The climb was legal, but he had to use a safety harness to comply with regulations.

HEART-STOPPING SPORT

Meaning "free from aid," free solo climbing involves climbing without ropes or safety equipment. Climber extraordinaire Alain Robert has reached the summit of the world's tallest buildings, often using just a pair of climbing shoes and his bare hands. Some of his stunts have been authorized, but he has also been arrested many times for scaling buildings without permission.

BASE jumping is similar to free climbing—only in reverse and much quicker. Adrenaline enthusiasts leap from a fixed point, such as a cliff or building. They free-fall before opening a parachute just in the nick of time to land safely.

At the top of their game

This pair of aces were hitting high during their breathtaking **tennis match** on the **helipad of a seven-star hotel** in Dubai. Switzerland's Roger Federer played the USA's Andre Agassi in a friendly game on the **world's highest court** in 2005.

Federer and Agassi were in training for the Dubai Duty Free Men's Championship when they gave this sky-high court a try.

GAMES WITH ALTITUDE

In 2007 FIFA (soccer's governing body) banned international soccer matches at high altitude. Playing at more than 8,200 ft (2,500 m) above sea level can be damaging to health. The thinner air gives an advantage to players used to such conditions. This field in Switzerland is at 6,560 ft (2,000 m).

> It is now possible to **get married** on the Burj Al Arab helipad—at vast expense.

FAST FACTS

The diameter of the helipad is just 79 ft (24 m).

Donut rings

An average Formula One car is 15 ft (4.5 m) long.

The Burj Al Arab helipad has also been home to other sports stunts. Formula One driver David Coulthard performed donuts in a race car in 2013—no easy feat in such a small space—and golfers Rory McIlroy and Tiger Woods have teed off from there.

The luxurious Burj Al Arab stands 1,053 ft (321 m) tall on a specially built island. Both players had the advantage when they saw the views of Dubai from the hotel's helipad, 692 ft (211 m) up. They smashed a few balls over the edge into the sea, but no one was eager to go retrieve them!

Basket **Building**

Although it looks like the food basket from a giants' picnic, this **basket-shaped building** is open for business. Completed in 1997, the award-winning **architectural achievement** in Ohio is the brainchild of basket entrepreneur Dave Longaberger.

The building measures 192 ft (58 m) by 126 ft (38 m) at its base and 208 ft (63 m) by 142 ft (43 m) at the roof.

ADVERTISER'S DREAM

The USA has lots of buildings designed to showcase the products on sale inside. Twistee Treat's ice cream outlets are shaped like cones, Kansas City Library's parking lot (above) resembles a bookshelf, and Furnitureland in North Carolina looks like a chest of drawers.

Founder of the Longaberger Company
Dave Longaberger dreamed up the idea to house his offices inside the world's biggest basket. The building is a scaled-up version of the handcrafted maple wood baskets manufactured and distributed by Longaberger. Inside the lavish seven-story building in Newark, Ohio, are marble floors, cherry woodwork, and a sweeping staircase.

Stucco (a cement wall covering) covers the building's steel frame so that it closely resembles a handwoven basket.

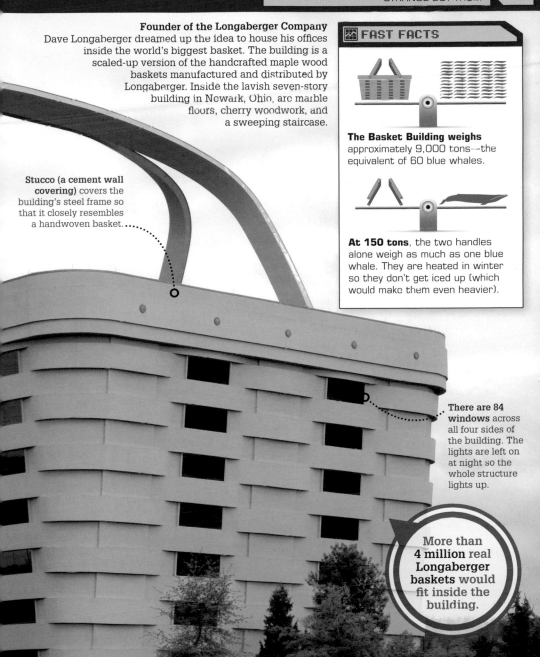

FAST FACTS

The Basket Building weighs approximately 9,000 tons—the equivalent of 60 blue whales.

At 150 tons, the two handles alone weigh as much as one blue whale. They are heated in winter so they don't get iced up (which would make them even heavier).

There are 84 windows across all four sides of the building. The lights are left on at night so the whole structure lights up.

More than 4 million real Longaberger baskets would fit inside the building.

Top trunks

Some trees are not just **part of the scenery**—they define the landscape with their **bizarre beauty**.

Tree of life
A prehistoric wonder in its native Africa, Australia, and Madagascar, the baobab is called "the tree of life." It can store huge amounts of water in its swollen trunk, enabling it to survive seasonal droughts.

Desert roots
The skinny and spiny Boojum tree soars above the other vegetation of the Sonoran Desert in California. Topping 50 ft (15 m), this species grows taller whenever there is rainfall, though it can survive for years without water.

Timber tunnel
Talk about a drive-through! This giant redwood named Chandelier Tree in Leggett, California, has a tunnel carved through its big base. Cars can pass through once a park entry fee has been paid.

Armed and deciduous

There's no better protected tree than the **Cannonball**. This **gargantuan grower** is found in South American forests and **attacks without warning**. Avoid being in the firing line when its weighty fruits **blast off**.

A member of the Brazil nut family, the Cannonball tree's proper name is *Couroupita guianensis*. Found in the rain forests of the Guianas (an area of northeastern South America) and in India, the tree's sweet-smelling flowers are used in perfumes and cosmetics. Its heavy fruits look like rusty cannonballs and when ripe, they fall to the ground and smash open with a bang. Locals use the fruit shells to craft containers and utensils.

TREE TREATMENT

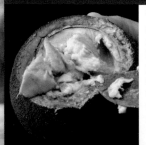

The Cannonball's bark, leaves, and fruit have been used in medicine for centuries. The beneficial bark is said to prevent colds and have antiseptic properties, while the leaves treat various skin diseases. The stinky fruit is used as a natural disinfectant for open wounds.

The tree towers up to **115 ft (35 m)** and each fruit can weigh about **6 lb (3 kg)**.

The flesh of the large, round fruits is edible, but it gives off an overpowering stench.

FAST FACTS

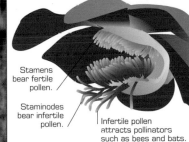

Stamens bear fertile pollen.

Staminodes bear infertile pollen.

Infertile pollen attracts pollinators such as bees and bats.

Flowers of trees in the Brazil nut family have a unique structure. The fertile stamens form a fleshy ring, with a secondary mass of infertile stamens, called staminodes, making a kind of hood. Only the strongest pollinators—large bees or some bats—can lift the hood and collect the infertile pollen. As they do so, they brush the stamens, carrying the fertile pollen to the next flower they visit.

Algae **attack!**

China's **Yellow Sea** has recently gone green, caused by the nation's greatest **algae growth** to date. Since 2007, algae have swamped the waters every summer, but 2013's **big bloom** covered a record-breaking **11,158 sq miles** (28,900 sq km).

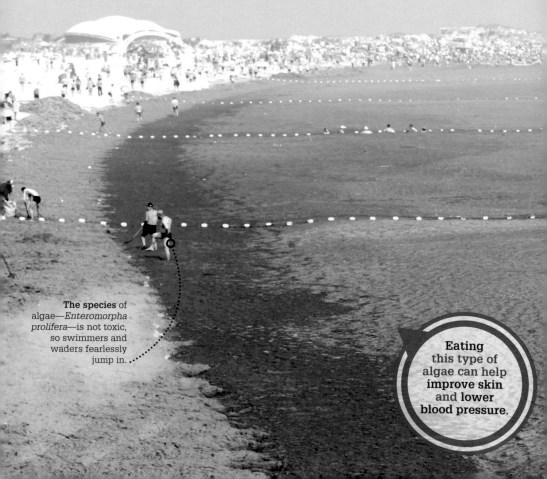

The species of algae—*Enteromorpha prolifera*—is not toxic, so swimmers and waders fearlessly jump in.

Eating this type of algae can help **improve skin** and **lower blood pressure.**

⊞ FAST FACTS

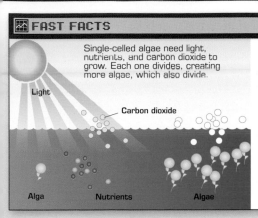

Single-celled algae need light, nutrients, and carbon dioxide to grow. Each one divides, creating more algae, which also divide.

Light

Carbon dioxide

Alga

Nutrients

Algae

Harmful algal blooms (HABs)

form where colonies of sea-inhabiting plants, called algae, develop at a rapid rate, causing devastation to local marine life. In the right conditions, a population of algae can double in hours.

Despite the fun and frolic on the beach at Qingdao in the eastern Shandong province, this thick covering of algae stops sunlight and oxygen from penetrating the water, which suffocates sea life. Scientists don't know why the tide has turned green, but they agree the carpet of algae comes from an ecosystem imbalance, and is probably the result of human activity, such as agricultural and industrial pollution.

More than 8,200 tons of algae had to be removed from the beaches by city officials using bulldozers.

BRING ON THE BLUES

Electric blue algal blooms off the coast of Hong Kong look brilliantly bioluminescent, but what lies beneath is toxic pollution. Harmful *Noctiluca scintillans*, or sea sparkle, is flourishing because of excessive fertilizer and sewage. This devastates the landscape, killing local marine life.

Foul flower

Even the greenest fingers stop at the **corpse flower**. The biggest bloomer on Earth, this species is also the **stinkiest**, pervading the atmosphere with the **stench of rotten flesh**. What a relief that it's one of the world's **rarest flowers**!

ITSY-BITSY BLOOM

At the other end of the floral spectrum is the Asian watermeal plant, or *Wolffia globosa*. The size of a grain of rice, this green grower is the world's smallest flowering plant, and can be found floating in streams and ponds.

The corpse flower features in Indonesian tourist brochures as a symbol of the region's vibrant rain forests.

Each flower is made up of red lobes with white spots, resting on a cup-like structure.

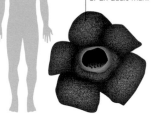

The diameter of the largest *Rafflesia* flowers is equivalent to half the height of an adult man.

Though other flowers have larger clusters of flower heads, the corpse flower is the largest single flower. It can reach 3 ft (90 cm) wide and weigh 22 lb (10 kg).

The **flower buds** are used in **traditional medicine** to aid recovery after childbirth.

Rafflesia arnoldii, as it is formally known, uses disgusting odors to lure flies and other insects to pollinate the plant. Native to the rain forests of Borneo and Sumatra, it takes up to 10 months to bloom fully before the flower dies a week later. The plant has no leaves or stem, but lives as a parasite inside a host plant, hidden from view until the flower bud bursts through and the giant bloom unfurls.

Freaky flora

The most **incredible plants** can grow from a humble seed. Around the world some **dramatically different** forms have **taken root**.

Size matters
The giant water lily grows year-round in its native Brazil. With leaves more than 8 ft (2.5 m) long, it can carry up to 100 lb (45 kg) in weight, so these pigeons are no problem.

Tree tumbo
Considered by many to be an ugly and unruly plant, the tree tumbo plant just keeps on growing. It can survive for 1,500 years on the dew found in its isolated patch of the Namib Desert.

Monkey cup

The *Nepenthes* pitcher plant, which grows in Australia, Madagascar, and Southeast Asia, is known as the "monkey cup" because monkeys like the fluid inside its pitchers. Insects fall into this carnivorous vine's tropical trap in pursuit of nectar—but end up getting eaten themselves.

Hanging bangers

The *Kigelia africana*, or Sausage tree, can be seen across Africa's wetter regions. This whopper of a species reaches 66 ft (20 m) in height, with strange sausage-like fruits up to 35 in (90 cm) long.

Bicycle **tree**

Whoever got on this bike definitely **reached the end of the road**. No one knows how these wheels got **stuck in a tree**, and the **mystery** still drives locals totally bonkers years later.

The tree appears to have grown around the bike, but many argue the tree could not have lifted the bike from the ground because trees grow from the top, not the trunk.

TEMPLE TREES

The Buddhist temples of Angkor Wat in Cambodia are a stunning structural spectacle, but trees are the star attraction at one crumbling temple. Ta Prohm is a fusion of nature and architecture, where the great roots of silk cotton and strangler fig trees grow through the ruined roof.

FAST FACTS

The outer and inner bark protect the cambrium from animals, fungi, and the weather.

Outer bark
Inner bark
A layer under the bark called the cambrium has living cells that make the tree grow.

A tree can grow slowly around an object placed on, in, or close by it. The tree cannot move away, so it has to stop growing, grow away, or grow around the object when its trunk increases in size. It takes decades for an object to be truly stuck.

The bicycle was once red, but it has turned to rusty ruins while lodged in the trunk of this fir tree.

Local author **Berkeley Breathed** wrote a children's book about the **bicycle mystery**.

The riddle of the bicycle up a tree is legendary in Vashon Island, Washington. One story goes that a boy tied his bike to the tree before going to war in 1914, while town sheriff Don Puz is sure he left the bike behind in the 1950s. Sceptics insist it is nothing more than a hoax.

Out of the blue

The picture-perfect islands of the **Maldives** are famed for white beaches lapped by the Indian Ocean. But **Vaadhoo Island** is most breathtaking after dark when tiny plants turn the water electric blue. In this natural phenomenon, the **sparkling sea** appears to **reflect the starry night**.

Many sea creatures feed on **phytoplankton**, including **whales**, **sea snails**, and **jellyfish**.

Microscopic marine microbes called phytoplankton live in the sea. When they are disturbed by oxygen, a chemical reaction called bioluminescence (biological light) takes place—a flashing blue light is produced by the phytoplankton. This usually happens at sea when ships shake up oxygen underwater. Vaadhoo is unusual because bioluminescence occurs on the shore.

FAST FACTS

A spine on the anglerfish's head is topped with a glowing lure.

The teeth are sharp and curved for stabbing prey.

Many deep-sea creatures have evolved to produce their own bright light in the darkness. The anglerfish uses a bioluminescent "lantern" to tempt prey. Dangling from the fish's head, this houses bacteria that use chemicals produced by the fish to glow.

Each wave releases a flash of glowing blue in the many millions of phytoplankton washed up on the sand.

GLOW IN THE DARK

The Waitomo Caves in New Zealand are a haven for glowworms. This unique species—*Arachnocampa luminosa*—produces a striking light in the darkness. Boat trips into the caves take tourists to visit the glimmering glowworms.

This caterpillar is the **larval stage** of the *Hemeroplanes triptolemus* moth.

Snake in the grass

When is a snake not a snake? When it's a **caterpillar**! This extraordinary disguise is **self-defense**. The snake mimic hawkmoth caterpillar does an **uncanny impression** of a scary snake to avoid its forest predators.

The brown area that forms the top of the "head" is actually the caterpillar's underside—its legs are visible if you look closely.

CAMOUFLAGE CATERPILLARS

Caterpillars use every trick in the book to deter an attack. Some resemble unappealing bird droppings (above), while others have false "eyespots" to make themselves appear more threatening. Other species develop prickly spines and hairy clumps to look less appetizing to predators.

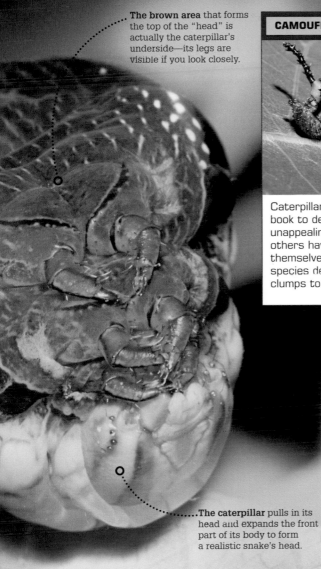

FAST FACTS

Clinging to a branch, the snake mimic hawkmoth caterpillar looks very ordinary.

If something alarms the caterpillar, it throws itself backward, twisting its body to show its underside.

The caterpillar then inflates the head-end of its body to create a realistic-looking snake's head.

The caterpillar pulls in its head and expands the front part of its body to form a realistic snake's head.

If this hawkmoth caterpillar feels threatened, it immediately takes on snake-like characteristics and behavior. Pulling in its legs and head, the caterpillar adopts a slithering motion. Its underside grows larger, giving the semblance of a snake's head. The body is large by caterpillar standards and covered in scales, ensuring this species is one convincing masquerader.

Flying figures

Considered a **sign of good fortune** in its native Central and South America, the **Callicore butterfly's** lucky numbers are **88** and **89**. Emblazoned across each wing, the **striking digits** help this species to **attract mates** amid the flora and fauna.

These high-speed fliers travel solo through their tropical rain forest homes.

WINDOW WINGS

You can see right through the Glasswing butterfly. Its transparent wings resemble panes of glass, helping the species evade predators in its Central American domain.

The 88'89 butterfly lands on people in summer to dine on their sweat.

FAST FACTS

Tiny scales scatter the light, creating beautiful iridescent colors.

Butterfly wings are covered with thousands of tiny scales made from a substance called chitin. These dusty scales give the insects their striking colors, as well as helping to regulate their body temperature.

The numerals 89 or 88 appear clearly on the underside of each wing.

The exact markings of the 88'89 butterfly depend on the specific subspecies. There are 12 types, with the markings taking a different form, color, and shape each time. Sadly, the number of Callicores is dwindling—they are often killed for their exotic wings, which are used in the production of tourist souvenirs.

Devil in disguise

Is it a leaf? Is it tree bark? No, it's the **Satanic leaf-tailed gecko**. Cleverly disguised as a rotting leaf, Madagascar's **camouflage king** has red eyes, pointy horns, and a taste for night hunting. It's nature's most **devilish deceiver**.

FAST FACTS

Geckos have sticky toe pads that allow them to cling to polished walls. Each toe is ridged and covered in thousands of tiny bristles, which are divided into billions of microscopic hairs. These hairs lock with irregularities in the surface the gecko is climbing, giving it grip.

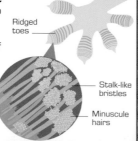

Ridged toes

Stalk-like bristles

Minuscule hairs

Leaf-tailed geckos have **no eyelids**. They use their **long tongues to wipe away dust**.

This mini-monster epitomizes survival of the fittest, having adapted gradually to become today's extraordinary leaf impersonator. Snakes and rats target the gecko—if the disguise fails, the brave battler falls to the forest floor, hoping to disappear in the foliage, or leaps to a higher branch for shelter.

MOSSY MASK

Madagascar's mossy leaf-tailed gecko is another master of disguise. Its color and markings make it look exactly like mossy tree bark. A fringe of skin flattens the gecko against the tree so that, when still, it blends seamlessly into its forest habitat.

The twisted body and veiny skin echo the detail of a dry leaf, which ensures the gecko blends in with its forest home.

The mottled tail appears to have sections missing, as though it has withered over time.

In hiding

Standing out from the crowd leaves you **vulnerable** in the **animal kingdom**. Where conflicts are fierce, food is scarce, and lives are on the line, **blending in** can be the best bet for **survival**.

Sly fox
As snowy white as its tundra home, the Arctic fox blends in easily with the icy winter surroundings. But this colored coat changes with the seasons. Summer sees the fox sport a reddish brown fur better suited to the bare rock and plants.

Tree mimic
The African scops owl uses its camouflaged plumage and twig-like ear tufts to conceal itself, then swoops suddenly on insects and rodents.

Secretive spider
Europe's green huntsman spider is the perfect shade to merge with nearby foliage. The arachnid can move virtually unseen by both predators and prey.

Armed attacker
This vivid inhabitant of Australia's Great Barrier Reef resembles part of the coral, but is actually a stonefish. With toxic spines ready, it waits to ambush passing prey.

Adaptable amphibian
The African red toad spends its days hiding under logs or on dead leaves, using its colors and patterned skin to keep safe, while nights are spent searching out insects.

Goat gymnasts

No kidding—the **goats of Tamri village** in Morocco show great agility when **searching for their favorite food**. These nimble nibblers claw, jump, and scramble up **argan trees** to reach their beloved berries, setting in motion a **practice** that's been around for centuries.

INTREPID IBEX

In 2010 a herd of Alpine ibex walked across the nearly vertical face of Italy's Cingino Dam. Despite the 164-ft (50-m) drop beneath them, the agile ibex searched for a snack—salt and lichen between the dam's stones.

Argan berries are a good source of income in this otherwise barren land. Goats gorge on them and pass the hard nuts in their droppings. Locals collect the droppings then remove and wash the nuts. These are ground and pressed to make expensive argan oil, used in salad dressings and cosmetic treatments.

The olive-like argan berry is perfect nourishment in an area where food is scarce.

The **Tamri goats** can climb 30 ft (9 m) up to the **treetops**.

Goats are curious by nature, revelling in opportunities to climb and explore.

FAST FACTS

Goats are good climbers because of their cloven hoofs. The two sides push apart to grip a surface. The hoof has a soft inner part that aids grip, while the animal's dewclaws help provide stability.

Dewclaws

Hard outer hoof

Hoof is cloven (split into two)

Soft inner part

Dance **fever**

The lord of the dance on the island of Madagascar is the **Verreaux's sifaka**. Fancy footwork has made this **species of lemur** a global sensation, but these moves have real purpose. **Whirling and twirling** through the forest helps them **evade predators**.

Sifakas have splayed feet, which make it difficult to walk. Instead, they "dance" by hopping sideways rapidly on their back legs.

PIG PARADISE

Pigs can't fly, but they can swim! A family of wild porkers enjoys an idyllic island lifestyle on Big Major Cay in the Bahamas. They take daily dips, heading for boats in case people drop food. Sailors are said to have left the pigs on the island, intending to return for a bacon bonanza, but they never did.

As dawn breaks, groups of Verreaux's sifakas perform a dazzling dance display. They swing, leap, and bound their way to the feeding grounds where they forage for food. Only in the safety of the treetops can they sit back to munch on a variety of plants unique to the African island.

The sifaka holds its arms up near its head for balance, while its springy step means it can escape fast, should a predator attack.

Verreaux's **sifakas** are named after their **distinctive noisy cry** that sounds like "shif-auk!"

📊 FAST FACTS

Sifakas are not only nimble on the ground. They also use their powerful hind legs and upright position to leap from tree to tree, often clearing distances of more than 30 ft (9 m).

In-flight fight

At first glance, **fur and feathers** appear to have forged an **incredible friendship** in this photograph. The weasel **hitches a ride** on the woodpecker's back as they soar the skies together. In reality, this picture catches on camera the **ultimate airborne animal attack**.

A **sign** now marks the spot where the **sensational snap** was taken.

ANIMAL ALLIANCES

The animal kingdom can be about forming friendships rather than fighting foes. In Ireland a dog named Ben and a dolphin named Duggie enjoy friendly swims together, while best pals Fum the cat and Gebra the owl were viewed playing together by more than eight million people on YouTube.

In 2015 amateur photographer Martin Le-May shot this image in Hornchurch Country Park, London, UK, but the picture doesn't tell the full story. The weasel attacked the woodpecker and refused to give up, even when the bird took flight. An aerial scrap ensued before the weasel tumbled and the woodpecker escaped.

The carnivorous least weasel typically attacks large prey, such as rabbits, mice, frogs, and birds.

FAST FACTS

The least weasel's body is just bigger than an adult hand.

The tail can be up to 3⅛ in (8 cm) long.

The least weasel is the world's smallest carnivore. Measuring only 4⅓–10⅕ in (11–26 cm) and weighing as little as ⁹⁄₁₀ oz (25 g), it has been known to kill prey up to 10 times its weight. It is found throughout Europe, North America, and parts of Asia.

The European green woodpecker often leaves itself vulnerable to attack because it forages on the ground for ants.

Dedicated **dad**

Assumptions about the **female of the species** giving birth are true of most creatures, but **reproduction** is **different** for seahorses. It's **the male** of this odd-looking fish species that **experiences pregnancy and childbirth**, to sighs of relief from female seahorses everywhere!

The young seahorses, or fry, emerge from the opening in the brood pouch.

Muscular contractions expel the young seahorses from the pouch.

SHARK SPAWN

The frilled shark has the longest gestation period of any species. Like seahorses, they are ovoviviparous—their young hatch from eggs inside the parent's body. Embryos then grow inside the mother for a staggering three and a half years before finally being born.

This male seahorse's pouch is full of fry. Smaller species may carry 50 offspring, while bigger types nurture up to 2,000.

The female seahorse makes the eggs inside her body. Male and female entwine tails and perform a long courtship dance that ends with the female depositing the eggs in the male's pouch. The male fertilizes the eggs and they hatch inside his pouch. The embryos take in everything they need, from oxygen to food, in a gestation period that lasts up to four weeks.

Fewer than **five** in **1,000** young seahorses **survive into adulthood.**

FAST FACTS

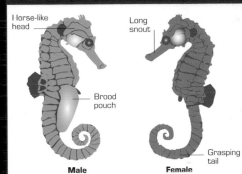

Horse-like head

Long snout

Brood pouch

Grasping tail

Male

Female

Seahorses are marine fish found in warm, shallow waters all over the world. Their bodies are protected by bony plates, rather than scales. Poor swimmers, they use their grasping tail to cling to vegetation and their long snout to suck up plankton.

Shoal-stopper

Millions of sardines cause an **amazing annual spectacle** by swimming in one **supersized shoal** along South Africa's eastern coastline, to the delight of hungry ocean predators. The **"Sardine Run"** is plagued with danger, and the reason for this **mega migration** is unknown.

MARINE MIGRATION

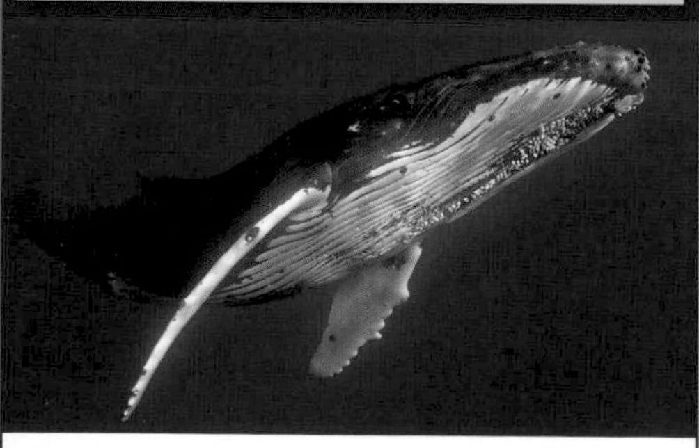

From small sardines to whopper whales, all kinds of marine life migrate. Humpback whales break the record for the longest mammal migration, covering 5,160 miles (8,300 km) from Pacific waters off Costa Rica all the way to Antarctica.

A baitball is 33–65 ft (10–20 m) in **diameter** and usually lasts only **10–20 minutes**.

Under threat, the sardines squash up into a neat baitball, so that no individual fish can be singled out.

FAST FACTS

The migrating sardines travel north along the east coast of South Africa, from their spawning ground of Agulhas Bank to the subtropical waters off the coast of Durban. The huge shoals can be 9⅓ miles (15 km) long.

Durban

South Africa

Cape Town

Agulhas Bank

Sardine run

Sardines are an integral part of the ocean food chain, with their sheer quantity sustaining many other fish species.

As the tiny fish make their journey, predators gather for a feeding frenzy. Dolphins round up the sardines into baitballs, while birds descend from the skies and sharks converge in the water. The risky migration's motive is unclear, but it may be that the southern waters become too cold for the sardines.

Bubbling under

On the surface, **Lake Abraham** in the **Canadian Rocky Mountains** is a photographer's dream. But beneath the frozen waters lie **towers of bubbles**, suspended in ice. These beautiful bubbles hide an ugly secret—they contain **harmful methane gas**.

Lake Abraham's methane bubbles are produced by bacteria on the lake bed feeding on dead plant matter. In the summer, the gas rises to the surface and escapes, but when the lake freezes over, the bubbles are trapped in the ice. Methane is a greenhouse gas, which traps heat in the atmosphere and contributes to global warming.

Methane gas forms in thousands of lakes. Lake Abraham has high levels because it was created by flooding a valley, so there is a lot of plant matter on the lake bed.

Lake Abraham is an artificial lake, created in 1972 by damming the North Saskatchewan River.

Stacks of methane **bubbles** pile up, as if a bubble-making machine has stopped in mid-flow.

FAST FACTS

Earth's atmosphere allows the Sun's heat to reach Earth but stops some from escaping. This is known as the greenhouse effect, and it warms Earth enough to support life. Increasing levels of methane and other greenhouse gases are contributing to the "enhanced greenhouse effect" by trapping more heat and causing Earth's temperature to rise.

Heat from the Sun passes through the atmosphere and warms Earth.

Some of the heat escapes into space.

Greenhouse gases trap some of the heat in the atmosphere.

EXPLODING BUBBLES

Methane is a colorless, odorless gas, but it is highly flammable. Scientists studying the frozen bubbles (above) may be unsure which gas they've found. Piercing the ice with a pick and igniting the gas produces explosive results—and proves the gas is methane.

Light show

When Earth's **magnetic field** is disturbed by the Sun's solar wind, the night sky lights up with **dancing streaks of color**. While the Northern lights (Aurora borealis) usually steal the show, **the Southern lights** (Aurora australis) are equally impressive but less accessible.

PLANETARY AURORAS

Intrepid explorers can spot auroras in space. Giant Jupiter has a strong magnetic field that reacts with its moons, producing vibrant lights. Saturn has an aurora on its south pole (above), while similar sights have been seen on Uranus, Neptune, and Mars.

This dazzing display of Aurora australis over Antarctica is seen from space.

Antarctica is surrounded by open water, so there is limited opportunity for people to find a viewing platform from which to enjoy the Aurora australis.

Auroras occur when the solar wind—electrically charged particles escaping the Sun—becomes trapped by Earth's magnetic field. The particles are funneled toward Earth's two poles, colliding with gases in the atmosphere. These collisions produce Aurora borealis at the north magnetic pole, around the Arctic Circle, and Aurora australis at the south magnetic pole, around the Antarctic Circle.

FAST FACTS

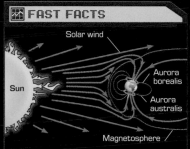

Solar wind

Sun

Aurora borealis

Aurora australis

Magnetosphere

Earth's magnetic field forms a protective layer around the planet. Called the magnetosphere, this deflects most of the solar wind particles. The particles that penetrate the magnetosphere are channeled toward the north and south magnetic poles. There, they interact with atmospheric gases to create brightly colored auroras.

An electron hits an oxygen atom, making it glow red.

Electrons enter Earth's upper atmosphere.

Above 400 miles (640 km)

Atom

When a nitrogen atom is hit by an electron, it glows blue.

Oxygen atoms glow green when electrons strike.

A nitrogen molecule glows crimson when it is struck.

Molecule

Below 62 miles (100 km)

As electrons enter Earth's upper atmosphere, they meet atoms of oxygen and nitrogen at altitudes high above Earth's surface. The color of the aurora depends on which atom is struck, and the altitude of the meeting.

In the past, auroras were considered a premonition of war or plague.

Spiky snow

Resembling an **overgrown garden**, with tall blades of green grass replaced by white snow, penitentes are the **coolest, sharpest snow formations** around. It was once wrongly believed that this **pointy Andes snowscape** was carved out by the biting mountain wind.

Spikes are most plentiful in the areas between Argentina and Chile.

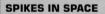

SPIKES IN SPACE

Jupiter's icy moon Europa is thought to be home to penitentes just like those on Earth. These ice blades stretch up to 33 ft (10 m) tall, posing a logistical nightmare for any future spacecraft attempting to land here.

Let's get right to the point—wind doesn't create penitentes. These spikes of hardened snow develop where air is cold and dry, allowing the sun to turn snow instantly into water vapor, without melting it first. This is called sublimation. Some areas sublimate quicker, leaving behind towering penitentes.

FAST FACTS

The sides of the depressions reflect heat, causing more snow to sublimate.

Tall spikes are created.

Snow sublimates unevenly, creating depressions.

Sunlight turns snow into vapor, creating depressions, which catch more sunlight and so sublimate quicker. The high sides of the depressions become spikes.

The height of penitentes ranges from 1 in (3 cm) up to 16 ft (5 m).

English naturalist **Charles Darwin** wrote about **penitentes** in **1839**.

Icebreakers

From **giant icebergs** to delicate **frost formations**, ice takes on some strange structures in the world's **coolest places**.

Frost beard
Frost beard resembles silky white hair growing on wood, like this log in Switzerland. Logs absorb rain, but when the water freezes in cold weather, it expands out onto the wooden exterior, exposing icy "hairs."

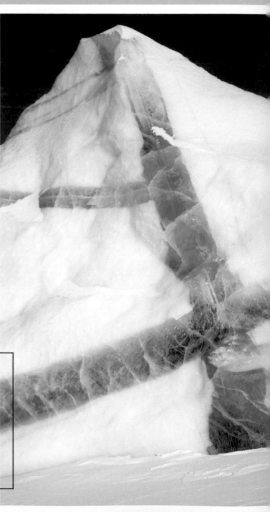

Ice stripes
Icebergs are usually white, but this one in Greenland seems to have blue veins! It is an example of striped ice, which occurs when algae, minerals, or sediment in seawater freeze onto the underside of an iceberg, creating streaks of blue, yellow, brown, or black.

Frost flowers
This pretty but fleeting phenomenon, seen here in the Canadian Rockies, occurs when plants carry water up from their roots to meet surrounding frozen air. Ice crystals form, which spread out and split the plant's stem open to reveal the frozen "flowers."

Polar pancakes
Less tasty than normal pancakes but much bigger, ice pancakes develop in polar regions when bits of foam floating on rivers and oceans freeze and knock into one another. Circular ice blocks result, enjoyed by these ducks on a river in sub-zero Belarus.

Alpine alley

The **Tateyama Kurobe Alpine Route**
is Japan's most spectacular scenic
journey. People traveling along
the **picturesque passageway** find
their view of the **lofty mountains**
suddenly obliterated by **towering
snow walls** on either side.

This panoramic route opened in 1971, and is open each year
from April to November. It is best known for the staggeringly
high snow walls of Murodo, which in some years are as tall as
a 10-story building. Other landmark sites along the route
include the Kurobe Dam and Hida Mountains.

**Diggers clear heavy
snow** to produce the
65-ft- (20-m-) high
Snow Corridor every
spring, which stretches
for 1,640 ft (500 m).

One million
tourists take
the Alpine
Route each
year.

SNOW TUNNELS

In 2015, heavy snowfall in North America resulted in locals digging their own snow tunnels to get out and about. Teams of diggers also constructed a variety of tunnels ranging in depth and length to help commuters and cyclists keep on the move.

FAST FACTS

Mt Tateyama
9,892 ft (3,015 m)
Murodo
Tengudaira
Midagahara
Tateyama
Highland Bus
Tateyama
Cablecar
Toyama
Chiho
Railroad

Tateyama Station

Bijodaira

Kurobeko

Kurobe-
daira

Kurobe
Cablecar

Kanden Tunnel
Trolleybus

Tateyama Tunnel
Trolleybus

Daikanbo

Tateyama
Ropeway

Kurobe
Dam

Ogizawa

Local
bus

Omachi
Onsenkyo

The terrain is tricky on many parts of the 56-mile- (90-km-) long Tateyama Kurobe Alpine Route so a number of different modes of transportation are used along the way, like trolleybuses, cable cars, and ropeways.

Morning glory

Like a magical highway running straight through the sky, **morning glory clouds** are an **extraordinary weather phenomenon**. A rarity in the rest of the world, they roll around regularly in **remote regions** of northern Australia, caused by wave-like currents in the air.

The spectacular sight can consist of one roll of cloud or as many as 10.

BUBBLING SKIES

When the sky appears to be covered in bubble wrap, it's most likely mammatus clouds. Usually associated with bad weather, these harmless clouds appear as a collection of droopy bulges underneath stormclouds.

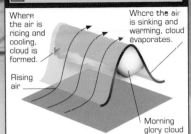

FAST FACTS

Where the air is rising and cooling, cloud is formed.

Where the air is sinking and warming, cloud evaporates.

Rising air

Morning glory cloud

These mysterious banks of cloud stretch across the sky from one horizon to the other. Appearing regularly in early morning between September and November, the clouds form in northeastern Australia's Gulf of Carpentaria, and roll in over Burketown, Queensland. The captivating clouds form on waves in the atmosphere created when moist sea air meets a layer of drier air.

Moisture-laden air blows in from the sea at night, pushing underneath a drier layer of air blown out from the land and creating a wave. Cloud is continuously formed in the upward current of the wave as the moisture-heavy air rises, cools, and condenses. In the downward current, the cloud evaporates. This continuous condensation and evaporation forms the roll-shaped bank of cloud.

The cloud rolls along at speeds of up to 37 mph (60 kph).

Morning glory clouds are a dream come true for hang gliders, who can "surf" them effortlessly, moved by the surrounding thermal winds.

Morning glory clouds can be **longer than 600 miles (1,000 km)**.

Snow chimneys

Winter wonderlands can be home to the unexpected sight of **snow chimneys**, or **fumaroles**, puffing steam into the sky. Occurring in **volcanic regions**, fumaroles are openings in Earth's surface from which **hot steam** and volcanic gases are emitted.

Carbon dioxide, sulfur dioxide, and hydrogen sulfide are often emitted from a fumarole, and a gas mask should be worn if confronting these dangerous gases.

SNOW ROLLERS

Another unusual eye opener is the snow roller. These giant cylinders develop naturally, as smaller pieces of snow blown by high winds gather more snow in a traditional snowballing effect. They are most commonly seen in cold regions of North America and Europe.

Close relations of hot springs and gushing geysers, fumaroles require heat and a gas or water source to burst forth. Volcanic magma (molten rock) under Earth's surface provides the heat and gases. When magma comes into contact with groundwater, the water boils and is released as steam.

Gas can be released for centuries or just a few weeks, depending on the heat source.

FAST FACTS

These steaming vents in Earth's surface always occur in regions with active volcanism. They work in a similar way to geysers: Underground water meets magma and is heated until it boils and bursts through cracks in the rock, making its way to the surface. A fumarole has a smaller reserve of water so emits only steam.

Volcanic eruption

Fumarole

Heated groundwater

Crack

Magma

In Arctic areas, the exiting steam freezes, forming vast snow chimneys around the volcanic opening.

In the line of firenadoes

Beware **blazing fires and whirling winds.** When two of nature's fiercest foes strike at the same time, they create firenadoes (**"fire tornadoes"**). Twisting flames leap high into the air in a **dangerous spectacle** that can quickly get out of control.

This firenado started on burning farmland in Chillicothe, Missouri, in 2014.

Shooting flames can stretch 100 ft (30 m) into the sky.

If hot air moves rapidly towards **cooler air**, it can generate a spiralling vortex (whirlwind). This can happen during a storm, causing a tornado. But a fiercely burning fire can create the same effect, with the added element of flames. These firenadoes do not usually last long, but they can be very destructive, hurling burning ashes over a broad area.

FIREBALL FRENZY

Science struggles to explain the regular occurrence of fireballs exploding from the Mekong River in Thailand. Locals believe that hundreds of "Naga fireballs" are released from the mouth of Naga, a legendary snake said to haunt the waters.

⊞ FAST FACTS

Tornado-like conditions can be created by a raging bush fire.

When violent updraughts generated by the fire meet cooler air above, the air starts to spin, forming a funnel.

When the hot updraughts meet cooler air, the air starts to spin.

The intense heat of the bush fire creates violent updraughts.

Oxygen strengthens the flames as the fire is sucked up into the funnel's center, creating a firenado.

Fire and combustible gases

are sucked up and fuelled by oxygen in the funnel's center. The funnel turns into a jet of flame—a firenado.

IT CAN'T BE TRUE!

Did you know that the colossal squid has eyes 11 times as wide as yours? Or that the longest mountain range lies under an ocean? It may seem hard to believe, but these amazing visual comparisons highlight the fantastic phenomena of our world.

Glass frogs are a group of South American tree frogs with unusually transparent undersides. When viewed from below, their blood vessels and internal organs are visible through the see-through skin of their bellies.

How much **blood** does a **heart pump?**

Oxygen-poor **blood** returns to the heart through veins (shown in blue).

The average **adult human heart** pumps about **10½ pints** (5 liters) of blood **every minute**, which is the **total amount** of blood in a **man's body.**

EXTREME PHYSIQUES

When cyclist Miguel Indurain won five Tours de France in the 1990s, his heart could pump 106 pints (50 liters) of blood a minute and his lungs could hold 17 pints (8 liters) of air. Average adult lungs hold less than 12¾ pints (6 liters).

The muscle that makes up the wall of the heart has its own blood supply.

FAST FACTS

The amount of blood pumped by the heart in a minute is known as "cardiac output." This can be used to measure a person's level of fitness. The more blood pumped, the more work their bodies can do.

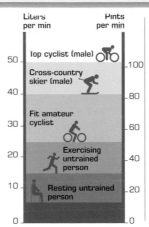

Liters per min		Pints per min
50	Top cyclist (male)	100
40	Cross-country skier (male)	80
30	Fit amateur cyclist	60
20	Exercising untrained person	40
10	Resting untrained person	20
0		0

Women	Men	Pregnant women
9½ pints (4.5 liters)	10½ pints (5 liters)	13¾ pints (6.5 liters)

On average, women have slightly less blood than men. An average pregnant woman, however, has more blood than a man. This extra blood is used to carry nutrients and oxygen to her baby.

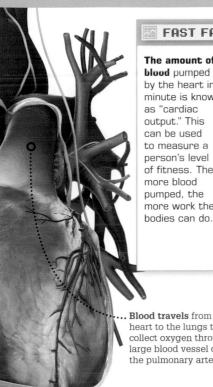

Blood travels from the heart to the lungs to collect oxygen through a large blood vessel called the pulmonary artery.

An **adult heart pumps enough blood** to fill **5.3 10,000-gallon (38,000-liter) road tankers every month.**

The heart has *a left* and a right side. The right side delivers blood to the lungs to pick up oxygen. The left side pumps this oxygen-rich blood around the body to deliver nutrients to all the body's cells. The cells absorb the oxygen, and the oxygen-poor blood returns to the heart to start its journey again.

The heart pumps oxygen-rich blood to the body through arteries (shown in red). This blood is bright red because it contains hemoglobin, the substance that carries the oxygen. Oxygen-poor blood is dark red.

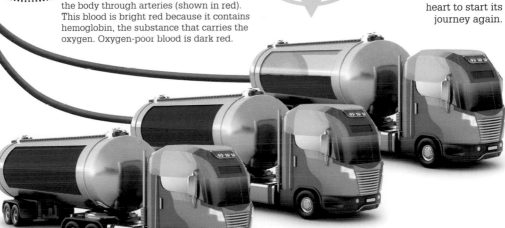

How **long** are your **blood vessels?**

It is estimated that there may be as many as **100,000 miles** (160,000 km) of blood vessels in an **adult's body,** and **60,000 miles** (97,000 km) in a **child's.**

There are three main types of blood vessel: arteries, veins, and capillaries. They cover such a great distance because they need to reach every cell in your body, delivering oxygen and nutrients and carrying away the cells' waste.

Blood leaves the heart and travels in arteries (shown in red) to the tissues and returns in veins (blue).

In the tissues, arteries (such as the two seen in each finger here) branch out into many smaller blood vessels, called capillaries.

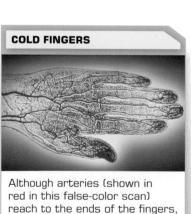

COLD FINGERS

Although arteries (shown in red in this false-color scan) reach to the ends of the fingers, sometimes hands can feel cold. This is because the body may restrict the blood flow to the hands to keep the rest of the body warm.

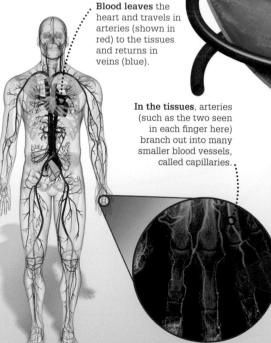

An
adult human's
network of
blood vessels
would **circle the
world four
times.**

Capillaries are thin—about 20 of the narrowest can fit across the width of a hair. These are just wide enough for one red blood cell to travel through at a time. Their thin walls let substances pass between the blood and the body tissues.

FAST FACTS

Capillary

Some capillaries are so narrow that only one blood cell at a time can pass through them. The widest blood vessel is an artery called the aorta. At its widest, the aorta is about 1¼ in (3 cm) across—about 6,000 times wider than the narrowest capillary.

There is more blood in the body's veins than in the arteries at any one time. Veins are wider inside than arteries (because they have thinner walls), and blood moves more slowly through them.

Veins 65% of blood volume

Arteries 35% of blood volume

London to Cologne
309 miles (498 km)

A red blood cell is thought to travel 2.5 miles (4 km) around your body every day. Over its lifetime of about 120 days, a cell will cover 300 miles (480 km)—that's just under the distance from London to Cologne, Germany.

How much air do you breathe in a lifetime?

Based on a life span of **70 years**, the average human breathes around **9.7 million cubic feet (275 million liters)** of air.

An average-sized **hot-air balloon**, capable of carrying three to five people, contains 616,000 gallons (2,800,000 liters) of air.

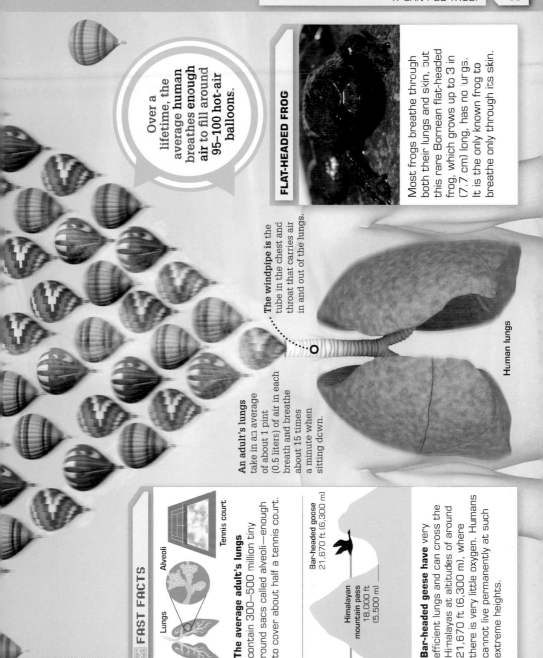

Over a lifetime, the average **human breathes enough air to fill around 95–100 hot-air balloons.**

FLAT-HEADED FROG

Most frogs breathe through both their lungs and skin, but this rare Bornean flat-headed frog, which grows up to 3 in (7.7 cm) long, has no lungs. It is the only known frog to breathe only through its skin.

The windpipe is the tube in the chest and throat that carries air in and out of the lungs.

An adult's lungs take in an average of about 1 pint (0.5 liters) of air in each breath and breathe about 15 times a minute when sitting down.

Human lungs

FAST FACTS

Lungs

Alveoli

Tennis court

The average adult's lungs contain 300–500 million tiny round sacs called alveoli—enough to cover about half a tennis court.

Bar-headed goose
21,670 ft (6,300 m)

Himalayan
mountain pass
18,000 ft
(5,500 m)

Bar-headed geese have very efficient lungs and can cross the Himalayas at altitudes of around 21,670 ft (6,300 m), where there is very little oxygen. Humans cannot live permanently at such extreme heights.

How **heavy** are your **bones?**

Bones are actually very **light**—your **skeleton** accounts for only about **15 percent** of your total weight.

The hyoid bone in the throat is one of the few bones that isn't joined to another.

INSIDE A BONE

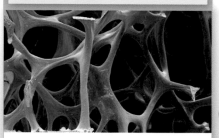

Although very strong, bones are light because they are not solid. Inside the hard, dense "compact bone" is "spongy bone," which looks like honeycomb (shown here in this false-colored image). The spaces in the bone are filled with jellylike marrow.

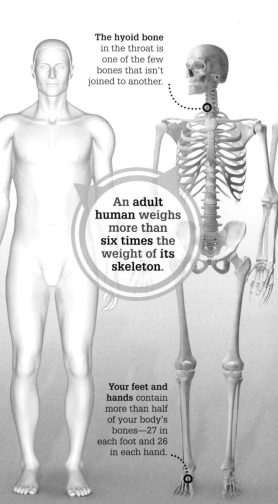

An **adult human weighs** more than **six times** the weight of **its skeleton.**

Your feet and hands contain more than half of your body's bones—27 in each foot and 26 in each hand.

FAST FACTS

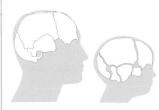

Adult skull   Baby skull

Babies are born with around 300 bones. As they grow up, many of the bones—such as those in the skull—fuse together, so most adults have 206 bones.

3,821 lb (1,733 kg)

Piece of bone

Bone is incredibly strong. A cube of bone measuring ½ in (1 cm) along each side would be able to support 3,821 lb (1,733 kg)—the weight of an adult male hippo.

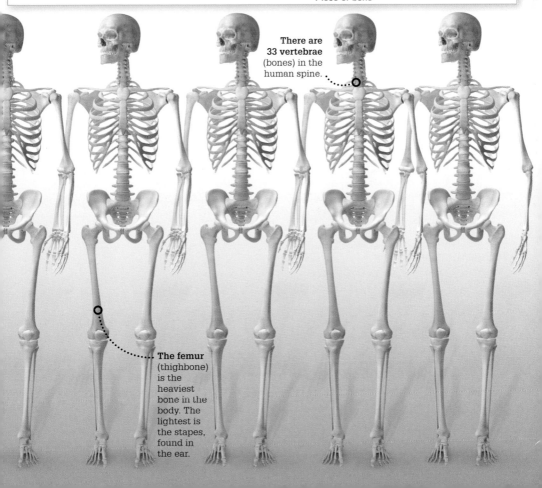

There are 33 vertebrae (bones) in the human spine.

The femur (thighbone) is the heaviest bone in the body. The lightest is the stapes, found in the ear.

FAST FACTS

Large eyes give animals the brightest, sharpest vision possible. Tarsiers have some of the largest eyes relative to their body size. They need them to hunt for insects in the rain forest at night. Each of their eyes is as big as their brain! A human's eyes are proportionally much smaller.

Tarsier brain and eye relative sizes

Human brain and eye relative sizes

What has the biggest eyes?

The **colossal squid**, a little-known species of squid bigger than the giant squid, has **eyes** up to **11 in** (27 cm) across in the few individuals measured.

PREHISTORIC VISION

Extinct reptiles called ichthyosaurs had eyes up to 12 in (30 cm) across. Like huge squid species, some probably hunted in the deep sea, their big eyes helping them to see in the dim light.

Human eyeball
1 in (2.5 cm)
across

Horse eyeball 1½ in
(4 cm) across

The lens of the colossal squid's eye is ball-shaped and about the size of an orange.

The largest **colossal squid eye** ever studied was a dead one that had the **same diameter** as **11 human eyeballs.**

Blue whale eyeball 6 in (15 cm) across

Colossal squid eyeball 11 in (27 cm) across. (Experts think the colossal squid's eyes may grow to 12—16 in (30—40 cm) across—as big as a beach ball!)

What has the biggest teeth?

African elephants have the **biggest teeth** of all animals. They have **enormous chewing teeth**, which crush vegetation, and two **huge front teeth** called **tusks.**

Up to 10 deep ridges line the top of the African elephant's molar, ideal for grinding tree branches.

The roots sit below the surface of the gum. When the molar first forms, the roots point down, but as the tooth moves forward in the jaw, the roots slant backward.

Around 65 human molars can fit on top of one elephant molar.

Human molars are on average ¾ in (2 cm) from the crown to the root. Humans grow only two sets of teeth in their lifetime.

VIPERFISH TEETH

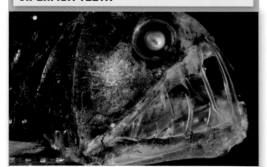

A viperfish's teeth are so long they curve around the outside of its head when it closes its mouth. The glassy daggers are perfectly suited for catching fish that live in the darkest depths of the ocean.

An elephant has four molars (back teeth) in its jaws at any one time. They grow up to 8¼ in (21 cm) long and 2¾ in (7 cm) wide, and weigh up to 9 lb (4 kg). Although tooth enamel is the hardest substance in a body, the teeth still wear down and are replaced six times during the elephant's life.

The crown is the part of a tooth that sits above the gum.

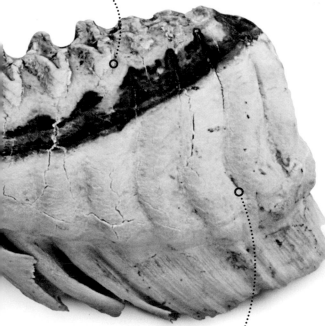

The creases in the root show that a molar is made up of a collection of up to 12 separate plates, or "tooth buds," that merged together as they grew.

A lion's back teeth are around 1¼ in (3 cm) wide. They are razor-sharp and work in pairs, like scissors, to slice through meat.

FAST FACTS

Tusks are front teeth used for defense while fighting, digging, lifting, or displaying. Walruses also use theirs like icepicks to haul themselves out of the water.

African elephant tusk 10 ft (3 m)

Narwhal tusk 9 ft (2.7 m)

Walrus tusk 3 ft 4 in (1 m)

Warthog tusk 18 in (45 cm)

Babirusa tusk 12 in (30 cm)

An ancient sharklike fish called *Helicoprion* had no teeth in its upper jaw and a unique set in its lower jaw—they were arranged like a spiral saw. No one is sure how the fish used them. Perhaps the teeth shredded the flesh of the fish as it pushed it toward its throat to swallow it.

Saw teeth spiraled out of its mouth

A great white shark has serrated teeth. The largest can grow to 2¾ in (7 cm) from base to tip.

What is the biggest living thing?

California's **giant sequoia** trees are the most **massive**, or heaviest, **life-forms**. They can weigh up to 2,105 tons (1,910 metric tons).

TUNNEL TREES

In the 1800s and early 1900s, people cut tunnels out of giant sequoias to allow carriages or cars to drive through them. These "tunnel trees" were tourist attractions, designed to advertise California's national parks. No new tunnels are cut today, but some old ones still exist.

Giant sequoias might grow even taller, but their height attracts lightning, which tends to kill off their upper branches.

Forest ecologist studying the top parts of the tree.

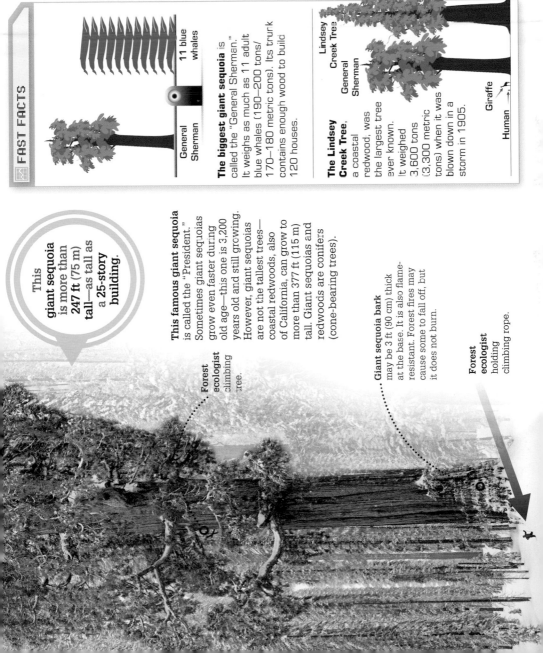

FAST FACTS

11 blue whales

General Sherman

The biggest giant sequoia is called the "General Sherman." It weighs as much as 11 adult blue whales (190–200 tons/ 170–180 metric tons). Its trunk contains enough wood to build 120 houses.

Lindsey Creek Tree

General Sherman

Giraffe

Human

The Lindsey Creek Tree, a coastal redwood, was the largest tree ever known. It weighed 3,600 tons (3,300 metric tons) when it was blown down in a storm in 1905.

This giant sequoia is more than 247 ft (75 m) tall—as tall as a 25-story building.

This famous giant sequoia is called the "President." Sometimes giant sequoias grow even faster during old age—this one is 3,200 years old and still growing. However, giant sequoias are not the tallest trees— coastal redwoods, also of California, can grow to more than 377 ft (115 m) tall. Giant sequoias and redwoods are conifers (cone-bearing trees).

Forest ecologist climbing tree.

Giant sequoia bark may be 3 ft (90 cm) thick at the base. It is also flame-resistant. Forest fires may cause some to fall off, but it does not burn.

Forest ecologist holding climbing rope.

How **big** is the **biggest animal?**

The **largest animal** on the **planet** is the **blue whale**, measuring **100 ft** (30 m). It is the **biggest** animal that has **ever lived**, including the **dinosaurs.**

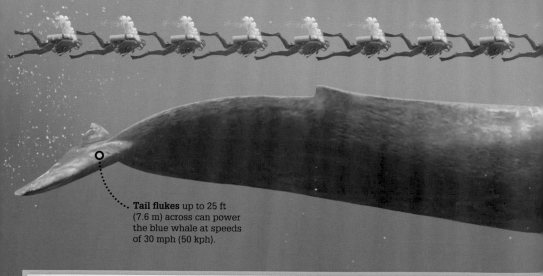

Tail flukes up to 25 ft (7.6 m) across can power the blue whale at speeds of 30 mph (50 kph).

FAST FACTS

A blue whale is longer than a basketball court and weighs up to 200 tons (180 tonnes)—the same as 15 school buses.

Blue whales make a noise louder than a jet aircraft taking off. Whales produce very low frequency sounds at a level of 188 decibels; these can be heard from thousands of miles away.

188 dB

140 dB

FILTER FEEDING

A blue whale can eat around 4 tons (3.5 metric tons) of krill (tiny sea creatures) a day. Taking 100-ton (90-metric-ton) gulps of water, the whale then filters the water out through baleen plates, comblike structures that hang from its jaw, trapping the krill.

The blue whale's heart is the size of a small car.

Its eyeball is 6 in (15 cm) in diameter.

Its tongue weighs as much as an elephant.

Its outer ear is the width of a pencil tip.

A blue whale is as long as 17 scuba divers swimming in a line.

A blue whale can blow 160 cu ft (4,500 liters) of air out of its blowholes at 300 mph (480 kph). The spray it produces reaches a height of 30 ft (9 m)—as tall as five men standing on each others' heads.

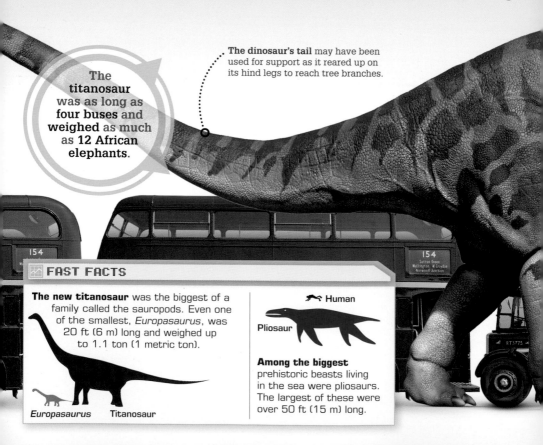

What was the biggest dinosaur?

The **fossil bones** of the **largest animal ever to walk on land** were unearthed in 2012. It is a type of **titanosaur** that **fossil hunters** estimate weighed **69 tons** (63 metric tons) and was **122 ft** (37 m) long.

The dinosaur's tail may have been used for support as it reared up on its hind legs to reach tree branches.

The titanosaur was as long as **four buses** and **weighed** as much as **12 African elephants**.

154

154
Sutton Green
Wallington W Croydon
Norwood Junction

RT3775

FAST FACTS

The new titanosaur was the biggest of a family called the sauropods. Even one of the smallest, *Europasaurus*, was 20 ft (6 m) long and weighed up to 1.1 ton (1 metric ton).

Europasaurus   **Titanosaur**

Human

Pliosaur

Among the biggest prehistoric beasts living in the sea were pliosaurs. The largest of these were over 50 ft (15 m) long.

BEFORE THE DINOSAURS

Long before the dinosaurs, there were no large animals on land—but there were in the oceans. *Pterygotus*, a giant sea scorpion that lived 400 million years ago, grew to 7 ft 6 in (2.3 m) long— bigger than an adult human.

The bones were discovered in Argentina in 2012 and the species was named *Patagotitan mayorum*. Its bones were not fully grown, so there could be even bigger dinosaurs out there!

The small head did not contain heavy jaws for chewing food— titanosaurs simply gulped it down.

Its long neck meant that the titanosaur could eat from the ground or from trees. It had to eat a lot—a dumpster full of vegetation every day.

154

LONDON TRANSPORT

RT3775

A 10

LONDON TRANSPORT

New titanosaur
122 ft (37 m) long

Double-decker bus
31.2 ft (9.5 m) long

What was the biggest land predator?

The **biggest predator** that ever lived **on land** was *Spinosaurus*, a **56-ft-** (17-m-) long fish-eating **dinosaur**.

Spinosaurus was the longest predatory dinosaur known. It lived around 100 million years ago in North Africa.

This adult man stands about 5 ft 11 in (1.8 m) tall.

A male polar bear is the biggest land predator today. It can grow up to 10 ft (3 m) in length and be 5 ft (1.5 m) tall at the shoulder.

Spinosaurus's size was enhanced by long spines extending up from its backbone, which probably created a tall crest or "sail."

Spinosaurus was more than five times the length of a polar bear.

SABER-TOOTHED CAT

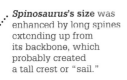

The dinosaur's **huge tail** balanced the weight of its head and forelimbs, allowing it to walk on its hind legs.

Smilodon was the biggest cat to walk the Earth. At 6 ft 6 in (2 m) long, it was big enough to attack and eat mammoths. The cat probably wrestled its prey to the ground, then killed it with its large canine teeth.

📊 FAST FACTS

Siberian tiger

Andrewsarchus

Mapusaurus

Giganotosaurus

Tyrannosaurus rex

Andrewsarchus, resembling a giant wolf, was the largest meat-eating mammal that ever lived. At about 11 ft (3.4 m), its body length was almost double that of the modern Siberian tiger.

Since *Spinosaurus* ate fish, it was not the largest meat-eater. That title is contested by *Tyrannosaurus*, *Giganotosaurus*, and *Mapusaurus*. All of these species may have topped 40 ft (12 m) in length.

What was the largest snake?

Titanoboa was an **enormous snake** measuring **48 ft** (14.6 m), or longer than a school bus. It lived around **60 million years ago** in the **jungle swamps** of modern-day **Colombia**.

Big snakes such as pythons can eat prey wider than themselves. The snake cannot chew, so prey must be swallowed whole. Digesting food uses so much energy, the snake is inactive for several days.

Like the jaws of today's snakes, the lower jaw would unhinge, enabling *Titanoboa* to swallow large prey.

Snakes breathe through a hole called the glottis. This can move to the side so that the reptile can breathe as it slowly swallows its prey.

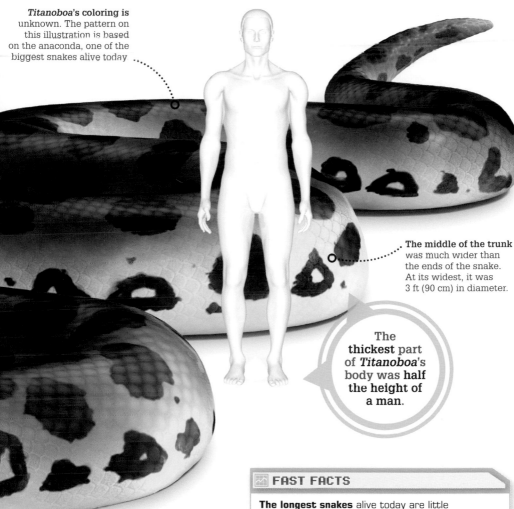

Titanoboa's coloring is unknown. The pattern on this illustration is based on the anaconda, one of the biggest snakes alive today

The middle of the trunk was much wider than the ends of the snake. At its widest, it was 3 ft (90 cm) in diameter.

The **thickest** part of **Titanoboa's** body was **half the height of a man.**

Titanoboa weighed more than 1 tonne (1 ton)—as much as a small family car and big enough to tackle giant turtles and crocodiles. Experts have argued that it grew so big because the world was warmer 60 million years ago, and reptiles today are usually bigger in warmer climates.

📊 FAST FACTS

The longest snakes alive today are little more than half the length of *Titanoboa*.

King cobra 18 ft (5.5 m)

Indian python 21 ft (6.4 m)

Green anaconda 29 ft (9 m)

Reticulated python 33 ft (10 m)

Megalodon's tail fin provided all the propulsion the shark needed while swimming and hunting.

How big was the biggest shark?

MOSASAUR

Megalodon was one of the world's biggest-ever hunters, but many other ocean predators have grown to monstrous lengths. The 49-ft (15-m) *Mosasaurus* lived around 65 million years ago.

The **largest shark** that ever lived was **megalodon**, which may have grown to **66 ft** (20 m) **long**. It died out more than **1.5 million years ago**.

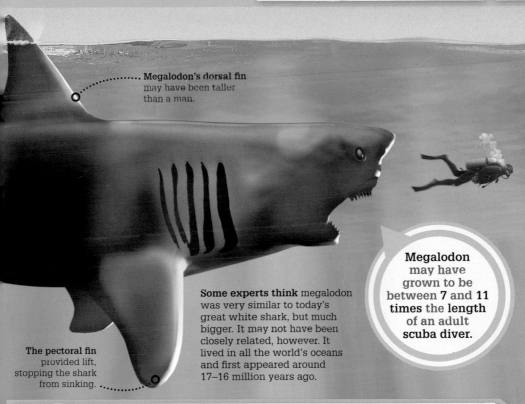

Megalodon's dorsal fin may have been taller than a man.

The pectoral fin provided lift, stopping the shark from sinking.

Some experts think megalodon was very similar to today's great white shark, but much bigger. It may not have been closely related, however. It lived in all the world's oceans and first appeared around 17–16 million years ago.

Megalodon may have grown to be between **7** and **11** times the length of an adult scuba diver.

FAST FACTS

Today's biggest shark is not the great white, but the whale shark, a gentle giant that feeds on plankton—tiny floating creatures. The great white is the biggest predatory shark—one that hunts down individual prey, such as fish.

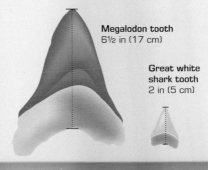

Megalodon
52–65 ft
(16–20 m) long,
55 tons (50 metric tons)

Whale shark
41ft 6 in (12.65 m)
long, 23.5 tons
(21.5 metric tons)

Great white shark
20 ft (6.1 m) long,
2 tons (1.9 metric tons)

Megalodon's huge teeth are the most common fossil remains of the creature. They are the same shape as the teeth of the great white shark, but more than three times the height.

Megalodon tooth
6½ in (17 cm)

Great white
shark tooth
2 in (5 cm)

The spider's leg span is measured from the tip of the first leg on one side to the tip of the fourth leg on the other.

Pedipalps are not legs—they are long mouthparts.

The spider's fangs, which are ¾ in (20 mm) long, are tucked under the hair-covered upper mouthparts.

The hairs covering the spider's body can cause rashes and swelling on human skin. This part, the abdomen, has hairs that the spider can flick at attackers to defend itself.

The Goliath bird-eater is a species of tarantula and lives in South America. It grows big enough to eat birds, although it mostly eats insects, rodents, bats, snakes, and lizards. It pounces on prey and injects it with venom from its fangs.

Goliaths can grow to be **bigger** than an **adult's hand** and can cover a **dinner plate!**

GIANT HUNTSMAN SPIDER

The longest spider legs are thought to belong to the giant huntsman spider of Laos, Southeast Asia. Its legs span up to 12 in (30 cm), although its body is just 1¾ in (4.6 cm) long.

How **big** can spiders grow?

The Goliath bird-eater rubs bristles on its legs to produce a hissing sound as a warning to predators.

The **heaviest type** of spider is the **goliath bird-eating spider**, which can **weigh** up to **6 oz** (175 g). The biggest one measured had a **leg span** of **11 in** (28 cm).

FAST FACTS

Darwin's bark spiders can spin webs up to 80 ft (25 m)—as wide a six-lane highway. Its silk is highly resistant to breaking and more than 10 times tougher than Kevlar (a material used to make body armor).

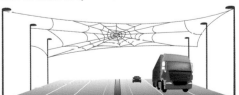

Most spiders are venomous, and some species have venom deadly enough to kill dozens of mice. Most spiders are harmless to humans, but these three demand respect.

Mice killed by **1 millionth of a gram of venom**

 Southern black widow 12.5 mice

Mediterranean black widow 37 mice

 Brazilian wandering spider 41 mice

What is the biggest insect?

There are several contenders, but the **Atlas moth** has the biggest wings, with a **span** of **10 in** (25 cm) and a **wing area** of **62 sq in** (400 sq cm).

The **Atlas moth** is much **bigger** than an adult **human** hand.

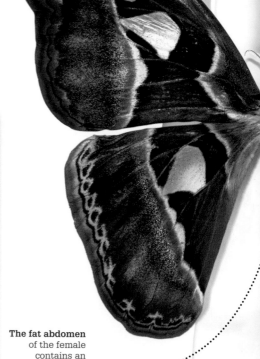

GIANT WETA

The giant weta, one of the world's heaviest insects, lives in New Zealand. Wetas gnaw roots and stems in their forest habitat and have grown to mouselike sizes. At 2½ oz (70 g), the largest are as big as three house mice.

The fat abdomen of the female contains an egg factory.

The Atlas moth of Southeast Asia is the biggest insect by wing area. However, the white witch moth of Central and South America has the widest wingspan, at about 12 in (31 cm).

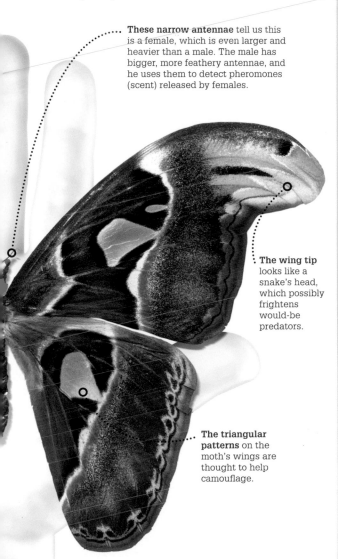

These **narrow antennae** tell us this is a female, which is even larger and heavier than a male. The male has bigger, more feathery antennae, and he uses them to detect pheromones (scent) released by females.

The wing tip looks like a snake's head, which possibly frightens would-be predators.

The triangular patterns on the moth's wings are thought to help camouflage.

FAST FACTS

There are other insects competing for the title of the biggest insect alive. Here are some of the contenders.

The titan beetle of South American rain forests grows up to 6.5 in (16.5 cm) long— as long as than the body of a rat. Its jaws can snap a pencil in half.

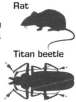

Rat

Titan beetle

Stick insects can be even longer. The record-breaking Chan's megastick of Borneo, Malaysia, is 22½ in (56.7 cm) long with outstretched legs. That's almost twice the width of this book.

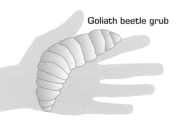

Goliath beetle grub

Some insects have really large grubs. One of the biggest and heaviest is that of Africa's Goliath beetle. It can grow up to 5 in (13 cm) long and weighs 3½ oz (100 g).

Running along the front edge of *Quetzalcoatlus*'s wing were the incredibly long bones of a single finger, which held the wing open.

The **wings** of *Quetzalcoatlus* stretched farther than those of a **Tiger Moth** biplane.

What had the **longest wings** ever?

The **largest flying creature** was a **pterosaur** called *Quetzalcoatlus*. It soared over its relatives, the **dinosaurs**, 68 million years ago. The largest had a **wingspan** of **more than 33 ft** (10 m).

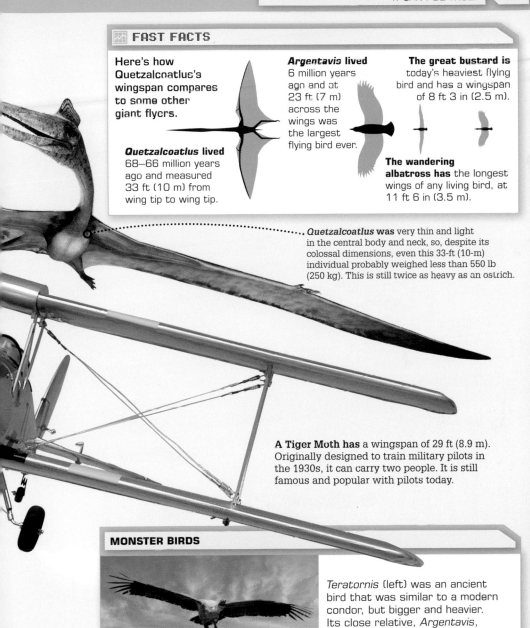

FAST FACTS

Here's how Quetzalcoatlus's wingspan compares to some other giant flyers.

Quetzalcoatlus lived 68–66 million years ago and measured 33 ft (10 m) from wing tip to wing tip.

Argentavis lived 6 million years ago and at 23 ft (7 m) across the wings was the largest flying bird ever.

The great bustard is today's heaviest flying bird and has a wingspan of 8 ft 3 in (2.5 m).

The wandering albatross has the longest wings of any living bird, at 11 ft 6 in (3.5 m).

Quetzalcoatlus was very thin and light in the central body and neck, so, despite its colossal dimensions, even this 33-ft (10-m) individual probably weighed less than 550 lb (250 kg). This is still twice as heavy as an ostrich.

A Tiger Moth has a wingspan of 29 ft (8.9 m). Originally designed to train military pilots in the 1930s, it can carry two people. It is still famous and popular with pilots today.

MONSTER BIRDS

Teratornis (left) was an ancient bird that was similar to a modern condor, but bigger and heavier. Its close relative, *Argentavis*, was gigantic and weighed as much as a person.

At only 2¼ in (5.5 cm) long, the bee hummingbird can perch on the end of a pencil.

The male bee hummingbird has a glossy pink head and throat and is even smaller than the female.

FAST FACTS

The bee hummingbird builds a cup-shaped nest about 1 in (2.5 cm) across from bits of cobwebs, bark, and lichen. Nests have been built on single clothes pins. The eggs are the size of peas.

In contrast, the heaviest living bird that can fly is the great bustard. At 46 lb (20.9 kg), it weighs as much as a six-year-old boy.

Great bustard

Today's heaviest bird, the ostrich, can weigh nearly twice as much as an adult person. However, a few hundred years ago, an even heavier bird—the elephant bird—lived in Madagascar. It weighed as much as three ostriches. It is now extinct.

Elephant bird   Ostrich   Human   Chicken

The bee hummingbird is a tiny but busy bird. It hovers by flapping its wings at 80 times a second, with its heart beating at an incredible 1,220 times a minute. To power this activity, the bird must feed every 10–15 minutes. It eats about half its own body weight in sugary nectar every day.

What is the smallest bird?

The **bee hummingbird**, which lives only in Cuba, is 2¼ in (5.5 cm) long and **weighs** just **0.06 oz (1.6 g)**.

THE SWORD-BILLED HUMMINGBIRD

Not all hummingbirds are tiny. Among the largest are sword-billed hummingbirds. Their bills alone measure the same as two entire bee hummingbirds!

Which bird laid the biggest egg?

Eggs of the extinct **elephant bird** were up to **13 in** (34 cm) **long.** Elephant birds lived in **Madagascar** until a few hundred years ago.

Emu eggs are unusually dark. They look like a huge avocado, at 5 in (13 cm) high.

Emu

A kiwi is 20 times smaller than an emu, but its eggs are almost the same size.

Hummingbird eggs are the smallest bird eggs. This one is from a ruby-throated hummingbird.

Rusty tinamou

Hummingbird

Chicken

Quail

Kiwi

Cormorant

Tawny owl

The most familiar eggs are laid by the domestic chicken.

King penguin

Common sandpiper

FAST FACTS

Elephant bird eggs are bigger than those of most dinosaurs. Even the eggs of sauropods (the biggest dinosaurs) are no more than 8 in (20 cm) long. Recent digs in China, however, appear to have turned up giant eggs of two-legged dinosaurs similar to *Oviraptor*.

24 in (60 cm)

13 in (33 cm)

8 in (20 cm)

Elephant bird 10 ft (3 m) tall

Sauropod up to 120 ft (36 m) long

Giant *Oviraptor* 26 ft (8 m) long

Elephant birds had died out by the 18th century, but a few of their eggshells still exist. Most shell remains, however, are found as fragments. Pieces found near the sites of ancient cooking fires suggest that people ate the eggs.

In terms of volume, an **elephant bird's egg** is as big as **200 chicken eggs** or **11 ostrich eggs**.

The shell of the egg is ¼ in (3.8 mm) thick and could bear the weight of about 90 bricks (550 lb/248 kg).

Ostrich

The ostrich is the world's largest bird, and it lays the biggest eggs today—although they are the smallest in relation to the size of the mother. They weigh on average just over 3 lb (1.4 kg)—more than 20 chicken eggs.

Elephant bird

Cetti's warbler

Guillemot

KIWI EGGS

Kiwis lay the biggest eggs in relation to their body size. One egg can be up to one-fifth of the weight of its mother.

Guillemot eggs roll in circles, so they don't fall off cliff ledges, where they are laid.

Great auk

Carrion crow

Curlew

Sparrowhawk

Cuckoo

Redshank

How **far** can a **bird fly?**

Bar-tailed godwits have been tracked flying **7,258 miles** (11,680 km) **nonstop** from Alaska to New Zealand on their **yearly migration.**

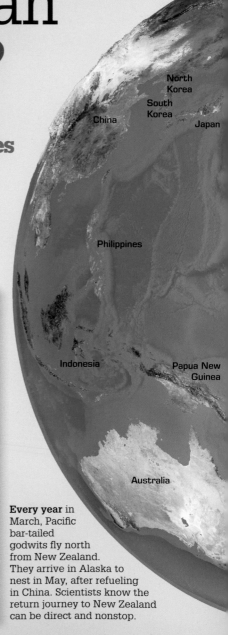

North Korea
South Korea
China
Japan
Philippines
Indonesia
Papua New Guinea
Australia

📈 FAST FACTS

Earth   Moon

Arctic terns migrate from the Arctic to the Antarctic and back every year. Single birds have been tracked flying 44,000 miles (70,900 km) in this time. In their 30-year lifetime, they can cover 1.3 million miles (2.1 million km), or more than two round trips to the Moon.

Glider 1,870 miles (3,009 km)

Airliner (Boeing 777 specially adapted for record attempt) 13,423 miles (21,602 km)

Breitling Orbiter balloon 25,361 miles (40,814 km)

Virgin Atlantic GlobalFlyer 25,766 miles (41,467 km)

An airliner can fly farther than any bird if it is specially adapted. Above are four human nonstop flight records involving different kinds of aircraft.

Every year in March, Pacific bar-tailed godwits fly north from New Zealand. They arrive in Alaska to nest in May, after refueling in China. Scientists know the return journey to New Zealand can be direct and nonstop.

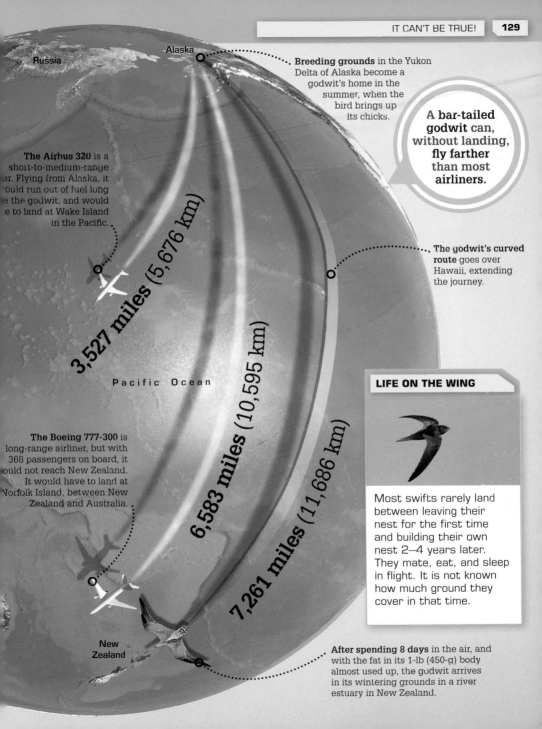

Russia

Alaska

Breeding grounds in the Yukon Delta of Alaska become a godwit's home in the summer, when the bird brings up its chicks.

A **bar-tailed godwit** can, without landing, **fly farther** than most airliners.

The Airbus 320 is a short-to-medium-range [air]er. Flying from Alaska, it [w]ould run out of fuel long [befor]e the godwit, and would [hav]e to land at Wake Island in the Pacific.

The godwit's curved route goes over Hawaii, extending the journey.

3,527 miles (5,676 km)

Pacific Ocean

6,583 miles (10,595 km)

LIFE ON THE WING

The Boeing 777-300 is [a] long-range airliner, but with 368 passengers on board, it [w]ould not reach New Zealand. It would have to land at [N]orfolk Island, between New Zealand and Australia.

7,261 miles (11,686 km)

Most swifts rarely land between leaving their nest for the first time and building their own nest 2–4 years later. They mate, eat, and sleep in flight. It is not known how much ground they cover in that time.

New Zealand

After spending 8 days in the air, and with the fat in its 1-lb (450-g) body almost used up, the godwit arrives in its wintering grounds in a river estuary in New Zealand.

How **old** is the **oldest tree?**

The world's **oldest living tree** started life in around 3050 BCE, making it more than **5,065 years old**. The tree is a **Great Basin bristlecone pine** in the White Mountains of California.

1804 First steam locomotive is built

c.800 CE Vikings raid northwest Europe

The **oldest bristlecone pine has lived through all of recorded human history.**

432 BCE Parthenon is completed in Greece

OLDEST SEED

While excavating King Herod's Palace at Masada, Israel, in the 1960s, archeologists found Judean date palm seeds that were at least 2,000 years old. In 2005, one seed successfully sprouted and was planted at Kibbutz Ketura. The tree has been nicknamed "Methuselah," after the Biblical man said to be the oldest person ever to live.

When the world's oldest tree sprouted from its seed, people wrote with pictures and symbols, not letters and words; the wheel was unknown in most of the world; and the great civilization of ancient Egypt was only just beginning.

c.3050 BCE The tree's seed sprouts

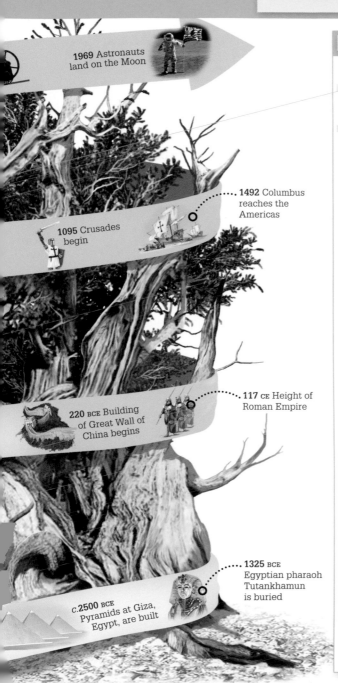

1969 Astronauts land on the Moon

1492 Columbus reaches the Americas

1095 Crusades begin

220 BCE Building of Great Wall of China begins

117 CE Height of Roman Empire

1325 BCE Egyptian pharaoh Tutankhamun is buried

*c.***2500 BCE** Pyramids at Giza, Egypt, are built

FAST FACTS

Bristlecone pine
Lifespan 5,000 years

Present day

Seagrass
Lifespan 100,000 years

A huge seagrass colony in the Mediterranean may be 100,000 years old, which would make it the oldest known life-form.

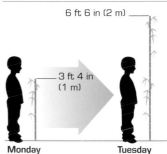

6 ft 6 in (2 m)

3 ft 4 in (1 m)

Monday   Tuesday

Bamboo can grow more than 3 ft 4 in (1 m) per day—faster than any other plant.

■ original size
■ after 100 years
■ after 200 years

Lichens are half-plant, half-fungi life-forms that grow as patches on rocks or trees. Some live for millennia, but they may grow less than 0.004 in (0.1 mm) per year.

How **old** are the **oldest animals?**

Ocean quahog clams are known to live for more than **500 years.** Scientists think some **sponges** may live **even longer.**

ANCIENT SPONGES

It is difficult to identify the age of a sponge, but Caribbean giant barrel sponges (left) have very long lives; one is believed to be 2,300 years old. Some Antarctic glass sponges may live for more than 10,000 years.

Ocean quahogs can live nearly **6 times** longer than **Asian elephants.**

Human
122 years

Rougheye rockfish
140–200 years

Most humans don't live 122 years, but there is a verified case of a woman who did.

Asian elephant
86 years

Olm
(a cave salamander)
100 years

Tuatara
111 years

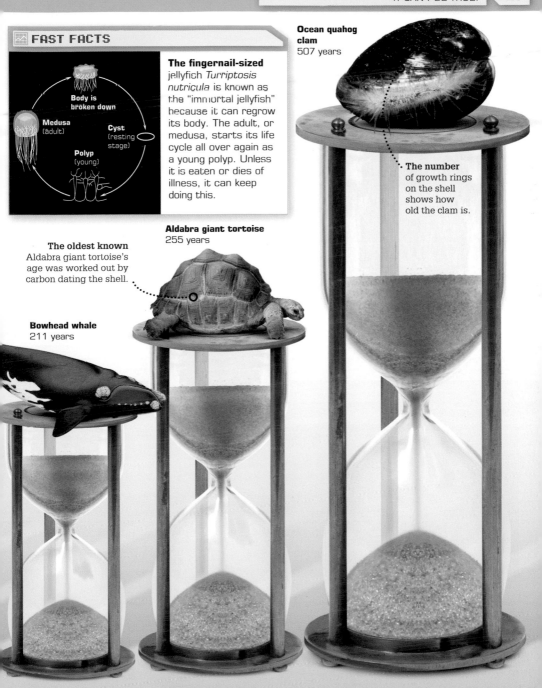

FAST FACTS

The fingernail-sized jellyfish *Turritopsis nutricula* is known as the "immortal jellyfish" because it can regrow its body. The adult, or medusa, starts its life cycle all over again as a young polyp. Unless it is eaten or dies of illness, it can keep doing this.

Body is broken down

Medusa (adult)

Cyst (resting stage)

Polyp (young)

Ocean quahog clam
507 years

The number of growth rings on the shell shows how old the clam is.

Aldabra giant tortoise
255 years

The oldest known Aldabra giant tortoise's age was worked out by carbon dating the shell.

Bowhead whale
211 years

What is the **fastest runner?**

The **cheetah** is the **fastest land animal**, but only over short distances. **Horses** are **slower**, but can run **much farther** before they get tired.

The fastest sprinters, running the 100 m in less than 10 seconds, reach their top speed usually during the 60–80 m stretch. If they could sustain this top speed throughout the race, they would run it in 8.4 seconds.

27 mph (43 kph)

WALKING ON WATER

Basilisk lizards can escape from predators by running across the surface of ponds and rivers. Running at a speed of around 4 mph (6 kph), they can cover a distance of 65 ft (20 m) before they start to sink.

At its **top speed**, a **cheetah** would finish a **100 m sprint** in around **3 seconds**.

A thoroughbred racehorse can gallop at up to 43 mph (70 kph) in races of 2 furlongs (0.25 miles/ 0.4 km). Running at this speed, the horse could complete the 100 m sprint in 5.15 seconds.

43 mph
(70 kph)

70 mph
(115 kph)

FAST FACTS

The cheetah's speed comes from its flexible spine. The cat hunches its spine at the start of a stride, bringing its back feet in front of the forefeet. As the back feet hit the ground and push off, its spine extends, giving the cheetah an extra-long stride.

- Snail 0.03 (0.05)
- Mouse 8 (13)
- Squirrel 13 (21)
- Elephant 25 (40)
- Human 27 (43)
- Domestic cat 30 (48)
- Greyhound 43 (70)
- African lion 55 (89)
- Pronghorn 62 (100)

Top speed in mph (kph)

The garden snail certainly takes its time to move around. However, the domestic cat is quite fast—it could beat an Olympic sprinter if it had to make a run for it.

A cheetah can sprint at incredible speeds to catch its prey, but the chase will only last for about 30–60 seconds, after which the cat gets too tired.

What animal can **jump** the farthest?

GLIDING MAMMALS

Some animals do not jump, but can glide for long distances. For example, the sugar glider of Australia, uses flaps of skin between its limbs to help it glide from tree to tree for 165 ft (50 m) or more.

The **snow leopard** of central Asia can **leap** the **farthest** in the animal kingdom. It can cover more than **50 ft** (15 m) in a **single jump**.

30 ft (9 m)

29 ft 4½ in (8.95 m)

9 ft (3 m)

The jerboa's long back legs help it to jump more than 25 times its body length.

⛰ FAST FACTS

The common flea is the most impressive jumping creature on the planet for its size. Fleas can be only 0.06 in (1.5 mm) long but can leap a distance of 13 in (33 cm)—220 times their body length. Fleas are parasites and spring onto mammals, sometimes including humans, to feed on their blood.

On a human scale, if a 5-ft 11-in (1.8-m) man could jump as far as a flea, he would be able to clear more than three soccer fields laid end to end.

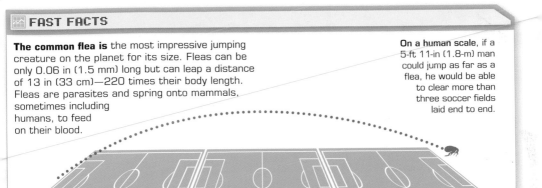

When it jumps, the red kangaroo can reach a speed of more than 40 mph (64 kph) with single leaps of up to 30 ft (9 m).

The **snow leopard** could easily clear **seven large family cars** in one leap.

The human world record for men's long jump was set by US athlete Mike Powell in 1991.

50 ft (15 m)

Snow leopards live in mountain habitats, where they leap to catch their prey of wild sheep and goats.

What is the fastest flyer?

In level flight, a **white-throated needletail** is the **fastest** bird in the air. It has a **top speed** of **105 mph** (170 kph).

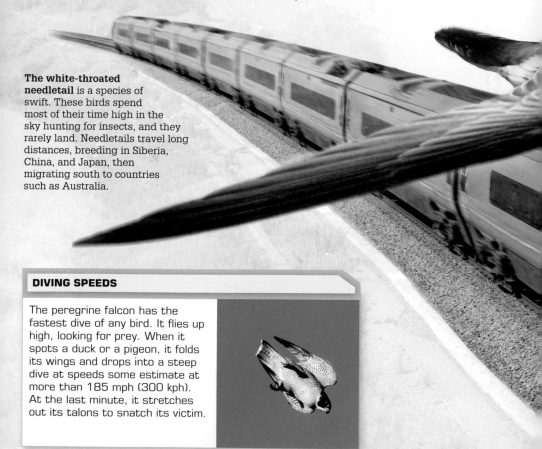

The white-throated needletail is a species of swift. These birds spend most of their time high in the sky hunting for insects, and they rarely land. Needletails travel long distances, breeding in Siberia, China, and Japan, then migrating south to countries such as Australia.

DIVING SPEEDS

The peregrine falcon has the fastest dive of any bird. It flies up high, looking for prey. When it spots a duck or a pigeon, it folds its wings and drops into a steep dive at speeds some estimate at more than 185 mph (300 kph). At the last minute, it stretches out its talons to snatch its victim.

FAST FACTS

Although they walk with a slow waddle, ducks and shorebirds are the fastest flying birds, other than swifts, that have been measured accurately. The great snipe has the fastest recorded migration.

Common swift
69 mph (111 kph)

Great snipe (a shorebird)
60 mph (97 kph)

Eider duck
47 mph (76 kph)

Birds are the fastest fliers, but among other animals, free-tailed bats are the quickest. Dragonflies are among the speediest insects.

Mexican free-tailed bat
40 mph (64 kph)

Flying fish
37 mph (60 kph)

Dragonfly
30 mph (50 kph)

A white-throated needletail flies fast enough to keep up with a high-speed train.

Long, curved wings slip easily through the air.

This high-speed train has a maximum speed of 125 mph (200 kph), but on a scheduled passenger trip, it averages about 106 mph (171 kph), including stops.

What is the fastest swimmer?

The **speediest swimmer**, the **sailfish**, could travel the length of an Olympic **swimming pool** in **1.6 seconds**—around **13 times faster** than the **human** record holder.

FAST FACTS

Sailfish
68 mph (110 kph)

Striped marlin
50 mph (80 kph)

Blue-fin tuna
44 mph (71 kph)

Blue shark
43 mph (69 kph)

Swordfish
40 mph (64 kph)

Dall's porpoise
35 mph (56 kph)

California sea lion
25 mph (40 kph)

Octopus
25 mph (40 kph)

Gentoo penguin
22 mph (36 kph)

Leatherback turtle
21.5 mph (35 kph)

The fastest swimmers are all fish. At the top is the sailfish, which is an amazing 18.5 mph (30 kph) quicker than its nearest rival, the striped marlin.

Some other sea animals swim fast. However, all are slower than the top five fastest fish, which have perfectly streamlined bodies with powerful muscles built for speed.

5.3 mph
(8.6 kph)

An Olympic swimmer can keep up his top sprint speed for only one length of the pool (164 ft/50 m).

Polar bears can swim very long distances. Scientists tracked one bear over a 420-mile (675-km) journey. It took nearly 10 days, and the bear didn't stop to eat or sleep.

67 mph
(108 kph)

The fastest personal watercraft can zoom across the water at about 12.5 times the speed of the Olympic swimmer.

A sailfish speeds through water at 68 mph (110 kph), faster than a personal watercraft.

68 mph
(110 kph)

A sailfish is a predator of the open ocean. It uses its speed and large dorsal fin to herd a shoal of fish into a ball. It then slashes its prey with its long bill.

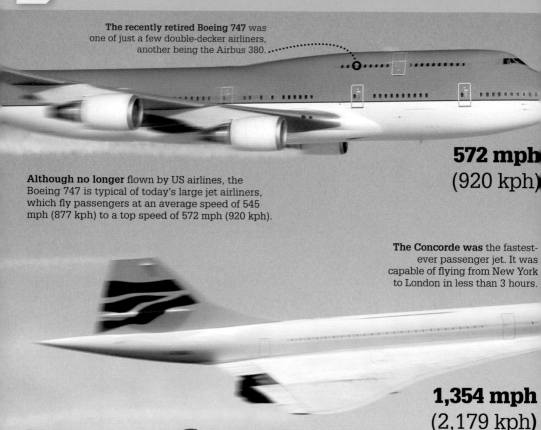

The recently retired Boeing 747 was one of just a few double-decker airliners, another being the Airbus 380.

572 mph
(920 kph)

Although no longer flown by US airlines, the Boeing 747 is typical of today's large jet airliners, which fly passengers at an average speed of 545 mph (877 kph) to a top speed of 572 mph (920 kph).

The Concorde was the fastest-ever passenger jet. It was capable of flying from New York to London in less than 3 hours.

1,354 mph
(2,179 kph)

How **fast** is the **fastest aircraft?**

The **X-15** was the fastest **manned airplane** ever to fly. Its **record speed** of **4,520 mph** (7,274 kph) was set in **1967** and has never been beaten.

FAST FACTS

Flyer
30 mph
(48 kph)

Mallard duck
65 mph (105 kph)

The first aircraft to fly, the Wright brothers' *Flyer*, reached a top speed of 30 mph (48 kph). This is less than half the speed of a mallard duck, which flies at 65 mph (105 kph).

4,520 mph (7,274 kph)
X-15—fastest manned aircraft

2,600 mph (4,184 kph)
SpaceShipTwo—fastest passenger spaceplane

2,193 mph (3,529 kph)
SR—71 Blackbird—fastest jet aircraft

700 mph (1,126 kph)
Cessna Citation X—fastest passenger jet

249 mph (400 kph)
Westland Lynx—fastest helicopter

The fastest aircraft fly to the edge of space. Tourists may soon travel there in supersonic space planes.

The **X-15** flew at nearly **eight times the speed** of a Boeing 747.

Bullet speeds vary, but a bullet from an M16 rifle is quicker than the fastest fighter jets.

2,125 mph
(3,420 kph)

HTV-2

In 2011, an experimental plane, the unmanned HTV-2, reached a speed of 13,000 mph (21,000 kph)—fast enough to travel from London to Sydney, Australia, in under an hour.

66671

The X-15 couldn't take off like an ordinary plane. The experimental aircraft was carried by a bomber to its cruising altitude. Only then did the X-15 fire up its rocket engines.

4,520 mph
(7,274 kph)

The LZ-130 *Graf Zeppelin II* could carry up to 72 passengers, plus a 40-man crew. With a top speed of 81 mph (131 kph), it had a range of 10,250 miles (16,500 km). The airship was filled with lighter-than-air gas and built to carry passengers across the Atlantic.

The **biggest Zeppelins were 3 times longer** and **6 times wider** than a Jumbo Jet.

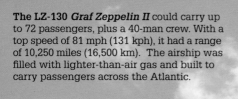

Graf Zeppelin

AIRBUS BELUGA

The Airbus Beluga is designed to carry large or awkwardly shaped cargo. This includes the parts for Airbus airliners, which are made in four different countries and then airlifted for assembly.

The control gondola contained separate control and observation rooms, plus a central navigation area.

Huge windows, which could be opened during flights, ran the length of the passenger decks.

What was the biggest aircraft?

At **804 ft** (245 m) **long**, the **Zeppelin airships** *Graf Zeppelin II* and *Hindenburg*, built in Germany in the 1930s, were the **largest aircraft** ever to take to the skies.

The Boeing 747-400D, launched in 1991, can carry up to 600 passengers, compared to the 72-person capacity of *Graf Zeppelin II*.

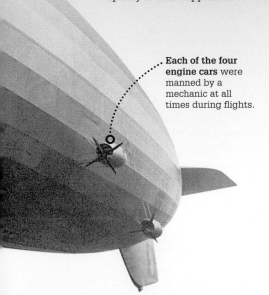

. Each of the four engine cars were manned by a mechanic at all times during flights.

FAST FACTS

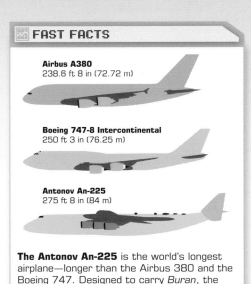

Airbus A380
238.6 ft 8 in (72.72 m)

Boeing 747-8 Intercontinental
250 ft 3 in (76.25 m)

Antonov An-225
275 ft 8 in (84 m)

The Antonov An-225 is the world's longest airplane—longer than the Airbus 380 and the Boeing 747. Designed to carry *Buran*, the Russian Space Shuttle, on its back, it now finds work transporting outsized cargo items.

How **fast** is the **fastest** watercraft?

A record of **318 mph** (511 kph) was set by a **speedboat**, the *Spirit of Australia*, in 1978. It has yet to be broken.

The *Spirit of Australia* is five times faster than *Hydroptère*.

FAST FACTS

Sometimes you can go almost as fast on a board as you can on a boat. The kitesurfing record of 64 mph (103 kph) is close behind the fastest sailing craft, *Sailrocket 2*, and is faster than *Hydroptére*'s 59 mph (95 kph). The fastest windsurfer is almost as fast.

Windsurfer
61.3 mph (99 kph)

Kitesurfer
64 mph (103 kph)

Vestas Sailrocket 2
75 mph (120 kph)

Under each side float of *Hydroptère* is a foil, or wing. Once the boat is at a certain speed, the foils lift it so that it almost flies above the water.

The personal watercraft, or water scooter, is one of the fastest vehicles on water. Its small size, fast speed, and ease of use make it ideal for use by police, lifeguards, and fun seekers.

l'Hydroptère

67 mph (108 kph)

Hydroptère was one of the fastest sailing vessels ever made. The boat was built for speed and its crew aimed to break sailing world speed records.

Hydroptère

59 mph (95 kph)

The *Spirit of Australia* was a jet-powered speed boat driven by Australian Ken Warby.

SPIRIT OF AUSTRALIA
THE WORLDS FASTEST BOAT

318 mph (511 kph)

FOSSEYS

KW2N

FAST FACTS

Harmony of the Seas
1,187 ft (362 m)

Knock Nevis
1,504 ft (458 m)

USS Enterprise (aircraft carrier)
1,123 ft (342 m)

Azzam
590 ft (180 m)

Statue
of Liberty
305 ft
(93 m)

The longest supertanker ever was the *Knock Nevis*, which was broken up in 2010. No longer in use, the USS *Enterprise* was the longest naval ship in the world, but was still shorter than the largest cruise ship, the *Harmony of the Seas*. The *Harmony* is nearly as tall as the Statue of Liberty, and twice the length of the *Azzam*, the largest private yacht.

How **big** is a **supertanker?**

The
TI Oceania is
the same **length**
as **29 yellow
school buses**
placed end
to end.

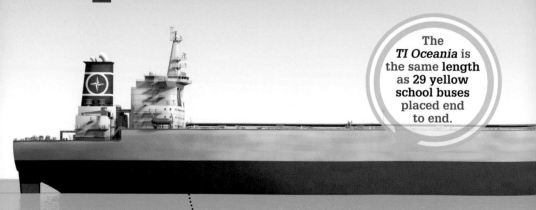

The *Oceania* and its three sister ships are among the largest ever oil tankers to have double hulls—the bottom and sides of the ship have two watertight walls to prevent oil spills in the event of an accident.

HARMONY OF THE SEAS

The world's biggest cruise ship, the *Harmony of the Seas,* can carry up to 5,479 passengers and 2,100 crew. Cruise ships are like floating towns, with movie theaters, stores, restaurants, and swimming pools. The *Harmony* even has a full-size basketball court!

The *Knock Nevis's* **anchor** weighed 40 tons (36 metric tons)—more than seven African bull elephants. It is the only part of the ship that remains.

At **1,246 ft** (380 m) **long** and **223 ft** (68 m) **wide**, the *TI Oceania* is one of the **biggest supertankers** afloat today. It can carry **3 million barrels** of **oil**, and when full it **weighs 486,764 tons** (441,585 metric tons).

TI Oceania **has a top speed** of 16.5 knots (19 mph/31 kph). At this speed it would take 46 seconds for the entire ship to pass someone watching from the shore.

TI OCEANIA

Protective red paint indicates the area of the hull that lies below the water when the supertanker is fully laden.

How **much** can a **ship carry?**

One of the **biggest container ships,** *MSC Oscar*, can carry **19,224** standard size **containers.** It is **1,297 ft** (395.4 m) **long.**

The bridge (from where the captain controls the ship) sits far forward so containers ca be stacked high without the captain losing visibili

MAERSK LINE

Standard containers are used to transport all kinds of goods all over the world, from fruit to clothes and TVs. Each standard container is 20 ft (6.1 m) long and 8 ft (2.44 m) wide, and can be lifted from the ship to fit directly onto a lorry or train.

FAST FACTS

The biggest tankers can carry even more cargo than container ships. The *Knock Nevis* supertanker was 1,504 ft (458 m) long and could hold 4.1 million barrels of oil—enough to fill 260 Olympic swimming pools.

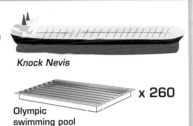

Knock Nevis

x 260

Olympic swimming pool

BLUE MARLIN

Heavy-lift ships, such as the *Blue Marlin*, transport huge structures such as oil rigs or aircraft carriers. The ship can submerge its deck to duck under the structure, then raise it again with the cargo on its back.

If every container were fully loaded, the boat would be too heavy to sail. It can carry a maximum 217,554 tons (197,362 metric tons), or 11 tons (10 metric tons) per container.

At 73 m (240 ft) tall, the *MSC Oscar* is as tall as a 25-story building. It is also 13 times longer than a blue whale, and seven buses could park end-to-end across its 59-m (194-ft) width. It sails between Asia and Europe.

Fully loaded, *MSC Oscar* could carry **38,448 cars** or **920 million cans of soup.**

How **powerful** was the **Space Shuttle?**

The **Shuttle's** three engines and two rocket boosters produced **6.8 million lb** (3.1 million kg) of **thrust**.

Fuel tank full of liquid hydrogen and liquid oxygen.

Two solid rocket boosters provided 71 percent of the thrust needed for liftoff.

The temperature inside the Shuttle's engines reached 6,000°F (3,315°C).

📈 FAST FACTS

The Space Shuttle's three engines could burn the equivalent of 2.4 swimming pools of liquid fuel in a minute—that's 1,000 gallons (3,785 liters) a second.

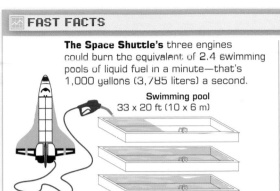

Swimming pool
33 x 20 ft (10 x 6 m)

Space Shuttle

Thrust SSC

The Space Shuttle took just under 40 seconds to reach a speed of 620 mph (1,000 kph). However, the holder of the world land-speed record, the *Thrust SSC* rocket car, reached this speed in 16 seconds—less than half the time taken by the Shuttle.

The Space Shuttle had the same power as 31 Jumbo Jets.

A Boeing 747, or Jumbo Jet, produces 224,000 lb (101,600 kg) of thrust at takeoff.

HEAVY LIFTING

The shuttle weighed around 2,200 tons (2,000 metric tons) at launch. Most of that came from the rockets and fuel needed to propel it fast enough to escape the pull of gravity and enter orbit.

How **far** have **people** been into **space?**

In **1970**, the crew members of the **Apollo 13 Moon mission** traveled a record distance of **248,655 miles** (400,171 km) **from Earth.**

3. A few hours before splashdown, the Service Module was detached and the crew saw for the first time the huge damage that had been caused by the explosion.

4. The Command Module reentered the Earth's atmosphere at a speed of 24,689 mph (39,733 kph).

The Lunar Module is the part of the spacecraft designed to detach in Moon orbit and descend to the Moon's surface.

The Command Module is where the crew sits during the journey to the Moon.

The Service Module contained a rocket motor, fuel, oxygen, and the electrical power supply.

FAST FACTS

Voyager 1 is the farthest-flung human-built object in space. It is 13.1 billion miles (21 billion km) from Earth, and in 2012 became the first craft to leave our solar system.

Solar system

Saturn Uranus Neptune

Pluto

Earth Distance
Solar system distances are measured in AU (Astronomical Units). One AU is the distance between the Earth and the Sun.

Apollo 13's mission was to orbit the Moon 69 miles (111 km) from its surface, traveling the same distance as previous Apollo Moon missions. Some crew members were going to land on the Moon's surface. When an explosion disabled the spacecraft, however, the mission changed. The spacecraft had to be sent on a new, longer path around the Moon, just to get the crew home safely.

2. Apollo 13 flew 164 miles (264 km) past the Moon before swinging back on its return path.

The **distance from Earth** reached by **Apollo 13** is equivalent to **10 circuits** of **Earth's equator.**

1. The craft was 204,000 miles (329,000 km) from Earth and 55 hours into its flight when an explosion crippled the Service Module's fuel, power, and oxygen supplies. The mission to land on the Moon had to be aborted.

MISSION CONTROL

In the Apollo 13 Service Module, a fan in an oxygen tank short-circuited, causing the tank to catch fire and explode. Mission controllers on Earth worked out that they could use the Moon's gravity to bring the craft back on course for home.

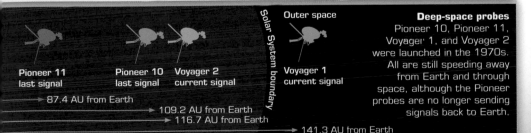

Pioneer 11 last signal

Pioneer 10 last signal

Voyager 2 current signal

Solar System boundary

Outer space

Voyager 1 current signal

→ 87.4 AU from Earth

→ 109.2 AU from Earth
→ 116.7 AU from Earth

→ 141.3 AU from Earth

Deep-space probes
Pioneer 10, Pioneer 11, Voyager 1, and Voyager 2 were launched in the 1970s. All are still speeding away from Earth and through space, although the Pioneer probes are no longer sending signals back to Earth.

Vehicle data

ON AND ON AND ON

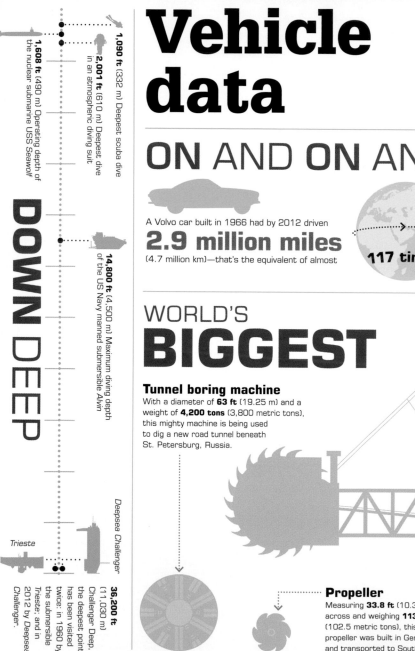

A Volvo car built in 1966 had by 2012 driven

2.9 million miles

(4.7 million km)—that's the equivalent of almost

117 times around the globe.

WORLD'S
BIGGEST

Tunnel boring machine
With a diameter of **63 ft** (19.25 m) and a weight of **4,200 tons** (3,800 metric tons), this mighty machine is being used to dig a new road tunnel beneath St. Petersburg, Russia.

Propeller
Measuring **33.8 ft** (10.3 m) across and weighing **113 tons** (102.5 metric tons), this giant propeller was built in Germany and transported to South Korea.

DOWN DEEP

1,090 ft (332 m) Deepest scuba dive

2,001 ft (610 m) Deepest dive in an atmospheric diving suit

1,608 ft (490 m) Operating depth of the nuclear submarine USS Seawolf

14,800 ft (4,500 m) Maximum diving depth of the US Navy manned submersible Alvin

Trieste

Deepsea Challenger

36,200 ft (11,030 m) Challenger Deep, the deepest point, has been visited twice: in 1960 by the submersible Trieste; and in 2012 by Deepsea Challenger.

LONGEST NON-STOP PASSENGER FLIGHTS

16 HOURS, 10 MINUTES

Doha, Qatar to Auckland, New Zealand: **9,032 miles** (14,535 km)

16 HOURS, 5 MINUTES

Auckland, New Zealand to Dubai: **8,825 miles** (14,203 km)

LONGEST **TRAIN**

• The world's longest train had **682 cars** and eight locomotives. It was used just once, to haul iron ore in Australia in 2001, and it measured **4.57 miles** (7.353 km) long. That's the length of **8.8 Burj Khalifas**, laid end to end.

• The longest passenger train—called the *Ghan*—runs in Australia. It is **0.68 miles** (1.1 km) long and is made up of two locomotives and **44 cars**.

TOTAL AMOUNT OF **RAILROAD** TRACK IN THE **WORLD**

More than **770,262 miles** (1,239,615 km)—over three times the distance from Earth to the Moon.

The three countries with the most railroad track are the US, China, and Russia. Among them, they have just under a third of all the world's track.

US: **139,679 miles** (224,792 km)

China: **75,186 miles** (121,000 km)

Russia: **53,400 miles** (86,000 km)

Land vehicle

An enormous excavator used in the German mining industry, the **Bagger 293** is **738 ft** (225 m) long, **315 ft** (96 m) high, and weighs **15,625 tons** (14,200 metric tons). It can fill 2,400 coal wagons a day.

Human

Animal
The blue whale measures **100 ft** (30 m) long.

How **small** is the **tiniest** computer?

A **miniscule computer** less than the size of a grain of rice can **read temperatures**, **take pictures**, and **record pressure readings**. It is small enough to be **injected into the body** or to **detect pockets of oil** in rock.

FAST FACTS

Computers are getting smaller each year. In 1993, to do 143 GFLOPS (143 billion calculations a second) you needed a computer 5 ft (1.5 m) tall and 25 ft (8 m) long. In 2013 just four laptops exceed this performance.

Intel Paragon supercomputer, 1993
143 GFLOPS

4 Intel i5 laptop processors, 2013
45 GFLOPS each

Moore's Law, invented by Gordon Moore, a founder of Intel, suggests that computers double in perfomance every two years. In fact, the average speed of the 500 fastest computers in the world more than doubled every two years during the decade 2002–2012.

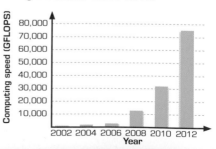

Computing speed (GFLOPS) vs Year, 2002–2012

This miniature device, called the Michigan Micro Mote, could have lots of different uses. As well as being inserted into the body to measure temperature or pressure, or used to find oil, it could also help us avoid losing things in our homes. Sticking the tiny computers onto keys or wallets could help us find these items using a central system.

The computer doesn't have a battery, but uses light as a source of power. It doesn't need to be natural sunlight, so the computer can work indoors.

It would take about 150 of these computers to fill a thimble.

MICROPROCESSORS

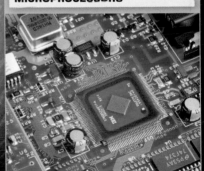

Computers became a lot smaller in 1971 with the invention of the microprocessor—the silicon chip that is the central processing unit of a computer. A silicon chip has a miniature electrical circuit printed on it. These printed circuits are smaller every year.

How many books can you fit on a flash drive?

A **1-terabyte (TB)** flash drive can store the text of **1 million books**. One terabyte is just over **1 million megabytes** (MB), or more than **1 trillion bytes.**

A flash drive weighs less than 1.1 oz (30 g) but can hold 1 TB of data. Flash memory can be erased and reprogrammed thousands of times.

A **1-TB** flash drive could store **1 million 200-page books.**

ATOMIC DATA STORAGE

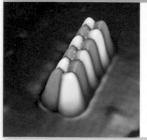

Seen here under a powerful electron microscope is the world's smallest data storage unit. Scientists have used just 12 iron atoms to hold one bit (the basic unit of information), and 96 atoms to hold a byte. A hard disk still needs half a billion atoms per byte.

FAST FACTS

The Library of Congress in Washington, D.C., is the biggest library in the world, containing 35 million books. All the text in those books could be stored on nine 4-TB hard disks.

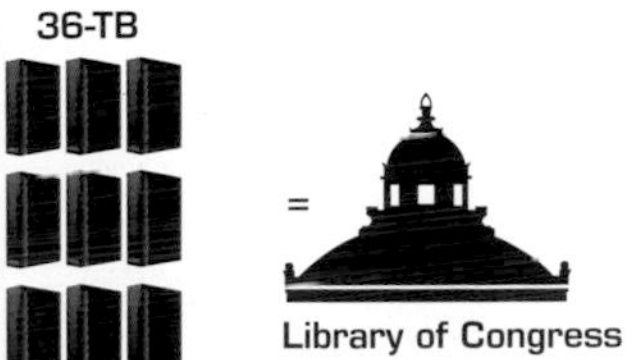

Storage media are getting more sophisticated every few years. Each piece of new technology stores many times more data than the previous one. They are also becoming faster and, because they have no moving parts, smaller and more durable.

3.5" floppy disk 1.44 MB

Zip disk 100 MB

CD 700 MB

DVD 4.7 GB

Dual-layer Blu-ray disk 50 GB

2-TB Flash drive 2 TB

Computer data

SOCIAL **NETWORKS**

In 2007, fewer than **500 million** people around the world used social networking sites, such as Facebook. As of 2017, this figure has grown to more than

2 BILLION.

VIDEO GAME DEVELOPMENT
COST$

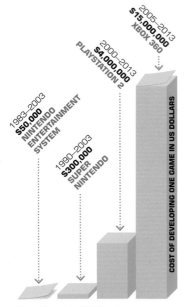

1993–2003
$50,000
NINTENDO ENTERTAINMENT SYSTEM

1990–2003
$300,000
SUPER NINTENDO

2000–2013
$4,000,000
PLAYSTATION 2

2005–2013
$15,000,000
XBOX 360

COST OF DEVELOPING ONE GAME IN US DOLLARS

Since the early 1980s, the **average cost of developing a video game** has increased by more than

30,000%.

COMPUTER MEMORY
GROWTH

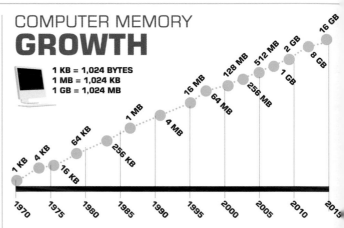

1 KB = 1,024 BYTES
1 MB = 1,024 KB
1 GB = 1,024 MB

1 KB, 4 KB, 16 KB, 64 KB, 256 KB, 1 MB, 4 MB, 16 MB, 64 MB, 128 MB, 256 MB, 512 MB, 1 GB, 2 GB, 8 GB, 16 GB

1970, 1975, 1980, 1985, 1990, 1995, 2000, 2005, 2010, 2015

SUPER
COMPUTER

One of the world's **fastest computers**, the **Tianhe-2**, uses **8,000 kW** of electricity when it is running at full speed. That's equivalent to **1 million** energy-saving 8-watt **lightbulbs**.

PERCENTAGE OF **PEOPLE ONLINE** IN EACH CONTINENT IN 20

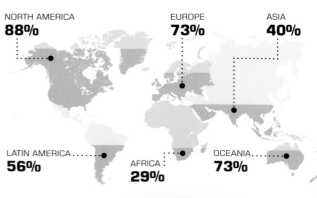

NORTH AMERICA
88%

EUROPE
73%

ASIA
40%

LATIN AMERICA.......
56%

AFRICA
29%

OCEANIA.......
73%

FLOOR SPACE

ENIAC, the world's **first electronic computer**, was built in 1946. It covered **1,798 sq ft** (167 sq m), and could perform

10,000 calculations per second.

Tianhe-2, **one of the fastest computers today**, covers **7,750 sq ft** (720 sq m), and performs

33,860 trillion calculations per second.

MOON LANDING

The **computer** on board the **Apollo 11** spacecraft that landed on the Moon in 1969 had just **72 kb** of memory, of which just **2 kb** was RAM.

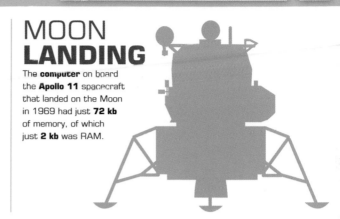

WEBSITE **GROWTH**

Since 1991, the number of websites has grown from 1 to more than 1 billion.

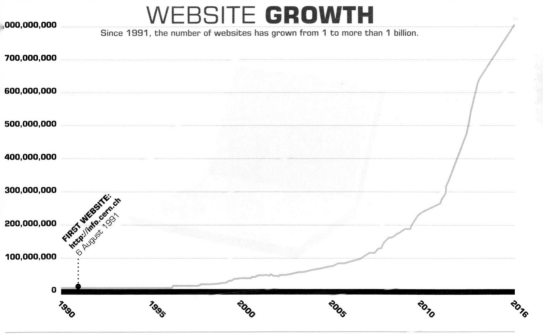

FIRST WEBSITE: http://info.cern.ch 6 August 1991

@YOU'VE GOT MAIL

The **first email** was sent by computer engineer Ray Tomlinson in Cambridge, Massachusetts, in **1971**.

E-BOOK**GROWTH**

Percentage of book sales in the US, the world's biggest book market, that were e-books

2002:	**0.05%**	2009:	**3.17%**
2006:	**0.50%**	2011:	**16.97%**
2008:	**1.18%**	2012:	**22.55%**

In 2012, online booksellers reported that e-books were outselling paper books for the first time.

The Burj Khalifa
has the longest
elevator ride.
You can go from
the lower ground
floor to the 124th
floor at a speed of
22.5 mph (36 kph).

**Express
elevator**
to the
124th floor

Cathedrals were the tallest buildings until the 20th century.
Ulm Minster is the tallest church in the world. Its steeple rises
to 530 ft (161.5 m) and contains 768 steps.

489 ft (149 m)	524 ft (160 m)	516 ft (157 m)	530 ft (161.5 m)
Old St. Paul's Cathedral, 1200	Lincoln Cathedral, 1300	Cologne Cathedral, 1880	Ulm Minster, 1890

The Burj is
nearly twice
as tall as the
**Empire State
Building.**

The Burj Khalifa
contains
6,210 miles
(10,000 km)
of steel and
is covered
in 26,000
glass panels.

How tall is the tallest building?

The **Burj Khalifa** in Dubai stands
2,716 ft (828 m) high. It has
163 floors, used for homes,
offices, and a hotel.

There are 1,860 steps
to the 102nd (top)
floor of the Empire
State Building.

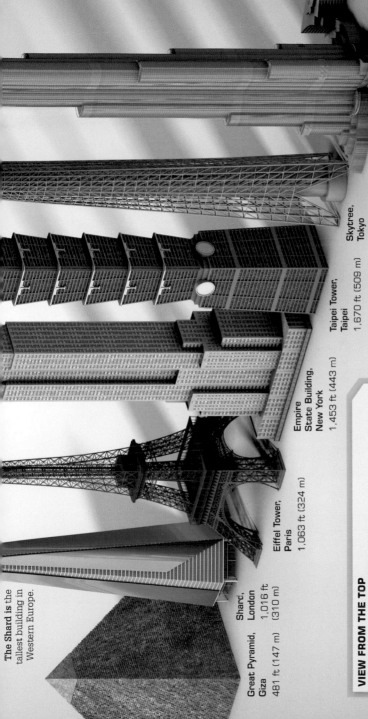

The Shard is the tallest building in Western Europe.

Great Pyramid, Giza
481 ft (147 m)

Shard, London
1,016 ft (310 m)

Eiffel Tower, Paris
1,063 ft (324 m)

Empire State Building, New York
1,453 ft (443 m)

Taipei Tower, Taipei
1,670 ft (509 m)

Skytree, Tokyo
2,080 ft (634 m)

Burj Khalifa, Dubai
2,716 ft (828 m)

Record-breaking buildings seldom hold their record for long. All the structures above were at one time the tallest of their kind. The Burj Khalifa broke all records when it was completed in 2010, but Tokyo's Skytree qualified as the world's tallest tower (because unlike the Burj, it is not strictly a building) when the builders finished it in 2011.

VIEW FROM THE TOP

This is the view from the top of the 700 ft (200 m) spire on the Burj. The spire was built inside the tower and lifted into place. In windy conditions the spire sways by as much as 4 ft (1.2 m).

Around the top of the roof of the London stadium, the lighting towers reach 197 ft (60 m) above the sports area.

You could fit **3 London Olympic stadiums** inside the factory walls.

The Boeing 747 is 64 ft (19 m) high and was the biggest aircraft in the world when the factory was built in the 1960s.

A huge mural on the side of the building covers six doors, each of which is 82 ft (25 m) high and the length of a National Football League (NFL) field.

How **big** is the **biggest building?**

Used for putting airplanes together, **Boeing's Everett Factory** in Seattle has a **volume** of **472 million cu ft** (13.4 million cu m).

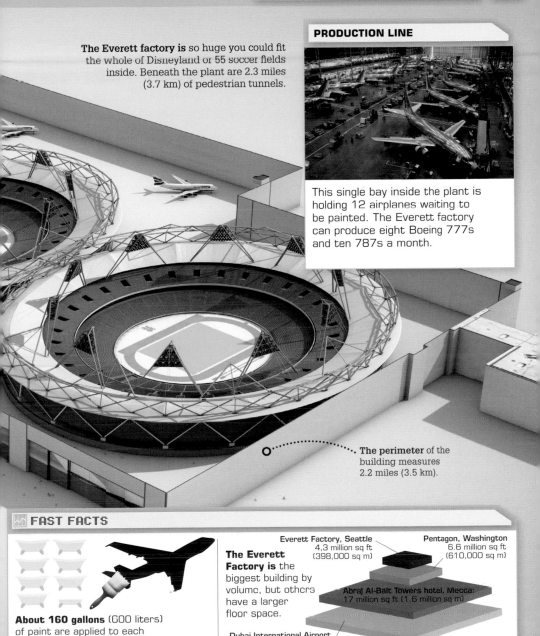

The Everett factory is so huge you could fit the whole of Disneyland or 55 soccer fields inside. Beneath the plant are 2.3 miles (3.7 km) of pedestrian tunnels.

PRODUCTION LINE

This single bay inside the plant is holding 12 airplanes waiting to be painted. The Everett factory can produce eight Boeing 777s and ten 787s a month.

The perimeter of the building measures 2.2 miles (3.5 km).

FAST FACTS

About 160 gallons (600 liters) of paint are applied to each Boeing 747—that is 7.5 bathtubfuls.

The Everett Factory is the biggest building by volume, but others have a larger floor space.

Everett Factory, Seattle
4,3 million sq ft
(398,000 sq m)

Pentagon, Washington
6.6 million sq ft
(610,000 sq m)

Abraj Al-Bait Towers hotel, Mecca:
17 million sq ft (1.6 million sq m)

Dubai International Airport,
Terminal 3: 18.4 million
sq ft (1.71 million sq m)

FAST FACTS

Millau bridge deck
40,000 tons
(36,000 metric tons)

5 x
Eiffel Towers

The bridge's steel deck contains enough steel to make five Eiffel towers. The deck was built in a total of 2,200 separate sections that were welded together into two halves, then pushed out toward each other from opposite sides of the valley.

Each of the longest cables on the viaduct is strong enough to withstand the thrust of eight Boeing 747 airliners at maximum thrust.

How **tall** is the **tallest** bridge?

The Millau Viaduct carries the road from Montpellier, in southern France, to Paris. The bridge is 8,070 ft (2,460 m) long and was opened in 2004.

The **Millau Viaduct**, which spans the valley of the **Tarn River** in **France**, is the **tallest bridge** in the world. Its **largest mast** is **1,125 ft** (343 m) above the base, where it meets the **valley floor**.

The tallest mast is 1,125 ft (343 m) tall. There are seven masts of different heights across the valley. Each holds 11 pairs of stays (metal cables). The stays support the road deck

The Empire State Building measures 1,250 ft (381 m) to its roof. If it sat in the bottom of the valley, the roof would be just 40 ft (12 m) above the bridge's highest point.

LONGEST BRIDGE

The world's longest bridge is the Danyang–Kunshan Grand Bridge in China, at 102.4 miles (164.8 km) long. The bridge is part of the Beijing–Shanghai High-Speed Railroad. Two more of the world's five longest bridges are part of the same railroad line.

The **Millau Viaduct** is almost as tall as the **Empire State Building**.

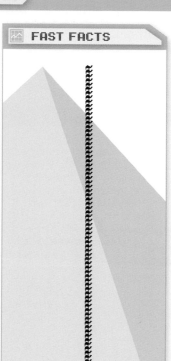

How **heavy** is the **Great** **Pyramid?**

Egypt's **Great Pyramid of Giza**, one of Earth's oldest buildings, weighs **5,750,100 tons** (5,216,400 metric tons).

The **Great Pyramid** weighs the same as 1 Empire Stat Buildings.

The world's tallest building for 3,800 years, the Great Pyramid measures 481 ft (147 m), the same height as a stack of 70 camels.

The largest of the 2,300,000 stones that make up the Great Pyramid weigh 69 tons (63 metric tons)—the weight of 20 African bull elephants.

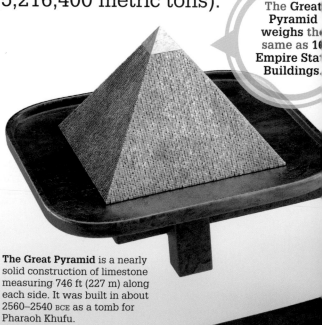

The Great Pyramid is a nearly solid construction of limestone measuring 746 ft (227 m) along each side. It was built in about 2560–2540 BCE as a tomb for Pharaoh Khufu.

The Empire State Building has a steel frame covered with concrete and glass. Unlike the pyramid, it isn't solid, being 102 floors of mainly office space.

To the top of its spire, the Empire State Building measures 1,453 ft (443 m) tall. When it was finished in 1931, it was the world's tallest building.

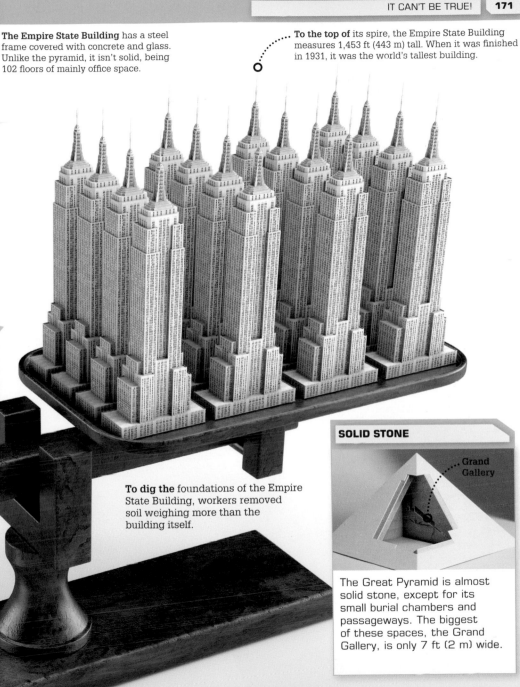

To dig the foundations of the Empire State Building, workers removed soil weighing more than the building itself.

SOLID STONE

Grand Gallery

The Great Pyramid is almost solid stone, except for its small burial chambers and passageways. The biggest of these spaces, the Grand Gallery, is only 7 ft (2 m) wide.

How **deep** can we **dig?**

The **deepest ever human-made hole** is the **Kola Superdeep Borehole**, which was begun in 1970. **By 1994**, when the project was abandoned, the hole was more than **7.5 miles** (12 km) **deep**.

The center of the Earth is 3,959 miles (6,371 km) below the surface. A journey there would begin with between 3 and 44 miles (5 and 70 km) of crust. Below this are the fluid rocks of the mantle and the liquid-metal outer core. Each of these layers is more than 1,200 miles (2,000 km) thick. The inner core is 794 miles (1,278 km) across.

The **deepest ever man-made hole** did **not even break through** the Earth's thinnest, outermost layer—the **crust**.

Kola Superdeep Borehole (Russia) 7.62 miles (12.262 km)

Mantle

Outer core

Inner core

Crust

Mantle

The boundary between the Earth's crust and mantle in Russia's Kola Peninsula is at a depth of about 22 miles (35 km).

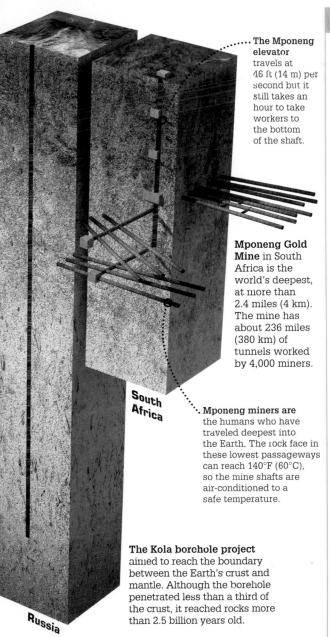

The Mponeng elevator travels at 46 ft (14 m) per second but it still takes an hour to take workers to the bottom of the shaft.

Mponeng Gold Mine in South Africa is the world's deepest, at more than 2.4 miles (4 km). The mine has about 236 miles (380 km) of tunnels worked by 4,000 miners.

Mponeng miners are the humans who have traveled deepest into the Earth. The rock face in these lowest passageways can reach 140°F (60°C), so the mine shafts are air-conditioned to a safe temperature.

South Africa

Russia

The Kola borehole project aimed to reach the boundary between the Earth's crust and mantle. Although the borehole penetrated less than a third of the crust, it reached rocks more than 2.5 billion years old.

FAST FACTS

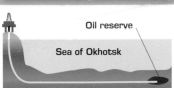

Oil reserve

Sea of Okhotsk

Kola is still the world's deepest borehole, but it is no longer the longest. In 2012, Exxon drilled an oil well 40,604 ft (12,376 m) long. Parts of it run horizontally, however, so it is not quite as deep.

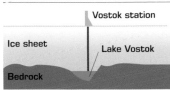

Vostok station

Ice sheet

Lake Vostok

Bedrock

In 1989, Russian scientists began a project to drill through 2 miles (3 km) of Antarctic ice to reach Lake Vostok, a freshwater lake that had lain sealed under the ice for more than 15 million years. In 2012, the scientists reached their goal.

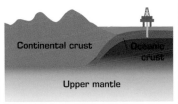

Continental crust

Oceanic crust

Upper mantle

Scientists almost broke through the crust where is it very thin, at less than 3.4 miles (5.5 km), in the ocean off Costa Rica. Oceanic crust is always thinner than continental crust, which forms the Earth's landmasses and is 15–45 miles (25–70 km) thick.

How **much** **gold** is there?

From **ancient times** to the **present day**, experts estimate that just **188,800 tons** (171,300 metric tons) of **gold** have been dug out of the ground.

GOLD NUGGETS

A nugget is a naturally occurring lump of gold. Most nuggets are small—but not all of them. This top shelf shows a model of the Welcome Stranger nugget, found in Australia in 1869 and weighing about 173 lb (78 kg).

A tennis court is 78 ft (23.78 m) long.

A ball the width of a tennis court might not sound big enough for 188,800 tons (171,300 metric tons) of gold, but gold is a very heavy metal. Two solid gold house bricks would weigh as much as an adult person.

The ball may look like a lot of gold, but this is all the gold that has ever been mined anywhere on Earth, since the beginning of history. Every day, the world produces enough iron to make more than 40 iron balls the same size!

All the world's **mined gold** would make a **solid ball 78 ft 9 in (24 m)** across.

FAST FACTS

Percentage of metals in Earth's crust

Aluminum 8.1%
Iron 5%
Gold 0.0000004%

Gold is much rarer than iron or aluminum, which make up large percentages of the Earth's crust. Gold is valuable because it is so rare, but also because it never rusts or tarnishes.

Gold left in the ground

Mined Gold

We have already mined about 80 percent of the world's recoverable gold. Only 51,000 tons (46,000 metric tons) of the gold left in the ground could be extracted with existing technology.

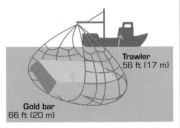

Trawler 56 ft (17 m)

Gold bar 66 ft (20 m)

Seawater contains dissolved gold. There may be up to 16,500 tons (15,000 metric tons) of it in the world's oceans. If this gold could be extracted, it would make a bar measuring 66 ft x 33 ft x 13 ft (20 m x 10 m x 4 m).

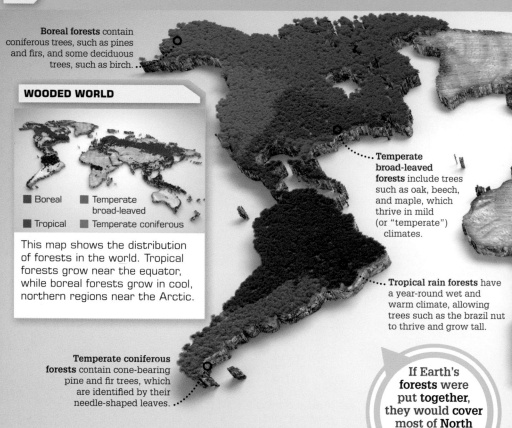

Boreal forests contain coniferous trees, such as pines and firs, and some deciduous trees, such as birch.

WOODED WORLD

- ■ Boreal
- ■ Temperate broad-leaved
- ■ Tropical
- ■ Temperate coniferous

This map shows the distribution of forests in the world. Tropical forests grow near the equator, while boreal forests grow in cool, northern regions near the Arctic.

Temperate broad-leaved forests include trees such as oak, beech, and maple, which thrive in mild (or "temperate") climates.

Tropical rain forests have a year-round wet and warm climate, allowing trees such as the brazil nut to thrive and grow tall.

Temperate coniferous forests contain cone-bearing pine and fir trees, which are identified by their needle-shaped leaves.

If Earth's forests were put together, they would cover most of North and South America.

How **many** **trees** are there?

Forests cover nearly **one-third** of our planet's land. There are an estimated **3 trillion** trees on Earth, but **billions** of trees are being **lost every year** through deforestation.

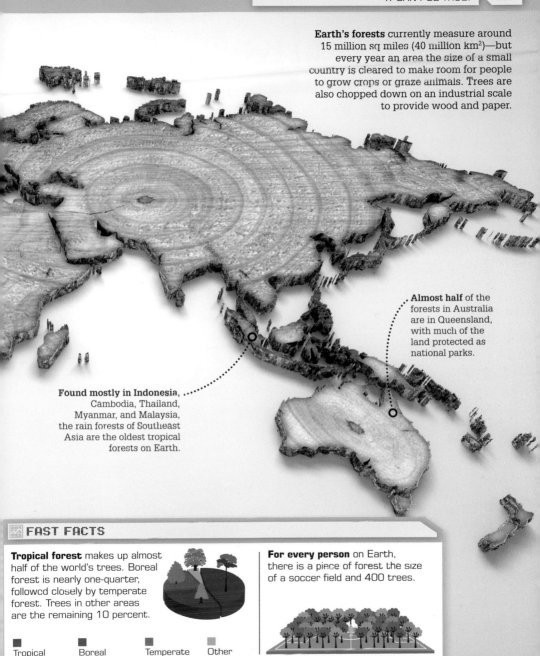

Earth's forests currently measure around 15 million sq miles (40 million km²)—but every year an area the size of a small country is cleared to make room for people to grow crops or graze animals. Trees are also chopped down on an industrial scale to provide wood and paper.

Almost half of the forests in Australia are in Queensland, with much of the land protected as national parks.

Found mostly in Indonesia, Cambodia, Thailand, Myanmar, and Malaysia, the rain forests of Southeast Asia are the oldest tropical forests on Earth.

FAST FACTS

Tropical forest makes up almost half of the world's trees. Boreal forest is nearly one-quarter, followed closely by temperate forest. Trees in other areas are the remaining 10 percent.

Tropical   Boreal   Temperate   Other

For every person on Earth, there is a piece of forest the size of a soccer field and 400 trees.

What's the **longest mountain range?**

The **Mid-Ocean Ridge mountain chain** is **40,400 miles** (65,000 km) long, but almost all of it lies **deep** in the ocean.

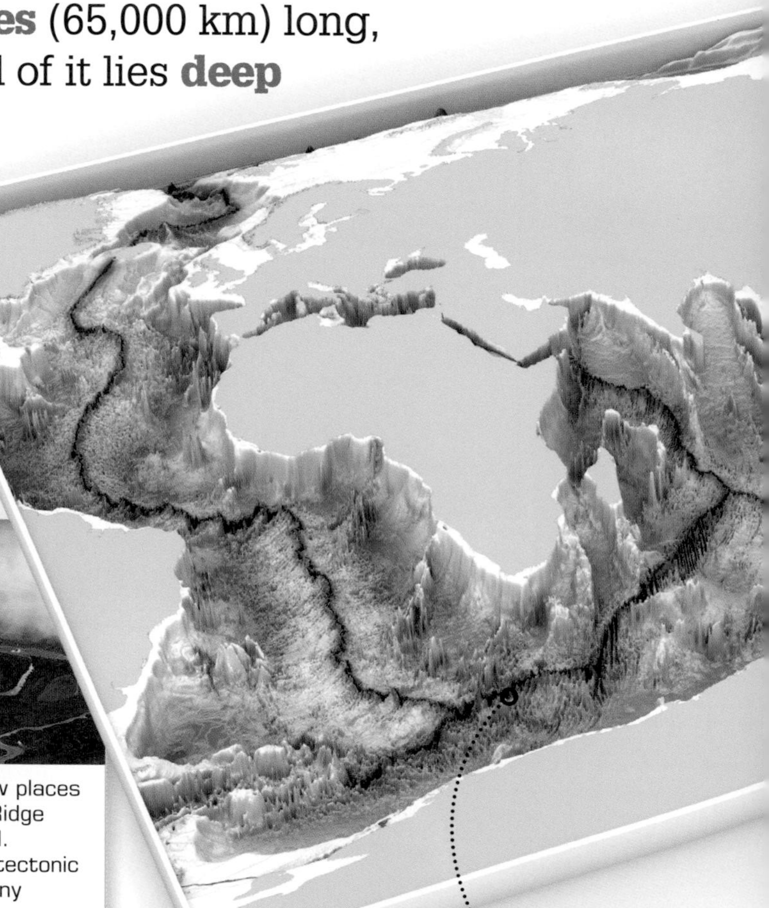

FIRE AND ICE

Iceland is one of the few places where the Mid-Ocean Ridge appears above sea level. Because of the ridge's tectonic activity, Iceland has many active volcanoes, such as Bardarbunga. This erupted for six months in 2014–2015.

Much of the Mid-Ocean Ridge remains unmapped, and existing charts may not be accurate because it is hard to map the seafloor.

The Mid-Ocean Ridge system formed along the joins between tectonic plates (sections of Earth's crust), which move continually. When the plates pull apart, magma from inside Earth's mantle comes to the surface and hardens into mountains.

The **Mid-Ocean Ridge system is** more than **nine times longer** than the **Andes.**

The Andes is the longest mountain range on land, stretching 4,350 miles (7,000 km) through seven countries in South America.

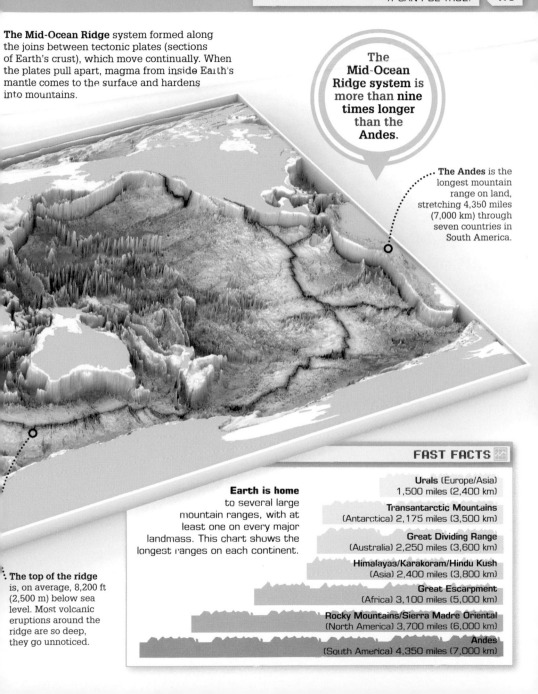

The top of the ridge is, on average, 8,200 ft (2,500 m) below sea level. Most volcanic eruptions around the ridge are so deep, they go unnoticed.

Earth is home to several large mountain ranges, with at least one on every major landmass. This chart shows the longest ranges on each continent.

FAST FACTS

Urals (Europe/Asia)
1,500 miles (2,400 km)

Transantarctic Mountains
(Antarctica) 2,175 miles (3,500 km)

Great Dividing Range
(Australia) 2,250 miles (3,600 km)

Himalayas/Karakoram/Hindu Kush
(Asia) 2,400 miles (3,800 km)

Great Escarpment
(Africa) 3,100 miles (5,000 km)

Rocky Mountains/Sierra Madre Oriental
(North America) 3,700 miles (6,000 km)

Andes
(South America) 4,350 miles (7,000 km)

How **big** is the **Pacific Ocean?**

The **Pacific** is Earth's **largest ocean**, covering about **one-third** of our planet's surface. Its area is about **62.5 million sq miles** (161,760,000 km²).

North America

South America

Pacific Ocean

All the continents on Earth could fit inside the **Pacific Basin**.

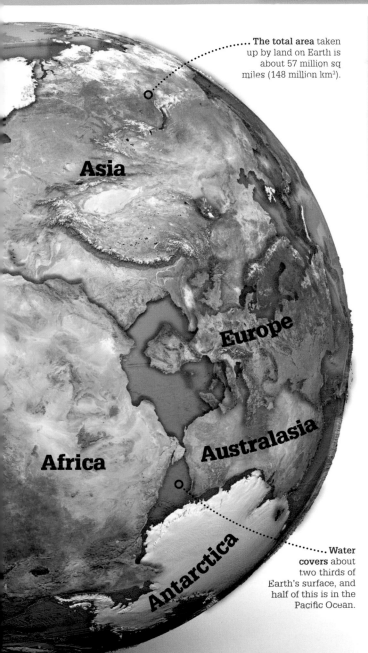

... **The total area** taken up by land on Earth is about 57 million sq miles (148 million km³).

Africa

Asia

Europe

Australasia

Antarctica

.... **Water covers** about two thirds of Earth's surface, and half of this is in the Pacific Ocean.

PLASTIC PACIFIC

The Great Pacific Garbage Patch is an area up to 7 million sq miles (15 million km²) that contains trash—mostly plastic—that has been dumped in the ocean and swept together by the currents.

The Pacific Basin is slowly shrinking due to tectonic movement: some of the plates (pieces of Earth's crust) that make up the ocean floor are sliding under the continental plates that make up the land.

FAST FACTS

The Ring of Fire is a zone around the edge of the Pacific that contains more than three-quarters of the world's volcanoes. Nine out of 10 earthquakes also take place here.

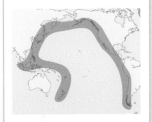

How much **salt** is in the **sea?**

If all the **salt** could be extracted from the **oceans** and put on **land**, it would cover the surface in a **layer** of salt **500 ft** (150 m) **thick**.

The world's oceans are salty because salt from the land enters the water as rivers pick up salt on the underlying rocks and soil and deposit it into the sea.

The total surface area of all the land on Earth is approximately 57.5 million sq miles (149 million km²).

FAST FACTS

Salt makes up about 0.4 percent of a person's body weight. A 110-lb (50-kg) person has about ½ lb (200 g) of salt—that's 40 teaspoons.

A huge salt mine lies under the city of Detroit, Michigan. It is deep enough for New York's Chrysler Building to fit inside.

1,200 ft (366 m)

A cup of water from the Dead Sea—the world's saltiest water—has seven times more salt than a cup of water from the world's oceans.

PALACE OF SALT

The largest salt flat in the world is Salar de Uyuni in Bolivia, measuring 4,086 square miles (10,582 km²). This abundance of salt has led to a hotel constructed entirely from salt blocks. Palacio de Sal ("Palace of Salt") opened in 2007 with walls, floors, ceilings, and furniture all made from salt.

> **Salt from the oceans could create a crust on land taller than the Great Pyramid.**

500 ft (150 m)

The salt crust would be the equivalent height of a 40-story office building.

The Great Pyramid of Giza in Egypt was completed in 2540 BCE.

Great Pyramid 482 ft (147 m) tall

How much rain falls in a year?

Planet Earth is a **wet world**, with a **total rainfall** of **121,000 cu miles** (505,000 km³). This includes other **precipitation**, such as sleet, snow, and hail.

When heavy rainfall makes a river burst its banks or causes water levels to rise, the resulting flood can destroy buildings and roads, and there is a risk to life.

Collected together, Earth's annual precipitation would form a ball 61.4 miles (98.8 km) high.

FAST FACTS

Raindrops are not drop-shaped.

They are round when they start falling from the sky...

... But they change to a shape more like a hamburger bun as they collect and absorb other droplets on their way down to the ground.

The average depth of rain across the whole planet for 1 year is almost 39 in (1 m)—about the height of a three-year-old child. However, less rain falls on land than over the oceans: on land, the average is 28 in (71.5cm).

Earth's **yearly rainfall** makes a **sphere 11 times** the **height** of **Everest**.

Mount Everest's summit stands 29,029 ft (8,848 m) above sea level. It is the *highest* peak on Earth, but not the *tallest*: that is Mauna Kea, which is more than 33,000 ft (10,000 m) tall, but stands on the seabed so rises only 13,800 ft (4,205 m) above sea level.

How **heavy** is a **cloud?**

Scientists estimate that the **weight** of **water vapor** in a fluffy white **cumulus cloud** is **0.02 oz** (0.5 g) for every **35 cubic feet** (1 cubic meter) of cloud. This means that a ¼ **cubic mile** (1 km³) cloud weighs **550 tons** (500 metric tons).

A typical **cumulus cloud weighs** slightly more than **two Boeing 787 Dreamliners.**

··· **The Boeing 787 Dreamliner** has a maximum takeoff weight of 250 tons (228 metric tons).

TURBULENT TIMES

Air rises and falls inside clouds, creating swirling hot and cold currents. This can cause turbulence when airplanes fly through them, making the craft wobble and lose altitude.

If a cloud is heavier than two aircraft, it is hard to imagine how it can float. The reason it does so is because the air underneath the cloud is denser than the cloud, and so holds it up. The weight of a cloud is spread out over billions of tiny water droplets. As these become heavier, the cloud breaks up and falls as rain.

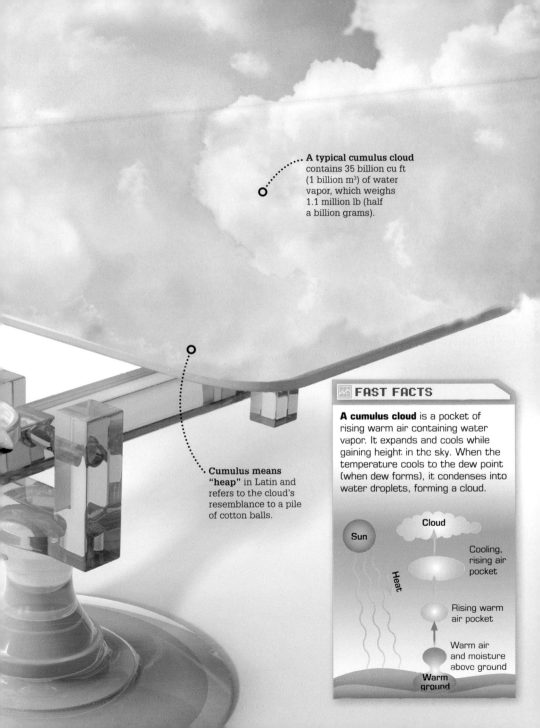

A typical cumulus cloud
contains 35 billion cu ft
(1 billion m³) of water
vapor, which weighs
1.1 million lb (half
a billion grams).

**Cumulus means
"heap"** in Latin and
refers to the cloud's
resemblance to a pile
of cotton balls.

📈 FAST FACTS

A cumulus cloud is a pocket of
rising warm air containing water
vapor. It expands and cools while
gaining height in the sky. When the
temperature cools to the dew point
(when dew forms), it condenses into
water droplets, forming a cloud.

Sun

Cloud

Cooling,
rising air
pocket

Heat

Rising warm
air pocket

Warm air
and moisture
above ground

Warm
ground

How much **electricity** is in a **lightning bolt?**

Physicists estimate that more than **5 billion joules (J)** of energy are released in a **lightning bolt**— enough to meet the **monthly needs** of a **household**.

Making toast from lightning bolts is an impossible dream because the energy cannot be harnessed. No one can predict where lightning will strike, and the energy cannot be stored and converted into the safe "alternating current" used in houses.

THUNDERSTORMS

Much of the energy in lightning is released as heat. This warms up the surrounding air, which expands quickly and creates the sound of thunder.

One **lightning bolt** could, in theory, toast **100,000** slices of **bread**.

FAST FACTS

At 30,000 Kelvin (53,540 °F/ 29,730 °C), a lightning bolt is five times hotter than the surface of the Sun, which is 6,000 Kelvin (10,340 °F/5,730 °C).

The electricity in lightning moves at a superfast speed of 62 million mph (38.5 million kph).

In theory, 5 billion joules could power a 1,000-watt toaster for 1,400 hours, which is 1 minute, 40 seconds to toast two slices.

How long would it take to fall to the center of Earth?

Even though it is a physical impossibility, calculations suggest it would take about **19 minutes** to fall to Earth's core, traveling at up to **18,000 mph (29,000 kph)**.

Why is it impossible? First, no one could dig a tunnel through Earth to its core. This calculation also assumes there is no air resistance in the tunnel: resistance would make the falling speed slower. Finally, if someone actually made it close to the center of Earth, the extremely hot temperatures would kill that person instantly.

Earth's crust consists of a variety of different types of rock on land and under the sea.

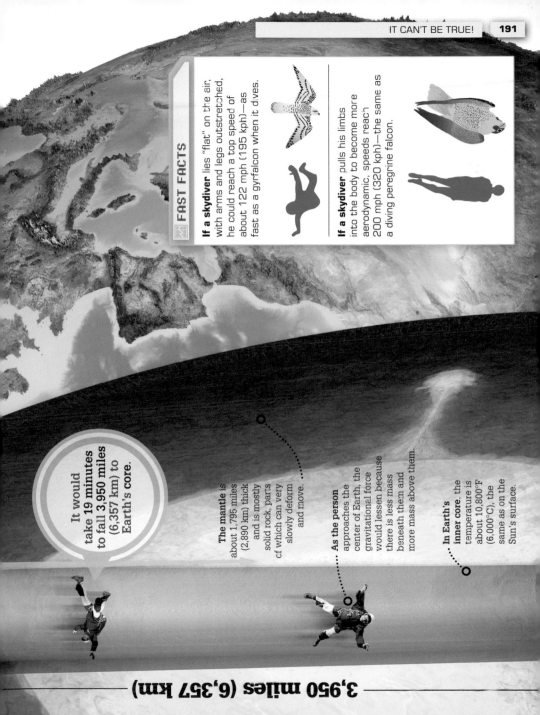

FAST FACTS

If a skydiver lies "flat" on the air, with arms and legs outstretched, he could reach a top speed of about 122 mph (195 kph)—as fast as a gyrfalcon when it dives.

If a skydiver pulls his limbs into the body to become more aerodynamic, speeds reach 200 mph (320 kph)—the same as a diving peregrine falcon.

It would take 19 minutes to fall 3,950 miles (6,357 km) to Earth's core.

The mantle is about 1,795 miles (2,890 km) thick and is mostly solid rock, parts of which can very slowly deform and move.

As the person approaches the center of Earth, the gravitational force would lessen because there is less mass beneath them and more mass above them.

In Earth's inner core, the temperature is about 10,800°F (6,000°C), the same as on the Sun's surface.

3,950 miles (6,357 km)

Earth data

MASSIVE VOLCANO

THE LARGEST SHIELD VOLCANO

on Earth is *under the Pacific Ocean,* **1,000 miles** (1,600 km) east of Japan. **Tamu Massif** covers *120,000 sq miles* (10,800 km²)—the same area as Thailand.

THE LARGEST ONLAND VOLCANO,

Mauna Loa, is one-sixtieth of Tamu Massif's size at **2,000 sq miles** (5,180 km³) in area.

Mauna Loa

EARTH'S *MAGNETIC* FIELD

▶ Earth's **magnetic field** is created by the molten iron in Earth's outer core moving around. As the molten iron moves, so does the magnetic field.

▶ Earth's **magnetic poles** move about 10 miles (16 km) a year. Since the early 19th century, magnetic north has moved northward by more than **600 miles** (1,000 km). In recent years the speed has increased to **24 miles** (40 km) per year.

▶ Every **few hundred thousand years**, the magnetic poles reverse. When this happens, if you held a compass with the needle *pointing to "N,"* it would actually be *pointing south.* These reversals take hundreds or thousands of years—the last one occurred about **780,000** years ago.

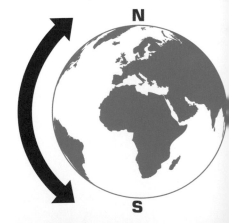

EARTH'S ROTATION

• The Earth takes **24 hours** to complete **one rotation** on its axis—in other words, one day. At the **equator** (24,900 miles/40,075 km long), the speed of the Earth's rotation is **1,040 mph** (1,675 kph)—roughly *twice the speed* of a cruising **airliner**.

• The time taken for each of Earth's rotations is **decreasing**, by about **1.4 milliseconds per 100 years**. At the moment, scientists adjust for this by adding **"leap seconds"** to standard time every few years.

Tajikistan is the highest country in the world, with an average elevation of **10,453 ft** (3,186 m) above sea level.

highest
AND
LOWEST

The world's **lowest country** is the Maldives, which is a tiny **6 ft** (1.8 m) above sea level—the height of an average man.

DRIEST PLACES

• The **driest** place on Earth is in **Antarctica**. The **McMurdo Dry Valleys** region has been almost completely swept free of ice by the extreme winds rushing over the landscape, melting any snow and ice.

• The **driest** non-polar area is the **Atacama Desert**, in Chile, which has an average of only 0.04 in (1 mm) of rain a year. Some parts of the desert have seen no rainfall for centuries.

BIOMASS

The biomass (the total mass of living things in a particular ecosystem) of adult humans on Earth has been estimated as **365 million tons** (332 million metric tons). We are **outweighed** by tiny Antarctic krill, which have an estimated total biomass of **420 million tons** (380 million metric tons).

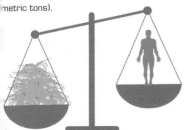

SPEEDY
TSUNAMI

A **tsunami** (which is Japanese for *"harbor wave"*) can cross the

Pacific Ocean

in less than a day. It zips across the water at up to

600 mph
(970 kph), which is faster than a

Boeing 777.

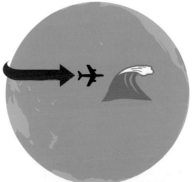

How far away is the Moon?

The average distance from Earth to the Moon is **237,675 miles** (382,500 km), but this can grow to **251,655 miles** (405,000 km) when they are at their **farthest apart**.

The rest of **planets in the solar system** could **fit between Earth** and the Moon.

Together with Earth, Mercury, Venus, and Mars are the four rocky planets.

From Earth...

Jupiter is a gas giant and the largest planet in the solar system. About 1,300 Earths could fit inside Jupiter.

FAST FACTS

The Moon's orbit around Earth is not circular, so its distance from Earth varies. If you drove to the Moon in a car at 70 mph (110 kph), it would take 133 days (4½ months) to arrive when the Moon is closest to Earth (at its perigee), or 149 days (5 months) when it is farthest away (at its apogee).

Perigee
233,700 miles
(360,000 km)

Apogee
251,655 miles
(405,000 km)

Added together, the diameters of Mercury, Venus, Mars, Jupiter, Saturn, Uranus, and Neptune total about 241,000 miles (388,000 km). They could easily fit between Earth and the Moon when they are at their farthest apart.

MOON FACE

Early astronomers mistook the dark areas of the Moon for water and called them "maria" (Latin for "seas"). They are ancient impact craters filled with solidified lava. The lighter areas are highland regions.

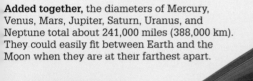

The Moon has about one-quarter of Earth's diameter.

Neptune is freezing cold, with some of the strongest winds in the solar system.

Uranus is blue because of methane gas in its atmosphere.

Saturn takes about 10 hours and 33 minutes to rotate on its axis. Earth takes 24 hours.

... to the Moon

How **high** can you **jump** in space?

The pull of **gravity** in **space** changes depending where you are. It's so weak on the **Moon**, you could **jump 5 ft 11 in** (181.4 cm) compared to just **12 in** (30 cm) on **Earth**.

The Moon has only one-eightieth of Earth's mass and its gravitational pull is 83 percent less.

Gravity on the Sun's surface is almost 30 times that on Earth. If you tried to jump, it would pull you back down.

Mercury has only about 38 percent of the gravity on Earth, so you can jump much higher.

Jumping on our planet results in a small lift before gravity pulls you back down to Earth.

SUN	**MERCURY**	**VENUS**	**EARTH**	**MOON**	**MARS**
0.42 inches	31 inches	13 inches	12 inches	71½ inches	31½ inches
(1.07 cm)	(79 cm)	(33.2 cm)	(30 cm)	(181.4 cm)	(79.8 cm)

FAST FACTS

Weight varies on other planets because of the gravitational pull: the stronger the pull, the more you weigh. This chart compares the weight of a 70-lb (32-kg) child in house bricks. On Earth he would weigh 14 bricks, but on the Sun he would weigh 28 times as much (if he could survive there).

Weight comparable in numbers of house bricks

400 — 350 — 300 — 250 — 200 — 150 — 100 — 50 — 0

Earth Moon Sun Mercury Venus Mars Jupiter Saturn Uranus Neptune

If everyone on Earth jumped at the same time, the force would move our planet the slightest amount—$1/100$ of the width of a hydrogen atom—before moving back to where it was!

You can jump higher on the Moon than on any planet in the solar system.

FLOATING FREE

An orbiting spacecraft falls toward Earth, pulled by gravity. It also has a horizontal speed, so it ends up circling Earth. Because no force opposes the falling, astronauts on board the craft feel weightless and seem to float.

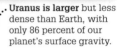

Uranus is larger but less dense than Earth, with only 86 percent of our planet's surface gravity.

On supersized planet Jupiter, gravity is more than twice that of Earth, pulling you back down after only a small jump.

Saturn's gravity is only slightly more than that on Earth, so the jumping height is about the same.

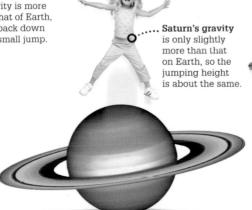

JUPITER
4¾ inches
(11.9 cm)

SATURN
11 inches
(28 cm)

URANUS
13½ inches
(33.7 cm)

NEPTUNE
10½ inches
(26.3 cm)

What is the hottest planet?

You might think that the **hottest planet** would be **Mercury**, as it is closest to the **Sun**, but the average surface temperature of **Venus** is **higher**, at **867.2°F (464°C)**.

This chart shows the average temperatures at the solid surface of the rocky planets (Mercury, Venus, Earth, and Mars) and near the top of the atmosphere for the gas giants (Jupiter, Saturn, Uranus, and Neptune).

Venus is so hot because its very thick atmosphere of unbroken clouds traps the Sun's heat.

The average temperature on Venus is 808.2°F (459°C) higher than on Earth.

Beneath Saturn's hazy surface are strong winds and fierce storms.

Earth is just the right distance from the Sun for water to be liquid. Oceans cover two-thirds of the planet's surface.

**Venus
867.2°F
464°C**

**Fahrenheit
°F**

**Mercury
332.6°F
167°C**

**Centigrade
°C**

900
800
700
600
500
400
300

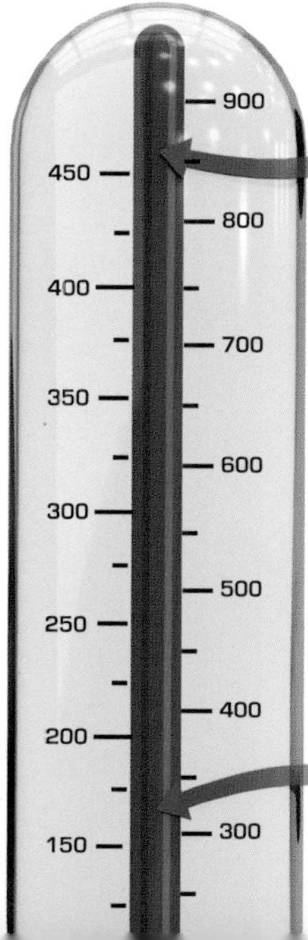

450
400
350
300
250
200
150

**Jupiter
–166°F
–110°C**

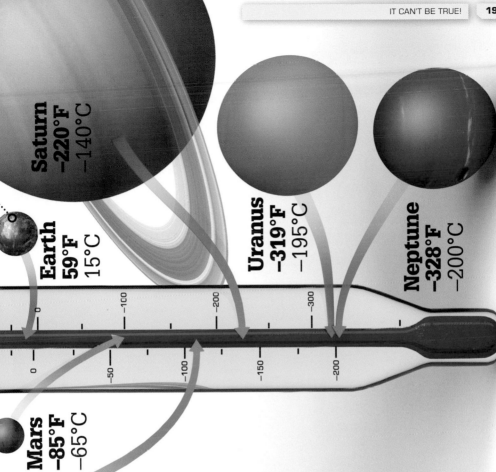

**Saturn
-220°F
-140°C**

**Earth
59°F
15°C**

**Uranus
-319°F
-195°C**

**Neptune
-328°F
-200°C**

**Mars
-85°F
-65°C**

Cloudy spots on Jupiter are storms, which can rage for years.

FAST FACTS

The hottest planet yet discovered outside our solar system, called KELT-9b, has a mind-melting surface temperature of 7,820°F (4,327°C) —hotter than most stars, and only slightly cooler than our Sun.

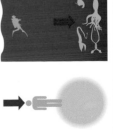

7,800°F (4,316°C)

KELT-9b

9,941°F (5,505°C)

Sun

The pressure of Venus's atmosphere at its surface is 92 times the pressure at Earth's surface. It is the same as Earth's water pressure at 3,000 ft (900 m) under the sea.

What's the most **massive planet?**

At **4,184,000,000,000,000,000,000,000,000 lb** (1,898,000,000,000,000,000,000,000,000 kg), **Jupiter** has the biggest planetary mass. If **Earth's mass** is represented by **one orange**, **Jupiter** is represented by **eight crates** of oranges.

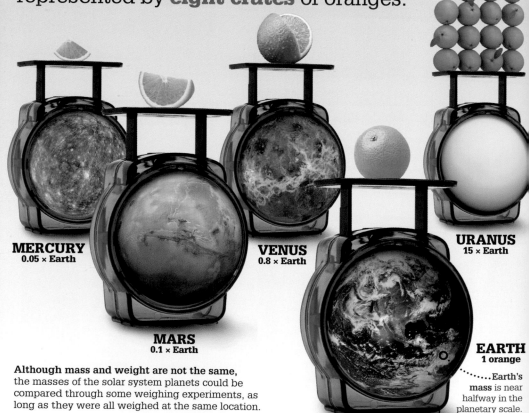

MERCURY
0.05 × Earth

VENUS
0.8 × Earth

URANUS
15 × Earth

MARS
0.1 × Earth

EARTH
1 orange

........Earth's **mass** is near halfway in the planetary scale.

Although mass and weight are not the same, the masses of the solar system planets could be compared through some weighing experiments, as long as they were all weighed at the same location.

FAST FACTS

The Sun is by far the most massive object in the solar system, making up 99.86 percent of the entire solar system's mass, including all the planets, asteroids, and moons. Its mass is 4,385,000,000,000,000,000,000,000,000,000 lb (1,989,000,000,000,000,000,000,000,000,000 kg) or 333,000 Earths.

Sun's mass

Mass of everything else in the solar system

Each crate here contains approximately 40 oranges.

JUPITER
318 × Earth

SATURN
95 × Earth

The most massive planet is **Jupiter**, which has **318 times** the mass of **Earth**.

NEPTUNE
17 × Earth

How **big** is **Pluto?**

Pluto is the **largest dwarf planet**, measuring **6,427,805 sq miles** (16,647,940 km²)— just **3.3 percent** of **Earth's area**.

Pluto is currently more than 3 billion miles (5 billion km) from Earth. A NASA spacecraft flew past Pluto in 2015, having set off from Earth in 2006. Light takes eight minutes to reach the Earth from the Sun, but at least four hours to travel from Pluto to Earth.

Pluto was downgraded from a planet to a dwarf planet—a round object in the solar system that is bigger than a comet or asteroid, but not planet-sized, and orbits the Sun. ...

📈 FAST FACTS

There are five recognized dwarf planets in the solar system. Pluto and Eris are almost the same size, but Haumea, Makemake, and Ceres are smaller. Experts estimate there may be more than 100 dwarf planets yet to be found.

Earth's Moon 2,158 miles (3,474 km)

Pluto 1,470 miles (2,372 km)

Eris 1,445 miles (2,326 km)

Haumea 892 miles (1,436 km)

Makemake 882 miles (1,420 km)

Ceres 592 miles (952 km)

Dwarf planet diameters

ICY WORLD

Pluto's icy surface is made of frozen gases. This dwarf planet is very cold, with average surface temperatures of −393°F (−236°C). A mix of rock and ice makes up the interior.

Pluto is small enough to fit between San Francisco, California, and Austin, Texas.

How **large** are **Saturn's rings?**

Saturn is the solar system's **second largest** planet, just over **nine times** the diameter of Earth. It is instantly recognizable by its **huge rings**, which are more than **174,000 miles** (280,000 km) wide.

There are seven main rings, with each one made up of hundreds of smaller ringlets.

The Cassini gap, named after its discoverer, is 2,900 miles (4,700 km) wide: big enough for Canada to fit inside.

Saturn's rings are made up of billions of pieces of ice and rock, ranging in size from tiny dust particles to huge lumps bigger than a house. Jupiter, Neptune, and Uranus also have rings, but they are much smaller.

📈 FAST FACTS

There is room to fit 764 Earths inside Saturn.

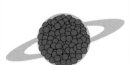

If you drove a car nonstop across Saturn's rings at 30 mph (50 kph), the journey would take 58 days.

Moon

Orbit | Saturn

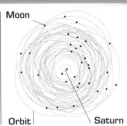

Saturn has 62 known moons. Many small, outer moons travel along tilted orbits far outside the planet's rings.

Beneath the haze around Saturn are strong winds and raging storms.

More than **21 Earths could fit across the diameter of Saturn's rings.**

RINGED WONDER

In 2009, a supersized ring of dust grains was discovered beyond Saturn's main rings. It covers an area almost 7,000 times larger than Saturn.

How **big** is **Comet P67/C-G?**

Comet P67/Churyumov Gerasimenko is **2.7 miles** (4.6 km) **long** and **2.5 miles** (4.1 km) **tall** at its biggest.

COMET COLOR

In space, the comet looks pale because it reflects sunlight in the darkness. If the comet were on Earth, it would appear dark against our lighter sky.

The comet's **highest** point is more than **12** times the **height** of the **Eiffel Tower** in Paris.

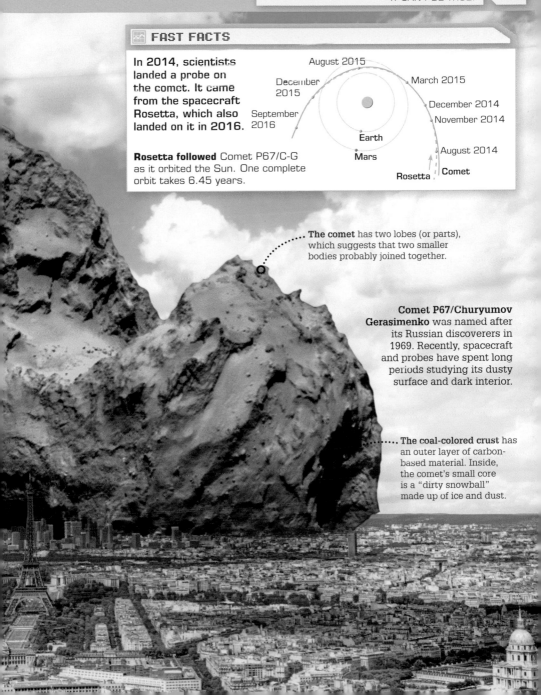

🖼 FAST FACTS

In 2014, scientists landed a probe on the comet. It came from the spacecraft Rosetta, which also landed on it in 2016.

August 2015

December 2015

March 2015

September 2016

December 2014

November 2014

Earth

Mars

August 2014

Rosetta | **Comet**

Rosetta followed Comet P67/C-G as it orbited the Sun. One complete orbit takes 6.45 years.

The comet has two lobes (or parts), which suggests that two smaller bodies probably joined together.

Comet P67/Churyumov Gerasimenko was named after its Russian discoverers in 1969. Recently, spacecraft and probes have spent long periods studying its dusty surface and dark interior.

The coal-colored crust has an outer layer of carbon-based material. Inside, the comet's small core is a "dirty snowball" made up of ice and dust.

How much **space junk** is there?

More than **150 million** pieces of space junk are currently orbiting Earth. They have an estimated total mass of nearly **7,000 tons** (6,300 metric tons). Let's talk trash!

A small fleck of debris orbiting near Earth would have the same impact as a 550 lb (250 kg) object traveling at 60 mph (100 kph).

SPINNING SATELLITES

More than 6,600 satellites have been launched into orbit in the history of space exploration. About half are still there, but only about 1,000 of them are currently operating.

There are more than **650,000** pieces of **debris** bigger than a **marble** orbiting Earth.

FAST FACTS

National space agencies have counted up the number of large objects they have in space. In 2017, Russia had the most.

6,515 objects
Russia

6,211 objects
USA

3,839 objects
China

The satellites and junk in space are influenced by gravity, which pulls them into traveling in orbits (paths) around Earth.

Earth

High Earth orbit 22,236 miles (35,786 km) from Earth

Mid Earth orbit 1,240–22,236 miles (2,000–35,786 km) from Earth

Low Earth orbit up to 1,240 miles (2,000 km) from Earth

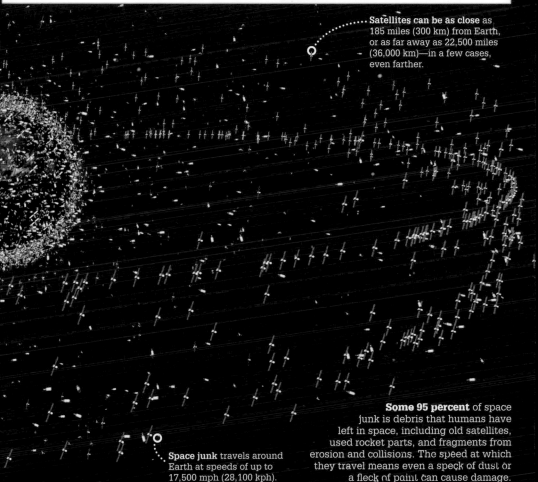

Satellites can be as close as 185 miles (300 km) from Earth, or as far away as 22,500 miles (36,000 km)—in a few cases, even farther.

Space junk travels around Earth at speeds of up to 17,500 mph (28,100 kph).

Some 95 percent of space junk is debris that humans have left in space, including old satellites, used rocket parts, and fragments from erosion and collisions. The speed at which they travel means even a speck of dust or a fleck of paint can cause damage.

Space exploration data

STARGAZING

On a **clear night**, with an unaided eye, it's possible to see around

2,500 STARS.

SPACE LIVING

The **International Space Station** orbits the Earth at about

17,500 mph (28,000 kph).

This means astronauts aboard the ISS see the **Sun rise and set** every 90 minutes.

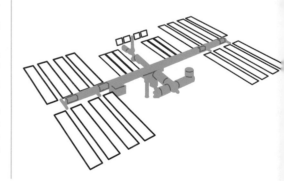

ASTRONAUT STATUS

The **World Air Sports Federation** (FAI) recognizes only those flights that reach an altitude of

more than 60 miles (100 km) as space flights. However, NASA awards astronaut wings to any astronauts who **travel above**

50 miles (80 km).

FIRST VOYAGES

····The world's first artificial satellite—**Sputnik**, a Russian communications satellite—is launched. Later that year **Sputnik 2** launches, carrying a dog called Laika: the first animal to orbit Earth.

····**Yuri Gagarin** becomes the first human in space and orbits the Earth once during a **108-minute** flight.

Neil Armstrong ···· becomes the first person to set foot on the Moon.

 1957

1961

196⸱

INESTIMABLY **HUGE** UNIVERSE

There are **more stars** in our universe than **grains of sand** on all of Earth's beaches.

ROCKET FUEL

The Space Shuttle was a spacecraft used to take astronauts into and back from space.

The Space Shuttle carried nearly **528,000 gallons** (2 million liters) of fuel just in its **external tank**. That's around **10,000 bathtubs of fuel**.

Each of the two **Solid Rocket Boosters** carried more than **1 million lb** (454,000 kg) **of solid propellant.**

SPACESUITS

• A space suit weighs **280 lb** (127 kg)—*without anyone in it!*

• It takes **45 minutes** to put on, including the *special clothes* worn underneath to keep the astronaut cool.

• An **oxygen supply** is *fanned* through the suit so the *astronaut can breathe.*

• The suit is **pressurized**—it squeezes the astronaut's body to stop his or her body fluids from *boiling in space*.

• The helmet's **visor** has a layer of *gold* to *protect against the Sun's rays*.

What's the smallest frog?

The *Paedophyrne amauensis* frog is small enough to sit on a dime.

The world's smallest frog, ***Paedophryne amauensis***, is just over ¼ in (7.7 mm) long—about the **size of a fly**. It is not only the smallest frog, but also the **smallest vertebrate** (animal with a backbone). It was discovered in Papua New Guinea in 2009.

FAST FACTS

The biggest species of frog is the Goliath, which comes from Africa. It is more than two-thirds the length of a house cat. It would take 41½ *Paedophyrne amauensis* frogs to make a line of the same length.

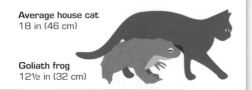

Average house cat
18 in (46 cm)

Goliath frog
12½ in (32 cm)

A dime is just under ¾ in (17.9 mm) wide. It is worth 10 cents, but costs more than five cents to make.

With back legs that are longer than its body when outstretched, the frog can jump 30 times its body length.

FREAKY FROG

The see-through skin of a glass frog's abdomen reveals its inner organs. Seen from above, the rest of its skin is lime-green—ideal camouflage among leaves.

Most frogs start life in water as tadpoles, but this species lives only on land. Its young do not have a tadpole stage but are born as "hoppers"—even tinier versions of the adult frog.

What's the biggest dog?

The tallest dog in the world was **Zeus**, a **Great Dane** towering **3¾ ft** (1.12 m) from the ground to his shoulders. A gentle giant, Zeus worked as a **therapy dog**, visiting schools and hospitals.

Although the average height of an adult male varies across the world, a rough average is 6 ft (1.8 m).

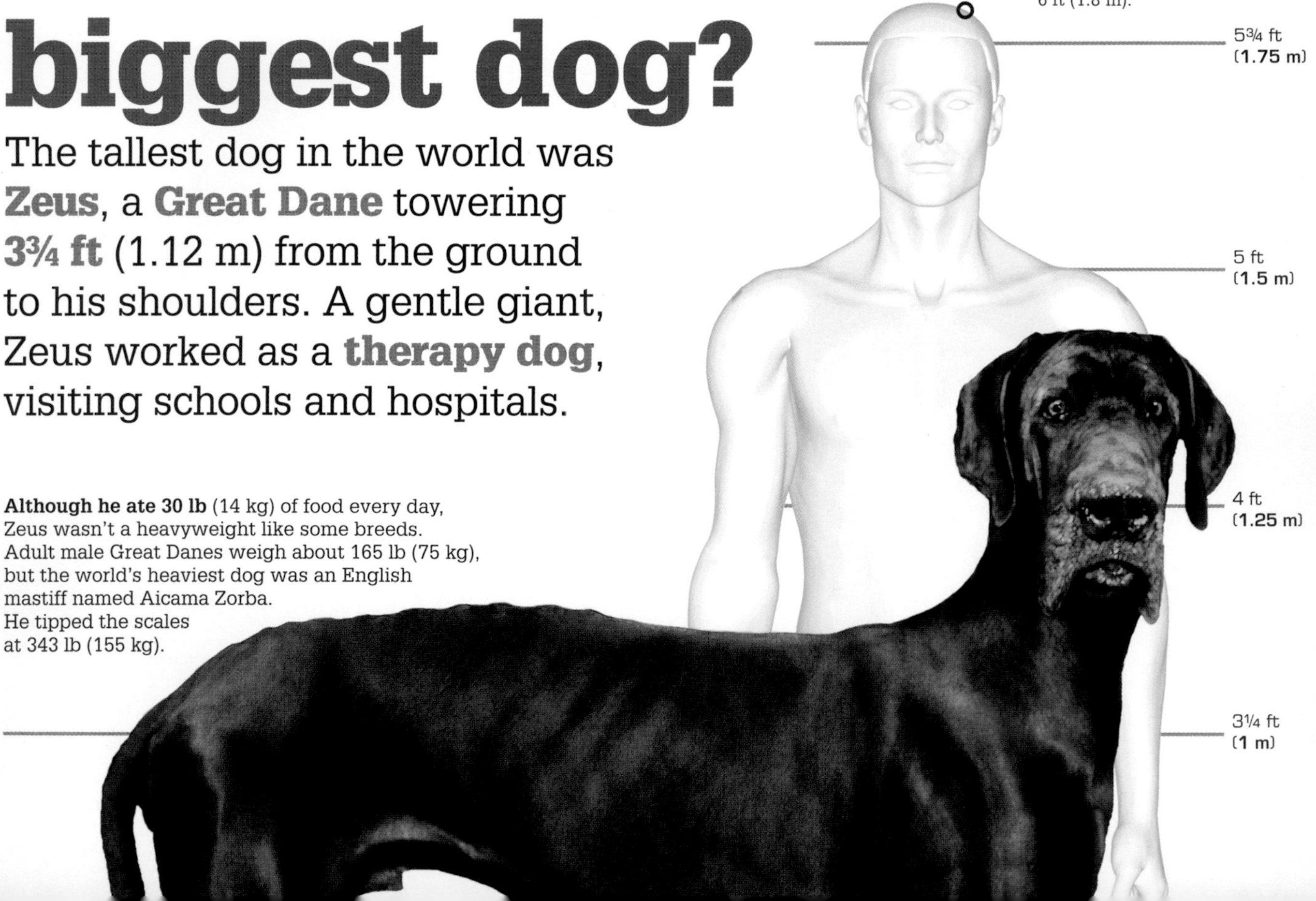

5¾ ft (**1.75 m**)

5 ft (**1.5 m**)

4 ft (**1.25 m**)

3¼ ft (**1 m**)

Although he ate 30 lb (14 kg) of food every day, Zeus wasn't a heavyweight like some breeds. Adult male Great Danes weigh about 165 lb (75 kg), but the world's heaviest dog was an English mastiff named Aicama Zorba. He tipped the scales at 343 lb (155 kg).

0.75 m

1½ ft
(0.5 m)

¾ ft
(0.25 m)

If Zeus stood up
on his hind legs,
he could reach
7¼ ft (2.24 m) tall.

Zeus
the Great Dane
is **seven times**
the height of
the **smallest
dog breed.**

Chihuahuas are the
smallest dogs, standing
6–9 in (15–23 cm) tall.

FAST FACTS

The smallest dog ever was
a female chihuahua named
Heaven Sent Brandy. She
was less than half the
length of the longest
ears on a dog.

Longest dog ears
13½ in (34.3 cm)

Smallest dog length
6 in (15.2 cm)

THUMBELINA

The world's smallest horse
is a dwarf miniature named
Thumbelina. At 17 in (43 cm)
tall, she's about the height of
a cocker spaniel and weighs
only 57 lb (26 kg).

What's the
biggest jellyfish?

Jellyfish are **marine creatures** with **small bodies**, but some have incredibly **long tentacles**. The **lion's mane jellyfish** has tentacles **120 ft** (36.5 m) long!

Jellyfish tentacles contain venomous stinging cells, used for self-defense or to catch prey such as fish and shrimp.

The tentacles of the lion's mane jellyfish are arranged in eight groups of up to 150, so a single jellyfish could have 1,200 tentacles. This type of jellyfish is only ½ in (1 cm) at birth, but grows up to 230 times bigger. Its life expectancy is one year.

It would take more than 40 scuba divers in a line to be the same length as the tentacles of the lion's mane jellyfish.

The tentacles of a lion's mane jellyfish are as long as 2½ blue whales.

The largest lion's mane jellyfish had a bell—or body—7½ ft (2.3 m) wide.

MOVING JELLY

Jellyfish have a nervous system, but no brain or eyes. They have three parts—the tentacles, bell, and oral arms. The bell is the pulsating jellylike body, which propels the jellyfish through water. Oral arms are used to direct food into the mouth opening.

A blue whale is a whopping 100 ft (30 m) in length.

FAST FACTS

Larger lion's mane jellyfish are darker than small ones. The smallest are cream or orange, and the biggest are deep red or purple.

The biggest lion's mane jellyfish can weigh 1.1 tons (1 metric ton), which is heavier than a polar bear.

How **long** can **animals** hold their breath in **water?**

DEEP BREATH

In the extreme sport of free diving, divers use no breathing equipment but hold their breath as they sink deep underwater.

Many **air-breathing animals** can hold their breath for **hours** underwater: the loggerhead turtle manages **7 hours** (420 minutes). Some animals dive to **find food**, while others stay underwater to **sleep**.

An average human can hold her breath for 30 seconds to 2 minutes; but the world record is 22 minutes. Do not try this at home!

Scuba divers can reach depths of 32 ft (10 m) for an hour if they have an adequate oxygen supply in the tank.

HUMAN

ORCA

EMPEROR PENGUIN

SCUBA DIVER

1 minute

20 minutes

27 minutes

60 minutes

FAST FACTS

Whales breathe through blowholes, spraying water in shapes that can be used to identify their species.

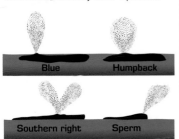

Blue | Humpback
Southern right | Sperm

Free diver Herbert Nitsch held his breath while sinking to record-breaking depths of 830 ft (253 m). The deepest scuba dive was by Ahmed Gabr, reaching 1,090 ft (332 m).

Loggerhead turtles dive to find prey such as crabs and sponges, and to escape predators, including sharks and orcas. They come to the surface to breathe in short bursts just 1–3 seconds long.

A human would need **7 scuba tanks** to stay underwater as long as a **loggerhead turtle.**

A Cuvier's beaked whale was recorded underwater for 138 minutes. This species of whale dives deeper than any other, with one tracked to 9,816 ft (2,992 m).

LOGGERHEAD TURTLE

CUVIER BEAKED WHALE

AMERICAN ALLIGATOR

ELEPHANT SEAL

120 minutes

120 minutes

138 minutes

420 minutes

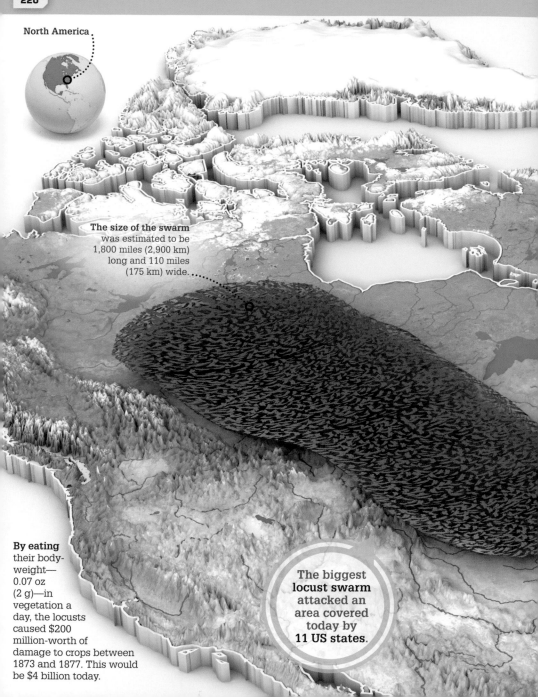

North America

The size of the swarm was estimated to be 1,800 miles (2,900 km) long and 110 miles (175 km) wide.

By eating their body-weight—0.07 oz (2 g)—in vegetation a day, the locusts caused $200 million-worth of damage to crops between 1873 and 1877. This would be $4 billion today.

The biggest **locust swarm** attacked an area covered today by **11 US states**.

FAST FACTS

There are 13 desert locusts for every person on Earth. They form today's biggest swarms, up to 460 sq miles (1,200 km²) in area.

Red-billed quelea form the biggest bird flocks. Numbers on the African plains can reach 10 billion.

One megacolony of Argentine ants stretches 3,700 miles (6,000 km) along Europe's Mediterranean coast.

How big is a locust swarm?

In 1875, **12.5 trillion** Rocky Mountain locusts descended on an area of **198,000 sq miles** (513,000 km²) in the western US.

North America

The density of locusts in this biggest-ever swarm led a witness to report that their "bodies hid the Sun and made darkness."

EXTINCT SPECIES

Fast wings for flight

Strong legs for jumping

Native to North America, the Rocky Mountain grasshopper (*Melanoplus spretus*) that swarmed in 1875 had died out by 1903.

How much **water** can an **elephant** hold in its **trunk?**

A large, male **African elephant** can suck up around **2½ gallons** (10 liters) of water in its trunk.

The two fingerlike projections at the end of the trunk are delicate and agile enough to pick up a peanut.

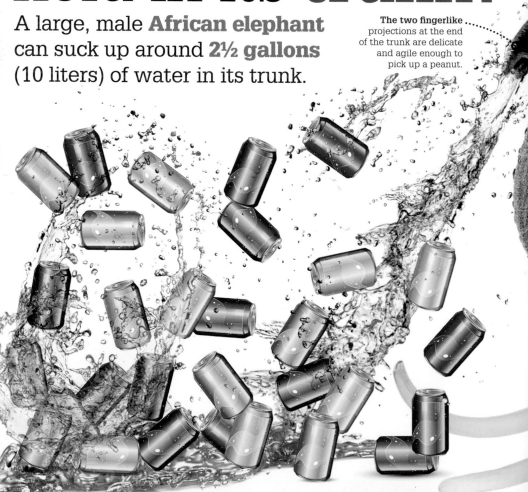

FAST FACTS

An elephant's trunk is up to 7 ft (2.1 m) long. With head raised and trunk extended, an elephant can reach up 23 ft (7 m) to pluck branches from trees.

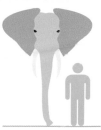

A trunk has five times the amount of smell receptors that are in a person's nose and can smell a banana from 165 ft (50 m) away.

165 ft (50 m)

The trunk is strong enough to lift 770 lb (350 kg), the same weight as 28 gold bars.

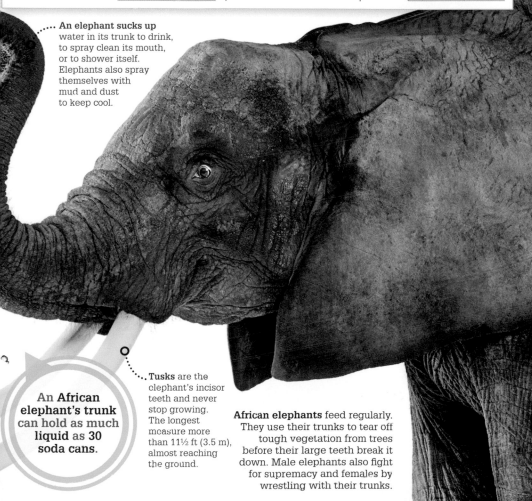

An elephant sucks up water in its trunk to drink, to spray clean its mouth, or to shower itself. Elephants also spray themselves with mud and dust to keep cool.

An **African elephant's trunk** can hold as much liquid as 30 soda cans.

Tusks are the elephant's incisor teeth and never stop growing. The longest measure more than 11½ ft (3.5 m), almost reaching the ground.

African elephants feed regularly. They use their trunks to tear off tough vegetation from trees before their large teeth break it down. Male elephants also fight for supremacy and females by wrestling with their trunks.

How **big** is a **hippo's mouth?**

A hippopotamus has a **very big** mouth, which can open to almost **180 degrees**. This creates an enormous **gape** of **4 ft** (1.2 m).

The name "hippopotamus" means "water horse," and most of this animal's time is spent in Africa's rivers and water holes. Its eyes have a protective membrane, which allows it to see underwater, and it can stay submerged without breathing for at least five minutes.

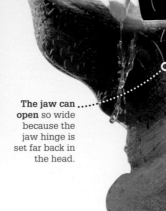

The jaw can open so wide because the jaw hinge is set far back in the head.

DISPLAY OF AGGRESSION

Hippos are the most dangerous large animal in Africa, killing 300 people a year. An open mouth is a sign of aggression, displaying canine teeth (tusks) up to 19 in (50 cm) long.

A hippo's jaw opens wide enough to fit a sports car inside.

The height of a Ferrari Modena car is 4 ft (1.2 m)—about as tall as a seven-year-old child.

The mouth opens wide when rival males are fighting or females are protecting their young.

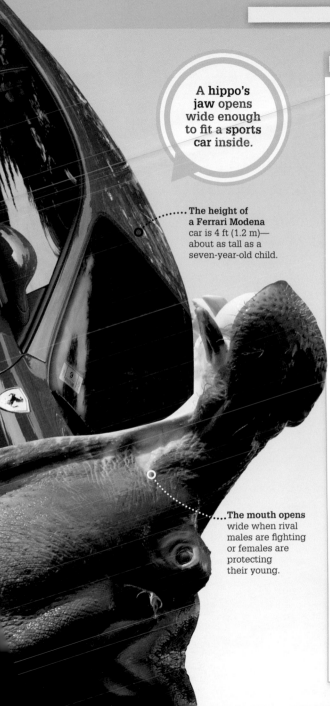

FAST FACTS

The biggest mouth of any animal belongs to the bowhead whale. The official world record is 16 ft (5 m) long, 8 ft (2.5 m) wide, and 12 ft (4 m) tall—three times bigger than a hippo's mouth.

The longest tongue relative to body size belongs to the tube-lipped bat. At 3½ in (85 mm) long, the tongue is 1.5 times the bat's body length and is extended into the tube flowers on which it feeds. When the bat is not feeding, the tongue retracts into the rib cage.

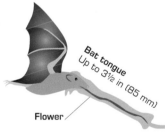

Bat tongue
Up to 3½ in (85 mm)

Flower

A woodpecker's tongue can be up to three times the length of its beak. The tongue curls up around its skull when not in use. The bird hammers its beak against trees, making holes for the tongue to probe inside the trunk for insects.

Tongue
Up to 6¾ in (170 mm)

What's the **ocean's deadliest animal?**

Many sea creatures deliver a **painful bite**, while others give a **deadly sting**. The deadliest of them all is the dreaded **box jellyfish**.

A box jellyfish has around 60 tentacles, each containing around 5,000 stinging cells.

From 2000 to 2015, 290 people died from "saltie" attacks

About 150 people a year are thought to die from sea snake bites, but not all bites are lethal

Fewer than 10 people per year die from shark attacks

World's most venomous fish, but deaths are rare

Stonefish

Great white shark

Sea snake

Saltwater crocodile

Just **1 oz (30 g)** of **box jellyfish venom** can kill 60 people in three minutes.

Box jellyfish

FAST FACTS

Box jellyfish venom is so powerful it can stop a human heart in seconds. These jellyfish have killed more than 5,500 people since 1954, which would fill an Airbus A380 passenger plane more than six times.

Airbus A380 carries 853 people per plane

STINGER SCARS

This picture shows the scars left from a jellyfish sting on human skin. Fortunately, the sting was treated and did not cause a painful death.

What's the most indestructible animal?

Tardigrades, also called water bears, are classed as **extremophiles:** creatures that can **adapt and survive** in the **harshest** conditions.

Tardigrades are about 0.02 in (0.5 mm) long.

In extreme environments, a tardigrade sheds more than 95 percent of its body water and shrivels into a blob, called a tun.

Tardigrades can survive more than 285 times the radiation a human can stand.

5,700 gray (Gy)

BORN SURVIVORS

This close-up of a tardigrade shows it has tiny claws at the end of its four pairs of stumpy legs. It is a tiny animal that lives in moisture, using its claws to clamber through moss, soil, or sand.

FAST FACTS

Tough tardigrades have survived in many extreme environments:

Existing in the vacuum of space for 10 days. A human can last only two minutes.

Freezing at -458°F (-272°C).

Heating to more than 300°F (150°C).

Pressure 6,000 times that of the deepest part of the ocean.

Tardigrades are almost impossible to kill. They can take in huge levels of radiation, measured in Gray (Gy), that would kill off any other creature. They first appeared more than 600 million years ago and have survived all five mass extinction events in Earth's history.

The Habrobracon wasp is a resilient insect, able to withstand 90 times more radiation than a human can.

Hardy cockroaches can survive for a few weeks without their heads.

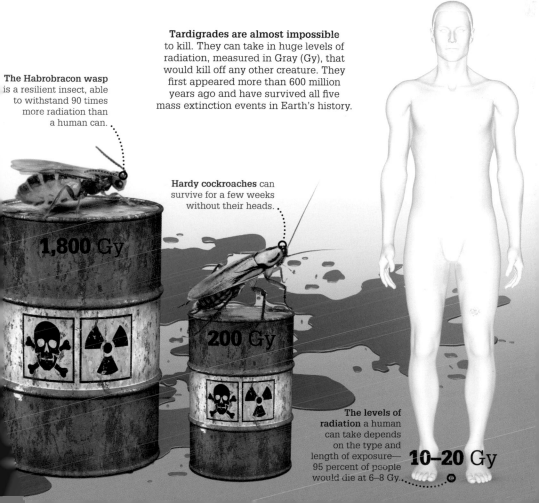

1,800 Gy

200 Gy

The levels of radiation a human can take depends on the type and length of exposure— 95 percent of people would die at 6–8 Gy.

10–20 Gy

In 2015, **a blue whale** washed up in Newfoundland, Canada, was the first to have its heart fully preserved for scientific study. The whale was 78 ft (24 m) long.

A blue whale's heart weighs as much a **motorcycle**.

The Honda CBR600FS weighs around 400 lb (180 kg) without fuel.

The aorta, or main artery, is so wide, a human head can fit inside.

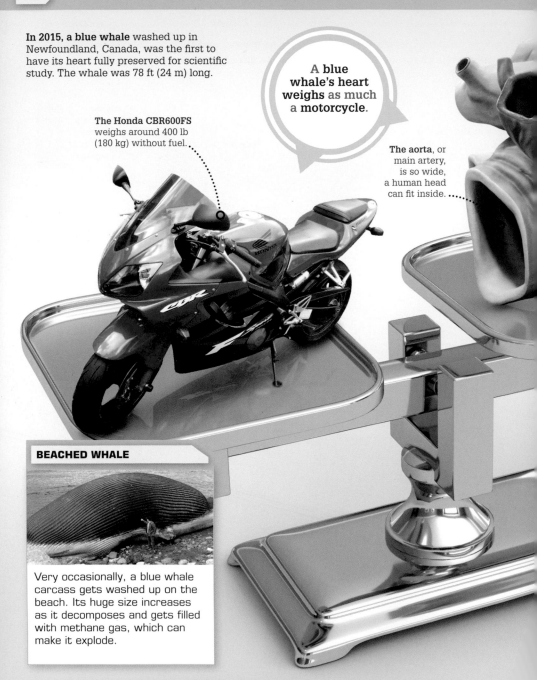

BEACHED WHALE

Very occasionally, a blue whale carcass gets washed up on the beach. Its huge size increases as it decomposes and gets filled with methane gas, which can make it explode.

FAST FACTS

The blue whale washed up in Canada had a heart that was the size of a golf buggy, at 5 x 4 ft (1.5 x 1.2 m).

A blue whale's heart pumps 232 quarts (220 liters) of blood per beat. The heartbeat is strong enough to be detected more than 2 miles (3 km) away.

The heart and arteries are huge to allow enough blood through to reach all areas of the whale's 100-ft (30-m) long body.

How **heavy** is a blue whale's **heart?**

The world's largest animal comes with a supersized **heart** that weighs **400 lb** (180 kg) and pumps **11 tons** (10 metric tons) of **blood** around the whale's body.

ENTRANCE HOLES

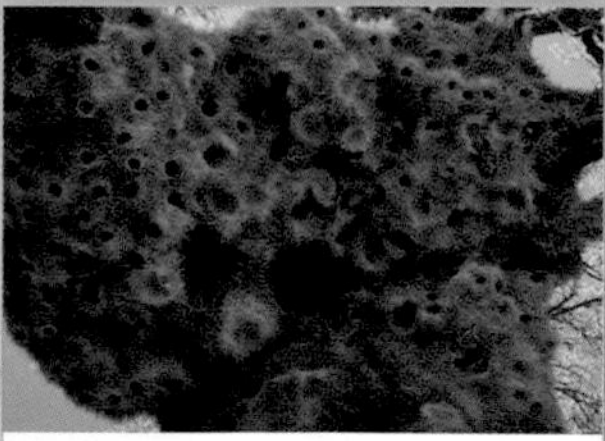

A sociable weaver's nest is dotted with entrance holes for the birds to access their own chamber within the nest. Straw is positioned in spikes around the holes to keep invaders out.

Nests are usually built in the safety of trees with high branches to avoid predators.

Which **bird** builds the **largest** nests?

The **sociable weaver** of southern Africa constructs the **largest** nests of any bird, building one giant nest for the **entire colony**. These intricate structures can be **13 ft** (4 m) in height.

Sociable weaver birds fill trees with **nests** large enough to house up to **400 birds.**

Grass and twigs are the main building materials.

Weaver birds live in the Kalahari Desert. Their nests are constructed so that the bottom part stays cool, providing respite from the desert heat.

The nest contains multiple entrances, measuring 10 in (25 cm) long and 3 in (7 cm) wide.

📊 FAST FACTS

A pair of bald eagles built the single largest bird nest. Created in 1963 in Florida, it was 9½ ft (2.9 m) wide and 20 ft (6 m) deep. That's big enough to fit a car inside!

Malleefowl birds lay eggs in mounds made of leaf-litter and bark. The eggs are covered in sand for warmth. The biggest known mound was 15 ft (4.6 m) tall and 35 ft (10.6 m) wide.

Egg chamber

Animal data

LUMINOUS ANIMALS

▶ Many **scorpions** are **fluorescent**—they have molecules on their body surface that glow in ultraviolet light

▶ When attacked, **Atolla jellyfish** emit a brilliant **burst of light** that can be seen up to **300 ft** (91 m) away.

▶ **Comb jellies** produce **blue** or green **light**, but moving their body can scatter the light to create multicolored moving patterns.

▶ Some **click beetles** emit a **bright light** to ward off predators; their light is so strong that you can read by it.

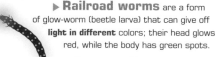

▶ **Railroad worms** are a form of glow-worm (beetle larva) that can give off **light in different** colors; their head glows red, while the body has green spots.

▶ **Sea sparkles** (*Noctiluca scintillans*) are tiny sea creatures that form huge colonies up to 80 miles (128 km) long. When disturbed, they flash **blue-green phosphorescent light** across miles of ocean.

UNUSUAL **EYES**

• The **chiton mollusk** has **more eyes than any other animal.** Embedded in its shell are thousands of eyes made of minerals, which can see light and shapes.

• The **tuatara lizard** has a so-called "**third eye**" on the top of its head, which **detects changes in light.**

• **Starfish** have basic **eye spots** at the **end of each arm** that can make out **light** and **large shapes**. Blue stars can see to a distance of **3 ft** (1 m), and each eye spot has a **170–220 degree** field of vision—slightly wider than that of a human.

• **Mexican tetra** fish species includes a blind variety that **lives in caves**. The lack of eyes means the **blind fish use 15 percent less energy** than the sighted ones.

NEEDLEWORK NEST

Tailorbirds curl up leaves to build nests inside. They make **tiny holes** along the edge of the leaf and use **plant fibers** or even **spider webs** to **stitch** the leaf in place.

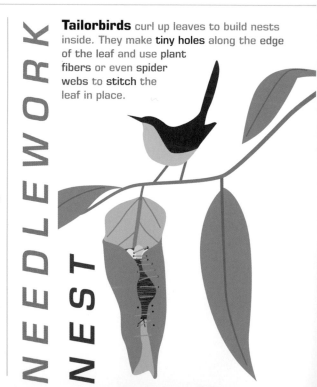

BLOOD COLORS

Not all **blood** is **red**.

Crabs have blue blood.

Earthworms and **leeches** have green blood.

Many invertebrates, such as **starfish**, have clear or yellowish blood.

ELECTRICITY GENERATORS

▶ **Platypuses** have electrical receptors in their snouts to detect prey animals.

▶ **Stargazer fish** shoot electric currents from their eyes to stun their prey or drive away predators.

▶ **Electric rays** can set their electric impulses to different settings. They use a mild pulse to ward off aggressors. To attack prey, they use the full setting of up to 220V—double that of an electrical appliance in your home.

▶ **Electric eels** can give off a charge of up to 650V—strong enough to kill people.

FASTEST AND SLOWEST HEARTBEATS

• A **blue whale's** heart beats at **6 beats per minute (bpm)**, while a **hummingbird's** heart beats at up to **1,260 bpm**.

1,260 bpm

6 bpm

SMARTEST ANIMALS

• **Ants** are skillful farmers. They cultivate "gardens" of fungi and keep aphids for the sweet honeydew they produce.

• **Crows** can solve complex problems and make tools from sticks and wire to help them reach food. Some are better at problem-solving than a 5-year-old child.

• **Octopuses** have 130 million nerve cells, 60 percent of which are in their arms. They can play with toys, solve puzzles, and even learn their own names.

• **Bees** carry a mental map of flowers up to 3 miles (5 km) away from their hive. They perform "waggle dances" to tell other bees where to go. The duration of the dance indicates the distance to food, while the angle shows the direction.

How **big** can a **snail** grow?

Although they have a reputation for being **slow**, snails are not always **small**. Meet the **giant Ghana snail**, the world's **largest** land snail. This creature's **shell** can grow to an incredible **12 in** (30 cm) long and **6 in** (15 cm) wide.

An eye is situated at the tip of each tentacle.

SPIRAL SANCTUARY

Snails are part of a group of mollusks called gastropods. Not all have shells, but those that do usually have spiral-shaped shells that the creatures hide inside, away from predators.

FAST FACTS

One mighty marine snail boasts an even bigger shell. The Australian trumpet snail has a shell three times longer than the giant Ghana snail; the shell weighs as much as a three-year-old child.

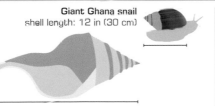

Giant Ghana snail
shell length: 12 in (30 cm)

Australian trumpet snail shell length: 3 ft (91 cm)

The biggest land snail was Gee Geronimo. At 15½ in (39.3 cm), its body was longer than a Dachshund.

Giant Ghana snails are native to several west African countries, not just Ghana. The average giant snail grows to around 8 in (20 cm) long and 4 in (10 cm) wide, but larger individuals can grow to 150 percent that size.

The striped shell gives the snail its other common name of giant tiger snail.

A giant Ghana snail is **longer** than a child's open palms put together.

How many eggs do animals lay?

EGG CARRIER

Midwife toads are experts at taking care of eggs. Once the female lays her eggs, the male carries them on his back legs until hatching time, when he deposits them in ponds.

A **chicken** lays **an egg a day**, but that's nothing compared to other creatures in the animal kingdom. **Fish** and **insects** tend to be the most prolific producers, especially the **African driver ant**, which can lay up to **4 million eggs** every 25 days.

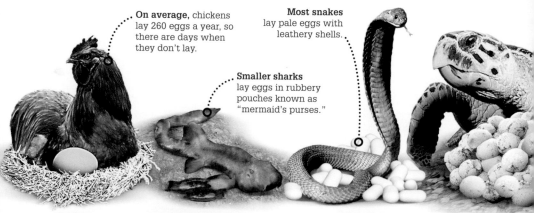

On average, chickens lay 260 eggs a year, so there are days when they don't lay.

Most snakes lay pale eggs with leathery shells.

Smaller sharks lay eggs in rubbery pouches known as "mermaid's purses."

Chicken
1 EGG

Brownbanded bamboo shark
2 EGGS

Cape cobra
20 EGGS

Hawksbill turtle
200 EGGS

🖼 FAST FACTS

The smallest eggs in the animal kingdom are laid by a fly called *Clemelis pullata*. The eggs are 0.0007 in x 0.001 in (0.02 mm x 0.02 mm).

You could line up 100 fly eggs across the width of this oval

Carpenter bees lay the largest insect eggs. The biggest ever found were ⅔ in (16.5 mm) long and 0.1 in (3 mm) across.

Carpenter bee and egg

Ostriches lay the most bird eggs in one nest. Up to 74 eggs can be in one nest, laid by all the females in the flock. An egg is laid every 2–3 days.

The eggs shown here are sized in relation to their mother animal. The numbers refer to the amounts laid at one time –a period that could be moments during one day or constant laying over many days.

The **African driver ant queen** lays **hundreds of thousands** of eggs in a day.

The gender of turtles' young depends on the temperature of the eggs at incubation. Up to 82°F (28°C) produces males, while over 90°F (32°C) produces females. Temperatures in between produce males or females.

A queen honey bee lays 200,000 eggs every year of her life, which can be up to 8 years.

In a lifetime, the gray grouper produces about 300 million eggs, with some spawning 200,000 at once.

Honey bee
2,000 EGGS

Gray grouper
200,000 EGGS

African driver ant
3–4 MILLION EGGS

What's the smallest living reptile?

The miniature chameleon species *Brookesia micra* was first discovered in **Madagascar** in **2014**. It is only **1 in** (29 mm) long from nose to tail.

Chameleons can change the color of their skin, depending on their mood. Spotted patterns appear when *Brookesia micra* is angry or stressed. This can also help them to merge with their surroundings and keep hidden from predators and prey.

Each eye can move independently, but also work together to track prey accurately.

FAST FACTS

The largest living reptile is the saltwater crocodile, which can reach a whopping 18 ft (5.5 m). This is the same length as lining up 190 mini chameleons.

Saltwater crocodile
18 ft (5.5 m)

Mini chameleon
1 in (29 mm)

The chameleon's tiny size and brown color are useful in keeping it hidden from predators as it wanders through leaf litter on the forest floor.

This **mini chameleon** is **small** enough to fit on the end of a **pencil**.

The tail wraps around branches for balance at night when the chameleon sleeps up in the trees.

TONGUE TRAP

Chameleons catch prey using their long, sticky tongue. The bearded pygmy chameleon's tongue is more than twice its body length of 3 in (8 cm). Some chameleons can fire their tongues at prey in one-hundredth of a second—1,000 times faster than a sports car can accelerate.

What's the most venomous snake?

The snake with the **most potent venom** is the **inland taipan**, native to Australia. Luckily, **attacks** are **rare** and have been **treated** successfully.

This snake's skin changes color with the seasons, turning lighter in summer and darker in winter.

Inland taipans can reach up to 8 ft (2.5 m) in length.

VENOMOUS STRIKE

Snakes kill small mammals by biting them and injecting venom through their hollow fangs. They can open their jaws wide enough to swallow prey whole.

One bite from an **inland taipan** contains enough **venom** to kill **100 adult men**.

Taipan snake venom contains potent neurotoxins, which are poisons that cause muscle weakness and paralysis.

FAST FACTS

Scientists estimate that the venom from an inland taipan could kill a person within 45 minutes.

The fangs of an inland taipan grow up to ¼ in (6.2 mm), but this is small compared to the snake with the longest fangs. The Gaboon viper's fangs can be 2 in (5 cm) long.

Gaboon viper

Taipan

There have been no recorded deaths from an inland taipan bite in Australia. In contrast, honey bees kill up to two people a year in Australia.

The bottles represent the number of people one bite could kill.

Despite also being known as the "fierce snake," the inland taipan is not aggressive. It lives in remote, semidesert regions, which are home to very few people.

How **big** can a **squid** grow?

The **largest** specimen of **giant squid** ever seen was **59 ft** (18 m) long and weighed in at a hefty **2,000 lb** (900 kg). They live in the depths of the oceans and are rarely seen.

The 59-ft (18-m) specimen is an unofficial record. Scientific studies put the squid's maximum length at 43 ft (13 m) from its mantle to its outstretched tentacles.

The mantle, or main body, covers the squid's internal organs, including its heart, stomach, and gills.

The eyes of the giant squid are the size of dinner plates. The only creature with bigger eyes is the colossal squid.

📈 FAST FACTS

A squid moves quickly by jet propulsion: it sucks water into its mantle, then pushes it out through its funnel. It uses its fins to move at slow speeds.

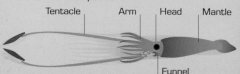

Tentacle   Arm   Head   Mantle

Funnel

LOOK AT THOSE SUCKERS

The squid's arms and tentacles have hundreds of rings of suckers. They are lined with teeth made from chitin, a similar substance to fingernails.

The squid has eight arms lined with suckers for gripping prey. It also has two tentacles, up to three times longer than its arms, used for pushing food into its mouth.

Three people can squeeze inside the 13-ft (4-m) long Triton 3300/3 submarine. It can explore down to 3,300 ft (1,000 m) deep.

The largest giant squid was 4.5 times longer than a Triton submarine.

How many **bees** make a jar of **honey?**

In its **lifetime**, an average bee will produce **one-twelfth** of a **teaspoon** of honey. It takes **800 bees**, collecting the nectar of **2 million** flowers, to make enough honey to fill **one jar**.

📈 FAST FACTS

Earth

Bees fly 55,000 miles (88,500 km)— more than twice around the world— to produce one jar of honey.

One honey bee visits up to 100 flowers in each flight, collecting nectar and pollen as food.

The world's most expensive honey comes from a cave 6,000 ft (1,800 m) deep in northeastern Turkey. Called Elvish honey, it sells for $2,500 per pound.

$2,500

A colony of honey bees is made up of a queen, up to 60,000 female worker bees, and hundreds of male, stingless drones.

Bee wings flap 230 times per second, creating a buzzing sound.

It takes **800 bees** to make enough **honey** to fill **a 1 lb (450 g) jar.**

Honey is the only food that never spoils. Perfectly preserved pots thousands of years old have been found in ancient Egyptian tombs.

POLLEN BASKETS

Bees feed on flower pollen and take it back to the hive for the colony. Using their middle legs, they brush pollen caught on their hairy body into "baskets" on their back legs.

Rotor blades move at high speed, creating a loud whirring noise that can be heard up to 5 miles (8 km) away. At 100 ft (30 m) away, the noise reaches 100 dB.

Humans can withstand 160 dB before sound levels split eardrums. A loud rock concert reaches 115 dB, while a jet engine gets up to 140 dB.

Unlike an aircraft, a helicopter can take off without a runway, move backward and sideways, and turn in midair.

How loud is an insect?

The **African cicada** (*Brevisana brevis*) is the world's **loudest insect**, with a call averaging **106.7 decibels (dB)** at a distance of **20 in** (50 cm) away.

FAST FACTS

The loudest noise in the animal kingdom is made by the tiger pistol shrimp. This is not a vocal sound, but the snapping of its claws. Blue whales also produce a loud noise, almost twice as loud as the African cicada's call.

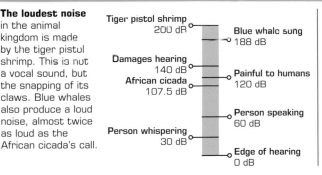

Tiger pistol shrimp
200 dB

Blue whale song
188 dB

Damages hearing
140 dB

African cicada
107.5 dB

Painful to humans
120 dB

Person speaking
60 dB

Person whispering
30 dB

Edge of hearing
0 dB

Scientists researching cicadas found the bigger the insect, the louder the noise. Most cicada species are 1–2 in (2–5 cm) long in the body, but the Empress cicada of Southeast Asia is 2¾ in (7 cm) long, so its call could be even louder.

African cicada   Empress cicada

The African cicada's call is louder than a helicopter.

Male cicadas make their deafening calls using two organs called tymbals, which are made up of a membrane stretched over ribs. The tymbal makes a clicking sound when the cicada contracts (squeezes) it and when it relaxes it. A cicada can produce 300–400 clicks every second.

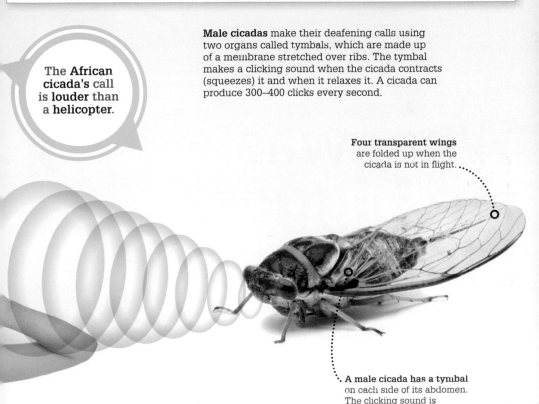

Four transparent wings are folded up when the cicada is not in flight.

A male cicada has a tymbal on each side of its abdomen. The clicking sound is amplified (made louder) by the insect's hollow body.

ANCIENT GIANTS

Prehistoric invertebrates (animals without a backbone), such as this millipede, grew to giant sizes because there was more oxygen in the atmosphere at the time. This enabled the bugs' body tissues to grow large. The bugs began to shrink when oxygen levels fell.

Compound eyes (eyes made up of many parts) provided multiple images, helping the insect detect movement and judge distances with amazing accuracy.

Biting jaws tore into ancient prey, including small reptiles and amphibians.

What was the **biggest insect** ever?

The **prehistoric griffenfly** *Meganeuropsis permiana* was about **17 in** (43 cm) long. This insect was the **ancestor** of today's **dragonflies** and damselflies.

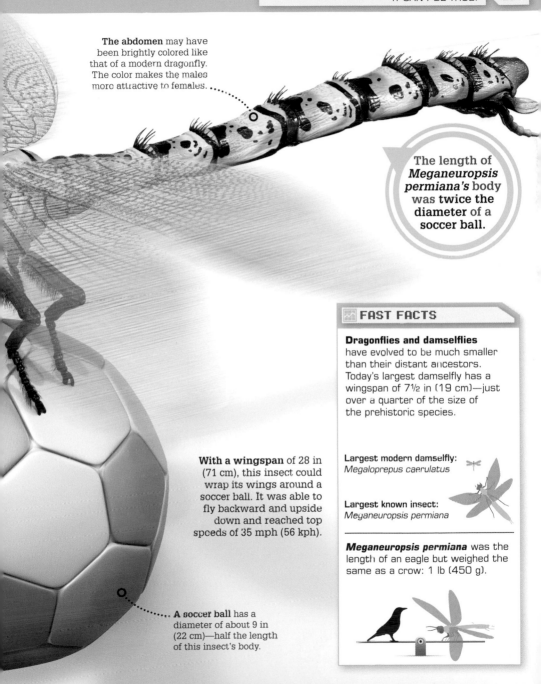

The abdomen may have been brightly colored like that of a modern dragonfly. The color makes the males more attractive to females.

The length of *Meganeuropsis permiana's* body was **twice the diameter** of a soccer ball.

With a wingspan of 28 in (71 cm), this insect could wrap its wings around a soccer ball. It was able to fly backward and upside down and reached top speeds of 35 mph (56 kph).

A soccer ball has a diameter of about 9 in (22 cm)—half the length of this insect's body.

FAST FACTS

Dragonflies and damselflies have evolved to be much smaller than their distant ancestors. Today's largest damselfly has a wingspan of 7½ in (19 cm)—just over a quarter of the size of the prehistoric species.

Largest modern damselfly:
Megaloprepus caerulatus

Largest known insect:
Meganeuropsis permiana

Meganeuropsis permiana was the length of an eagle but weighed the same as a crow: 1 lb (450 g).

What's the smallest insect?

The **smallest**, fully grown adult **insect** is a **male fairyfly** (a parasitic wasp) of the species *Dicopomorpha echmepterygis*. These blind, wingless insects are only **0.005 in** (0.139 mm long.

ESSENTIAL EGGS

The fairyfly is a parasite that lives in the egg of a bark louse (shown above). The male fairyfly dies in the egg, but the female chews her way out so she can lay her own eggs in other hosts before she dies.

A typical grain of rice is ⅛ in (4 mm) long and 0.1 in (2.5 mm) wide.

Parasitic wasps have no stinger and are completely harmless to people. There are hundreds of different varieties: most are tiny in size and brown or black in color. They have two pairs of wings and long antennae.

FAST FACTS

The male wasp is just one-eighth the size of the female (by volume). Females range in length from 0.015 in to 0.022 in (0.39 mm to 0.55 mm).

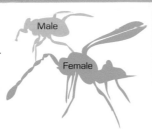

Male

Female

Some of the tiniest animals of all are lociferans, which live between grains of sand. At 0.0004 in (0.01 mm) long, the smallest lociferan is 200 times smaller than a grain of sand.

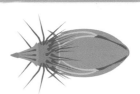

Shown at 2000 times its real size

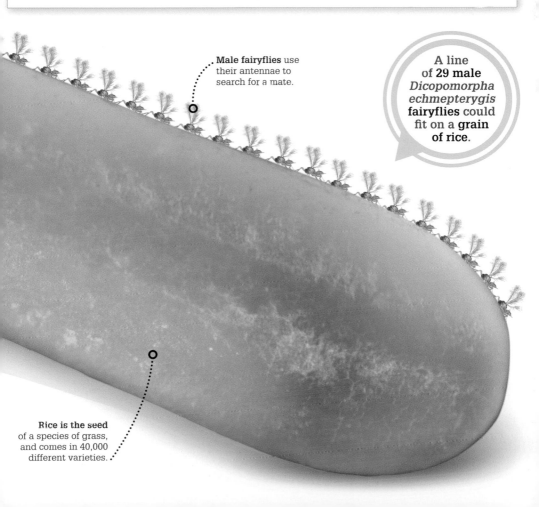

Male fairyflies use their antennae to search for a mate.

A line of **29 male** *Dicopomorpha echmepterygis* **fairyflies** could fit on a **grain of rice.**

Rice is the seed of a species of grass, and comes in 40,000 different varieties.

FAST FACTS

Beavers are rodents. Their largest ancestor, *Castoroides* or ancient giant beaver, was the size of a grizzly bear.

Human 6 ft (1.8 m) tall

Castoroides 8 ft (2.5 m) long

Modern beaver 4 ft (1.25 m) long

The **beaver dam is wider** than **two Hoover Dams**.

The Hoover Dam is 1,205 ft (367 m) wide at the top.

Water makes turbines spin, creating hydroelectric power. The more water, the more energy is produced.

How big can beaver dams get?

The Hoover Dam contains 17 generators that produce in excess of four billion kilowatt hours of electricity every year.

One of the largest structures ever built by animals is a **beaver dam** in Alberta, Canada. It contains two beaver lodges and measures **2,800 ft** (850 m) **wide**.

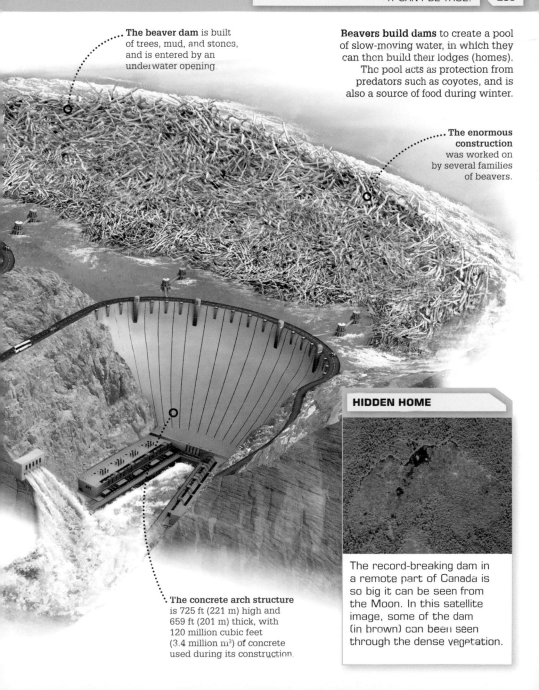

The beaver dam is built of trees, mud, and stones, and is entered by an underwater opening.

Beavers build dams to create a pool of slow-moving water, in which they can then build their lodges (homes). The pool acts as protection from predators such as coyotes, and is also a source of food during winter.

The enormous construction was worked on by several families of beavers.

HIDDEN HOME

The record-breaking dam in a remote part of Canada is so big it can be seen from the Moon. In this satellite image, some of the dam (in brown) can been seen through the dense vegetation.

The concrete arch structure is 725 ft (221 m) high and 659 ft (201 m) thick, with 120 million cubic feet (3.4 million m³) of concrete used during its construction.

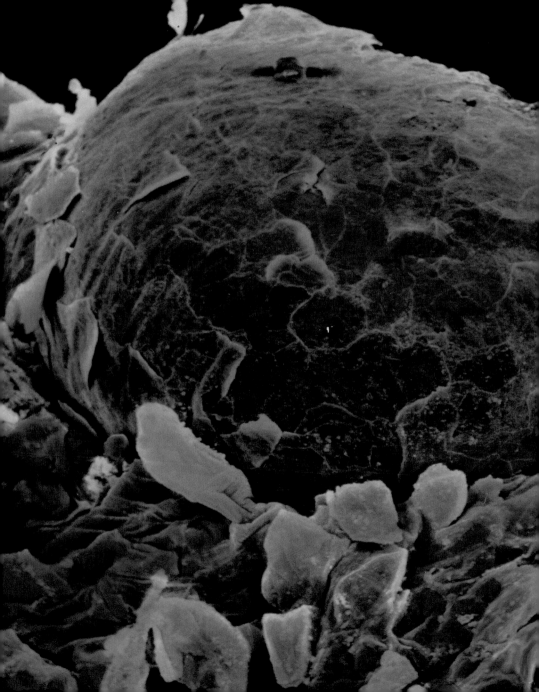

TRUE OR FALSE?

Uncover the myths behind some terrible truths and find out which facts were really right all along. Is the Earth round? Was Napoleon really short? Test yourself on more questions along the way, with the answers revealed in the back of the book.

This microscopic mound is a fungiform papillae—a tiny lump on your tongue where taste-detectors lie. Thousands of these taste buds are found across the tongue and can identify all the flavors of food.

TRUE or FALSE? Your **irises** are as **unique** as your fingerprints

The iris is so complex and multilayered that even your right and left eyes are different. Identical twins also have different iris patterns.

Here's an **eye-opener**—everyone has a unique iris pattern. This **colored ring** around the pupil is as individual as your fingerprints, ensuring that we're all complete **one-offs**.

IRIS RECOGNITION

Since every person has a unique iris pattern, iris recognition software has been developed for identification purposes. A scan of the pupil converts the iris pattern into a digital code, which is stored in a database with other people's unique codes.

What do all blue-eyed people have in common?

The tough outer layer is the sclera, responsible for maintaining the shape of the eye.

Sight is the most important sense, enabling us to view the world. Light from exterior objects is automatically focused onto a layer of light receptors at the back of the eye. These receptors then send messages to the brain about the patterns of light. The brain interprets these messages, enabling us to see 3-D, moving color images of what is going on around us.

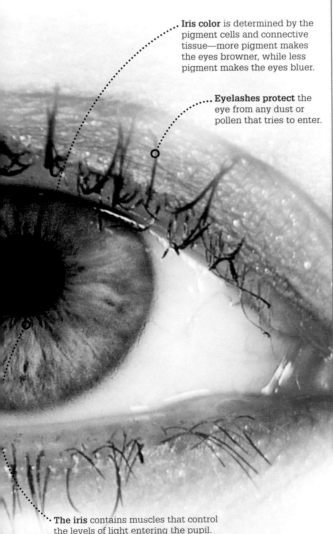

Iris color is determined by the pigment cells and connective tissue—more pigment makes the eyes browner, while less pigment makes the eyes bluer.

Eyelashes protect the eye from any dust or pollen that tries to enter.

The iris contains muscles that control the levels of light entering the pupil.

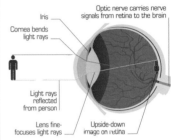

The **tongue** taste zones

Taste maps took off in the 20th century, when it was thought the tongue could be divided into **taste zones**. But then scientists discovered that different tastes can be **detected everywhere** on the tongue—so there really is no accounting for taste!

TASTE BASE

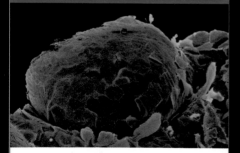

The tongue is covered in microscopic bumps called papillae. Many are filiform papillae, which help the tongue grip food. Other types of papillae house sensors called taste buds, which detect tastes in food. Fungiform papillae (pictured) detect the full range of tastes, while about ten big circumvallate papillae at the back of the tongue are more sensitive to bitter tastes.

Umami comes from a Japanese word, translated as "pleasant, savory taste." It was scientifically indentified in 1908 by Kikunae Ikeda, a professor at Tokyo Imperial University.

Olives are often considered "an acquired taste"—they are disliked at first but then liked after trying them a few times.

Various parts of the tongue were thought to be exclusively responsible for different tastes. This zone was thought to detect salty tastes.

Sweet sensations are detected by the taste buds and recognized as enjoyable by the brain.

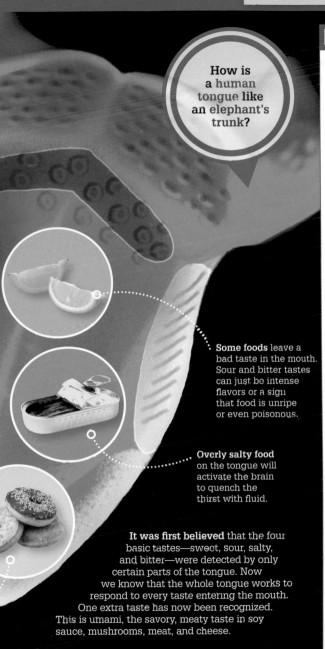

How is
a human
tongue like
an elephant's
trunk?

Some foods leave a
bad taste in the mouth.
Sour and bitter tastes
can just be intense
flavors or a sign
that food is unripe
or even poisonous.

Overly salty food
on the tongue will
activate the brain
to quench the
thirst with fluid.

It was first believed that the four
basic tastes—sweet, sour, salty,
and bitter—were detected by only
certain parts of the tongue. Now
we know that the whole tongue works to
respond to every taste entering the mouth.
One extra taste has now been recognized.
This is umami, the savory, meaty taste in soy
sauce, mushrooms, meat, and cheese.

FAST FACTS

80% OF THE FLAVOR SENSATION
WE GET FROM FOOD COMES FROM ITS SMELL

The nose can detect more than one trillion
different odors, but when it is blocked
food becomes almost flavorless. Try eating
something while holding your nose shut. Food
will be almost tasteless.

WOMEN'S SENSE OF SMELL IS STRONGER THAN MEN'S

Not only have women shown
that they can smell better than
men; their sense of taste is
stronger too. Women are also
better at finding the words to describe
what they are smelling and tasting.

THE MOUTH HAS ONE MILLION TASTE RECEPTOR CELLS

There are up to 100 of these specialized cells in
each of the taste buds. Tiny taste "hairs"
attached to each receptor cell detect taste
molecules dissolved in saliva. Receptor cells
then send messages to the brain, which
identifies tastes in food.

TRUE or FALSE? Head lice like **dirty hair**

Head lice don't care about **bad hair days**. These critters aren't choosy. Whether your **crowning glory** is clean or dirty, these bad boys jump in and make themselves at home. But bring on the **chemical treatments** and the problem will soon be washed away!

Head lice pass quickly from head to head, so children at school are most at risk.

MICROSCOPIC MITES

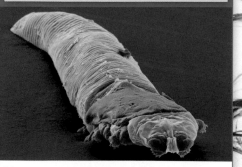

You may not realize it, but living in your eyelash follicles are microscopic mites like this one. They feed on dead skin cells and oily secretions from your scalp. They are too tiny to see and there's no way to get rid of these uninvited but harmless guests.

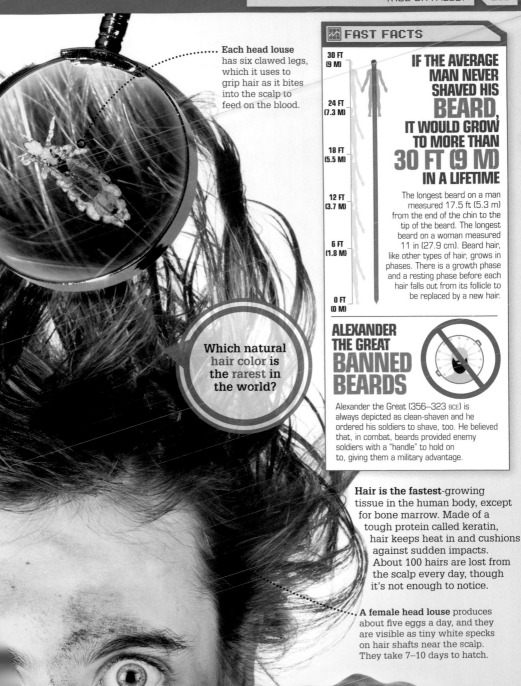

Each head louse has six clawed legs, which it uses to grip hair as it bites into the scalp to feed on the blood.

FAST FACTS

30 FT (9 M)
24 FT (7.3 M)
18 FT (5.5 M)
12 FT (3.7 M)
6 FT (1.8 M)
0 FT (0 M)

IF THE AVERAGE MAN NEVER SHAVED HIS BEARD, IT WOULD GROW TO MORE THAN 30 FT (9 M) IN A LIFETIME

The longest beard on a man measured 17.5 ft (5.3 m) from the end of the chin to the tip of the beard. The longest beard on a woman measured 11 in (27.9 cm). Beard hair, like other types of hair, grows in phases. There is a growth phase and a resting phase before each hair falls out from its follicle to be replaced by a new hair.

ALEXANDER THE GREAT BANNED BEARDS

Alexander the Great (356–323 BCE) is always depicted as clean-shaven and he ordered his soldiers to shave, too. He believed that, in combat, beards provided enemy soldiers with a "handle" to hold on to, giving them a military advantage.

Which natural hair color is the rarest in the world?

Hair is the fastest-growing tissue in the human body, except for bone marrow. Made of a tough protein called keratin, hair keeps heat in and cushions against sudden impacts. About 100 hairs are lost from the scalp every day, though it's not enough to notice.

A female head louse produces about five eggs a day, and they are visible as tiny white specks on hair shafts near the scalp. They take 7–10 days to hatch.

TRUE or FALSE? You catch a **cold** from being **cold**

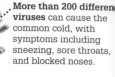

More than 200 different viruses can cause the common cold, with symptoms including sneezing, sore throats, and blocked noses.

While it is true that colds are more **common in winter** and cold air can create **runny noses**, this statement gets the **cold shoulder**. The only thing that causes a cold is a **cold virus**.

ANTIBIOTIC REVOLUTION

Antibiotics can help the body fight infections. These wonder drugs target and kill specific bacteria, but they cannot cure a cold. This is because colds are caused by viruses, and antibiotics work only against bacteria.

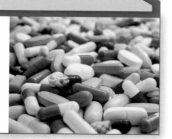

As the cold invaders advance, the nasal lining fights back by producing mucus—a sticky trap for catching viruses, dust, and pollen.

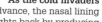

📊 FAST FACTS

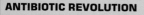

IT IS POSSIBLE TO SNEEZE WITH YOUR EYES OPEN

The eyelids snap shut naturally during a sneeze, but if they are held open it is still possible to sneeze—and contrary to popular legend, your eyes won't pop out! It is believed that our eyes close as protection from the microorganisms and particles contained in the sneeze.

SNEEZES CAN REACH TOP SPEEDS OF 100 MPH (160 KM/H)

It is the force and magnitude of the sneeze that allow germs to spread so quickly, infecting others wherever the water droplets land.

COMPUTER KEYBOARDS ARE DIRTIER THAN TOILET SEATS

Other household items such as remote controls, telephones, and door handles also contain more bacteria than the average toilet seat. Since toilet seats tend to be disinfected, they are often one of the cleanest surfaces in the house.

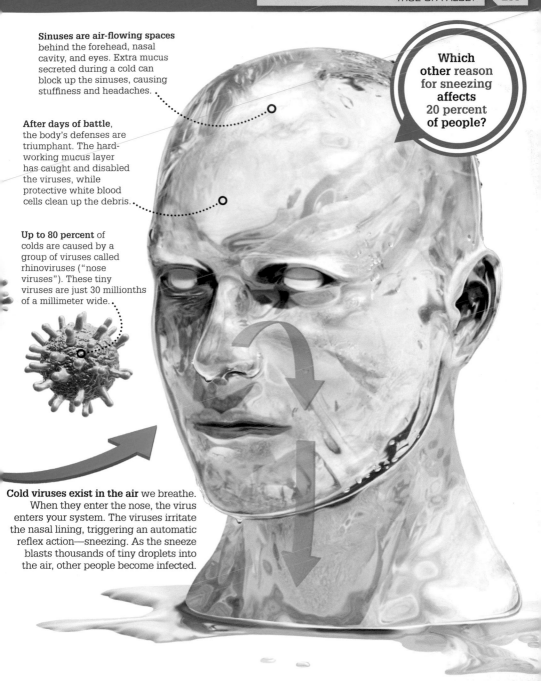

Sinuses are air-flowing spaces behind the forehead, nasal cavity, and eyes. Extra mucus secreted during a cold can block up the sinuses, causing stuffiness and headaches.

After days of battle, the body's defenses are triumphant. The hard-working mucus layer has caught and disabled the viruses, while protective white blood cells clean up the debris.

Up to 80 percent of colds are caused by a group of viruses called rhinoviruses ("nose viruses"). These tiny viruses are just 30 millionths of a millimeter wide.

Which **other** reason for sneezing **affects** 20 percent of people?

Cold viruses exist in the air we breathe. When they enter the nose, the virus enters your system. The viruses irritate the nasal lining, triggering an automatic reflex action—sneezing. As the sneeze blasts thousands of tiny droplets into the air, other people become infected.

TRUE or FALSE? Spinach makes you strong

Spinach **wins the gold** in any food contest, making other vegetables **green with envy**. Although it packs a punch in the nutrition department, spinach is more of a **weakling** when it comes to iron. Instead, red meat and seafood **muscle in** to steal first place for truly **cast-iron content**.

Fresh, leafy, organic spinach without any pesticide treatment is the best to eat.

SWEET TREAT

Made from cocoa beans, dark chocolate has multiple benefits. Its antioxidants protect against diseases and delay the signs of aging, while flavonoids control blood-sugar levels. Phenylethylamine triggers the brain to release endorphins—chemicals responsible for feeling happy. So go on, treat yourself!

🖼 FAST FACTS

SUGAR DOESN'T
MAKE YOU HYPER

Sugar is commonly linked with hyperactivity because adults perceive that children behave hyperactively when they eat it. However, sugar is often consumed during special occasions, such as birthday parties, when children tend to become more excited and energetic anyway.

THE SMELL OF TOAST HAS BEEN PROVEN TO MAKE PEOPLE HAPPIER

Many people link the smell of toast with happy memories of weekends and family. When memories are triggered by smell, it is known as the "Proust effect." This can be used to help sell things. For example, when a house smells like baking bread and fresh coffee, it can make potential buyers feel more at home.

Cooking spinach improves its health benefits, with just half a cup of cooked spinach providing three times the nutrition of one cup of raw spinach.

Which vitamin is a must-have for your bones?

Like other green vegetables, spinach has high levels of vitamin B_6, which helps the body make proteins and release energy.

An iron-rich diet is essential for staying strong, but spinach is average in terms of iron levels. However, spinach is crammed with vitamins and minerals. As a source of beta-carotene, spinach is a warrior in the fight against serious disease. Its properties protect the heart, improve the skin, boost eye health, and keep the digestive system functioning.

TRUE or FALSE? We share 96% of our DNA with chimps

There's **monkey business** going on at the **gene pool**. All living organisms come from the **same family tree** and that's why everything uses DNA to store its **genetic instructions**. Chimpanzees are our **closest relatives**, with almost identical genes.

Mouse: 75%

This primate is closest to humans because it shares 96% of the same DNA.

Chimpanzee: 96%

BACK TO THE START

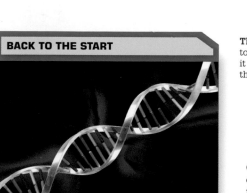

Each body cell contains long molecular strands of deoxyribonucleic acid (DNA) in a double-helix formation. Our DNA holds the instructions for building and operating a living human being. These instructions are written in code using combinations of four "letters."

Genetic testing companies can examine your DNA to trace your ancestors, creating personalized family trees. A much more mind-boggling family tree comes from going back in time to find common ancestors with humans. All kinds of living things share surprisingly large sequences of DNA with us, as shown here.

Which group of people has radioactive DNA?

Human: 100%

Fruit fly: 60%

Cow: 80%

Cat: 90%

Banana: 50%

TWO BROWN-EYED PARENTS CAN HAVE A
BLUE-EYED CHILD

As long as both parents carry the gene for blue eyes, it is possible for them to have a blue-eyed child. Human eye color is determined by multiple genes and the process is so complex that almost any parent-child combination can occur.

ALL HUMANS HAVE
UNIQUE DNA—
EVEN IDENTICAL TWINS

Almost all (99.9 percent) of human DNA sequences are the same in every person. However, our genetic make-up is made of more than three billion letters, so the remaining 0.1 percent leaves room for a lot of differences. Identical twins begin life with the same DNA but, as they grow and letters are copied, different "typos" happen in each twin, meaning their DNA is not exactly the same.

ALL LIVING HUMANS CAN BE TRACED BACK TO ONE COMMON ANCESTOR
IN AFRICA

"Mitochondrial Eve," who lived up to 200,000 years ago, was the most recent ancestor of all humans alive today, if their ancestry is traced through the female line (mitochondrial). English naturalist Charles Darwin was the first to propose the common descent of all living organisms.

TRUE or FALSE? Your **ears** and **nose** keep **growing** as you age

Have you **heard** this one before? **Cartilage tissue** in the ears and nose **continues to grow** as you age. The earlobes also **elongate** as **gravity** pulls them downward.

Saggy ears can be the result of the skin's elasticity losing its firmness.

LONGEST LIVING LADY

The world's oldest person was Jeanne Calment (1875–1997). The French cycling enthusiast died at the age of 122 years, 164 days. She claimed the secret to longevity was being calm and carefree.

The skin of older people is often wrinkled because the dermis produces far less collagen and elastin fibers that keep the skin of younger people firm and wrinkle-free.

The effects of time catch up with all of us eventually. While the ears and nose keep growing, the rest of the body starts slowing. Cells and tissue become worn out, and the skin thins and wrinkles. Eyesight and hearing both deteriorate.

The hippocampus (the area of the brain that helps store memories) may function less effectively, so elderly people can become more forgetful and confused.

What did **long earlobes** mean to the ancient Chinese?

📊 FAST FACTS

THE AVERAGE HUMAN LIFE EXPECTANCY HAS DOUBLED IN THE LAST 200 YEARS

In 2013 average life expectancy in Hong Kong, Japan, and Switzerland topped the charts at 83 years. At the bottom, however, is Sierra Leone, where life expectancy is just 45 years.

YEARS: 90 80 70 60 50 40 30 20 10 — **45** — **83**

LIFE EXPECTANCY IS INFLUENCED BY 70% ENVIRONMENTAL FACTORS AND 30% GENETICS

There is a lot that you can do to influence how long you will live. It is well known that people who smoke, eat foods high in cholesterol, don't exercise enough, and lead stressful lives will most probably die younger.

30% Genetics

70% Environmental

Osteoporosis—a disease that makes bones less dense and more fragile—is common in the elderly, with 8.9 million fractures annually. That's one every three seconds.

Aches and pains in the joints build up over time, but gentle stretching and walking can relieve discomfort.

Body talk

WOW, THAT'S **LONG!**

The **longest bone** in the body, the femur (thigh bone) is one-quarter of your height.

The **DIGESTIVE TRACT** is a **30 ft** (9 m) tube running from your mouth to your bottom. That's almost the length of a **school bus.**

If the **DNA** from **ONE CELL** was stretched out, it would be about **6.5 ft** (2 m) in length. That's about as tall as an adult man.

HANG ON A MINUTE

Every minute, you:

- produce **120 million** red blood cells in your bone marrow

- shed about **40,000** skin cells

- make **180** tiny eye movements

- have **70** heartbeats

- take **20** breaths

- process **2.1 pints** (1,200 ml) of blood in your kidneys, making **0.002 pints** (1 ml) of urine

THE HARD STUFF

The **SMALLEST** bone in your body is the size of a grain of rice. It is called the **STIRRUP** and is one of three bones in the ear.

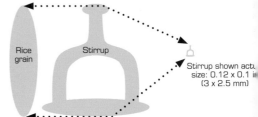

Rice grain

Stirrup

Stirrup shown actu[al] size: 0.12 x 0.1 i[n] (3 x 2.5 mm)

A fingernail would grow about **90 ft** (28 m) if it was never cut.

That's about the length of **four** elephants.

ON THE
MOVE

An adult's network of blood vessels is
100,000 miles
(160,000 km) long. That's long
enough to **wrap around the
world four times.**

The fastest nerve signals can
travel about **250 mph** (402 km/h).
That's faster than a peregrine falcon
and a **Formula 1** race car.

FORMULA 1 CAR	**PEREGRINE FALCON**	**NERVE SIGNAL**
240 mph	**242 mph**	**250 mph**
(386 KM/H)	(389 KM/H)	(402 KM/H)

You are born with **300** bones, but when you are fully grown you have only **206.**

The enamel of your teeth is the **HARDEST** substance in the body. It has no living cells, so your body cannot repair it once it's damaged.

GETTING
SLEEPY

A hormone called melatonin peaks at night
to make people feel sleepy.

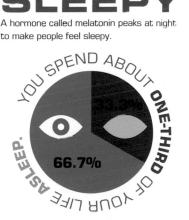

YOU SPEND ABOUT **ONE-THIRD** OF YOUR LIFE ASLEEP.

33.3%

66.7%

Teenagers don't produce **melatonin** until 1am. This is much later than most adults, which may be why it's hard to get teenagers out of bed in the morning!

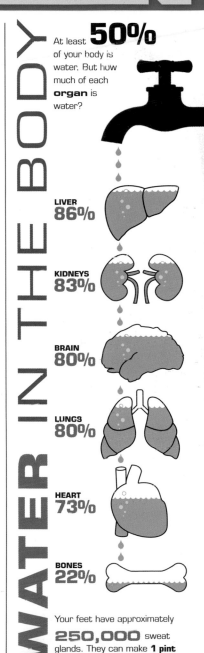

WATER IN THE BODY

At least **50%** of your body is water. But how much of each **organ** is water?

**LIVER
86%**

**KIDNEYS
83%**

**BRAIN
80%**

**LUNGS
80%**

**HEART
73%**

**BONES
22%**

Your feet have approximately
250,000 sweat glands. They can make **1 pint** (0.5 liters) of sweat each day.

TRUE or FALSE? Mice like cheese

Cheese is the food of choice for **cartoon mice**, but not for **real rodents**. While a hungry mouse will devour **virtually anything**, a choosy mouse opts for **fruit, grain, and seeds**.

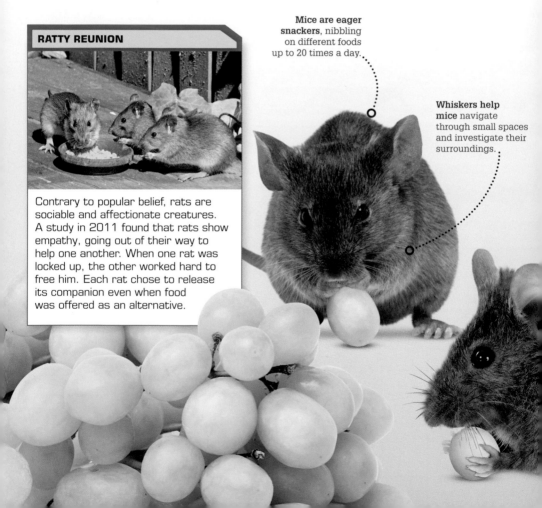

RATTY REUNION

Contrary to popular belief, rats are sociable and affectionate creatures. A study in 2011 found that rats show empathy, going out of their way to help one another. When one rat was locked up, the other worked hard to free him. Each rat chose to release its companion even when food was offered as an alternative.

Mice are eager snackers, nibbling on different foods up to 20 times a day.

Whiskers help mice navigate through small spaces and investigate their surroundings.

The country with the highest cheese consumption per capita is Greece.

OTHER MAMMALS 60%

RODENTS 40%

ABOUT 40% OF ALL MAMMAL SPECIES ARE RODENTS

Rodents are possibly the most successful group of animals of all time—they have survived for about 160 million years and remain abundant today.

THE ROMANS THOUGHT WHITE RATS WERE LUCKY

But if a black rat ate your lunch, it was believed to be a bad omen. Also, the Hindu Karni Mata Temple in Rajasthan, India, is dedicated to rats—about 20,000 live there, and if a human kills one, he or she must replace it with a solid gold statue of a rat.

THE LONGEST RAT IS THE SIZE OF A CAT

The Bosavi woolly rat was discovered by a television crew shooting a documentary about Mount Bosavi, an extinct volcano in Papua New Guinea. At about 32 in (82 cm) long, it is slightly longer than the average domestic cat, which is 30 in (76.2 cm) long.

What is unusual about the incisor (front) teeth of mice?

Mice hide out near food sources. These accomplished climbers, jumpers, and swimmers navigate their way around homes and yards easily. A recent study revealed that male mice sing love songs to females, but they are so high-pitched that we can't hear them. If things go well, a female house mouse can have up to 120 babies a year!

Mice love to explore, squeezing down small to fit through tiny gaps and biting clean through obstacles to keep moving.

TRUE or FALSE? Bees **die** when they **sting** you

Honeybees **sting you and die**, but wasps can sting **again and again**. Confusion over the two types of stinger can give some people **a bee in their bonnet**. To spot the difference if there's a buzz going on in your garden, bees are generally the **fatter**, **laid-back** ones, while wasps are **thinner and much angrier**!

Honeybees use sight and smell to locate flowers and find nectar.

BEE THERAPY

Some alternative therapists believe bee venom can help those suffering from diseases such as arthritis or multiple sclerosis. The affected area is deliberately stung to reduce pain and swelling. This treatment must be advised by a doctor because bee venom can cause anaphylactic shock, leading to sudden death, in a minority of allergic people.

Worker honeybees undertake various tasks, depending on their age and the requirements of the colony.

What do bees and turtles have in common?

Honeybees don't die when they sting other insects, but stinging a mammal, such as a human, causes the barbed stinger to become lodged in the skin. As the honeybee flies away, part of the digestive system, muscles, and nerves are torn out with the stinger. It is impossible for the honeybee to survive this loss. By contrast, wasps and other bees have a smooth stinger, allowing it to sting multiple targets repeatedly.

📊 FAST FACTS

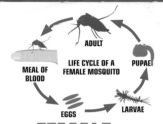

MEAL OF BLOOD • LIFE CYCLE OF A FEMALE MOSQUITO • ADULT • PUPAE • LARVAE • EGGS

ONLY **FEMALE** MOSQUITOES **BITE**

Female mosquitoes need nutrients from blood to produce eggs. Males prefer flower nectar because they don't make eggs. Once the females have laid their eggs, they die.

FIRE ANTS COORDINATE THEIR

BITES WHEN THREATENED

Nobody quite knows how they do it, but if you bump into a fire ant nest, the counterattack by the ants is organized so that all the ants will bite you at once. The effect is what gives the ants their name, since it feels like being on fire. Ouch!

RATING	INSECTS
1.0	Southern fire ant (*Solenopsis xyloni*)
2.0	Honeybee, Africanized bee, bumblebee, yellow jacket
3.0	Velvet ant, paper wasp
4.0	Tarantula hawk (*Pepsis* wasp)
4+	Bullet ant (*Paraponera clavata*)

THE **STARR STING** PAIN SCALE RANKS STINGS FROM ONE TO FOUR

Created by insect specialist Christopher Starr, this scale describes the pain of stings from bees, wasps, and ants. The bullet ant is the king of the stingers—its name says it all.

TRUE or FALSE? **Goldfish** have three-second memories

Goldfish are more gifted than people think. Studies have found them to be **fast learners** and **punctual timekeepers**, with the ability to remember colors, music, and other cues months later, **sinking this myth** to the bottom of the fishbowl.

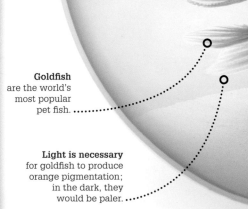

How do goldfish save the lives of people?

SALMON SWIMMERS

Adult salmon nearly always return to the river in which they spent their early life to breed. Once they're close to home, these speedy swimmers detect minerals in the water and trace them to their birthplace, where they go to lay eggs. Tagged salmon swam almost 2,000 miles (3,220 km) in 60 days along the Yukon River in Canada and Alaska.

Goldfish are the world's most popular pet fish.

Light is necessary for goldfish to produce orange pigmentation; in the dark, they would be paler.

Researchers have played the brain game with goldfish, finding they have a memory span of between three and five months. Taught to fetch balls, push levers, solve mazes, and limbo under bars, these multitalented marine creatures also enjoy routine, recognizing accurately when their daily feeding time will be.

FAST FACTS

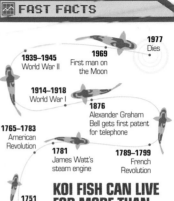

1977
Dies

1969
First man on the Moon

1939–1945
World War II

1914–1918
World War I

1876
Alexander Graham Bell gets first patent for telephone

1765–1783
American Revolution

1781
James Watt's steam engine

1789–1799
French Revolution

1751
Born

KOI FISH CAN LIVE FOR MORE THAN 200 YEARS

Like a tree, the age of a fish can be guessed by counting growth rings on its scales. Most koi fish die at about 50 years old, but legend has it that the oldest koi fish, called Hanako (meaning "flower maid"), was 226 years old when she died in 1977.

SOME LIPSTICK CONTAINS FISH SCALES

Pearl essence is a silvery substance that is found in fish scales and used in lipstick and nail polish to give a shimmery effect. The scales are one of the many by-products from the commercial fish processing industry and are primarily obtained from herring. Synthetic versions of pearl essence have also been developed.

TRUE or FALSE? A **cockroach** can **live for three days** without its **head**

Surviving the **extinction of the dinosaurs**, these **hardcore critters** take toughness to the next level. They can live **without air** for 45 minutes and **without their heads** for at least three days. Be afraid—be very afraid!

Antennae, or **feelers,** provide the cockroaches' sense of smell.

BUTTERFLY BRAIN

Developments in CT scanning have allowed scientists to study caterpillars during their metamorphosis into butterflies. They found that adult butterflies remembered things that happened to them while they were caterpillars. In a series of tests, butterflies reacted to bad smells in the same way they did as caterpillars, proving they remembered them.

The oldest fossil from a roachlike insect dates back to 315 million years ago. These superstrong miracles of nature can go for at least a month without food or water. They breed like wildfire and strike fear in people's hearts in the event of a home infestation. But very few species of cockroaches live in cities. Most dwell in forests and caves a long way from civilization.

📈 FAST FACTS

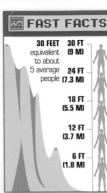

30 FEET	30 FT (9 M)
equivalent to about 5 average people	24 FT (7.3 M)
	18 FT (5.5 M)
	12 FT (3.7 M)
	6 FT (1.8 M)

TERMITE MOUNDS CAN REACH 30 FT (9 M) IN HEIGHT

The master builders of the insect world create their towering homes from a mixture of wood, soil, mud, saliva, and poop. Termites use openings at the base of the mound to enter and exit the nest, while workers add new tunnels and repair damage.

CANADA

UNITED STATES

MEXICO

SOME MONARCH BUTTERFLIES FLY 1,750 MILES (2,800 KM) IN THEIR LIFETIME

Flying south to Mexico, some monarch butterflies travel far to escape cold weather. In addition to being great fliers, they use special sensory organs on their feet and heads to identify their favorite plant, milkweed. They live for up to eight months.

There are 4,600 named species of cockroaches.

These scavengers eat virtually anything to survive.

Could cockroaches survive a nuclear explosion?

Their six legs carry them at speeds up to 3.4 mph (1.5 m/s).

TRUE or FALSE? We swallow **eight spiders** a **year** in our **sleep**

This thought is a **nightmare** for those suffering from **arachnophobia** (fear of spiders), but it is nothing more than a **tangled web** of nonsense. The possibility of this situation ever happening is **highly unlikely**, and there are **no examples** in scientific or medical records.

WONDER WEBS

In 2012 scientists used computer simulations to find out how well spiderwebs withstood a range of stresses. Some could even survive hurricane-force winds! This superstrength helps the web stay intact when prey is trapped within it.

Common house spiders trap flies and other bugs in their webs before rushing out to consume them.

The leg span of a Goliath bird-eating spider is about the same size as a dinner plate.

Jumping spiders have eight eyes and can leap up to 50 times their own body length.

FAST FACTS

THE DIVING BELL SPIDER CAN STAY UNDERWATER FOR 24 HOURS

The only spider known to live entirely underwater, the diving bell spider weaves a silk container to trap air on the surface, which it then uses to breathe when it's underwater. Their supply usually lasts a day.

SPIDERWEBS CAN SPAN RIVERS

The largest spiderweb crafted by a single spider measured 82 ft (25 m). It was made by a Darwin's bark spider in 2010 and crossed a river in Andasibe-Mantadia National Park on the island of Madagascar.

SOME SPIDERS LOVE GASOLINE

The yellow sac spider likes the smell of gasoline so much that it builds webs in car engines. Over time the webs could cause blockage and a buildup of pressure. In 2014 Mazda recalled 42,000 cars over fears the webs could clog fuel tanks, causing fires.

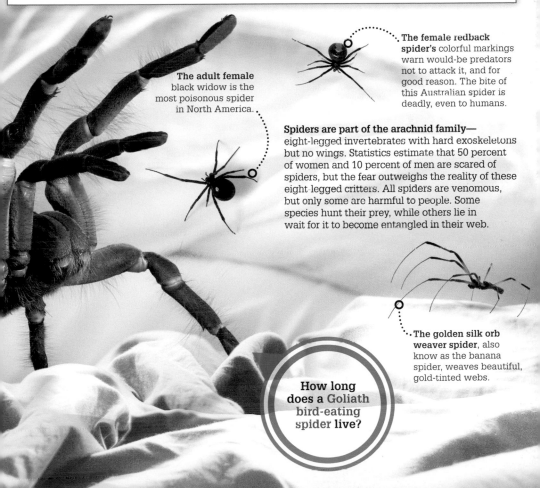

The female redback spider's colorful markings warn would-be predators not to attack it, and for good reason. The bite of this Australian spider is deadly, even to humans.

The adult female black widow is the most poisonous spider in North America.

Spiders are part of the arachnid family— eight-legged invertebrates with hard exoskeletons but no wings. Statistics estimate that 50 percent of women and 10 percent of men are scared of spiders, but the fear outweighs the reality of these eight-legged critters. All spiders are venomous, but only some are harmful to people. Some species hunt their prey, while others lie in wait for it to become entangled in their web.

The golden silk orb weaver spider, also know as the banana spider, weaves beautiful, gold-tinted webs.

How long does a Goliath bird-eating spider live?

TRUE or FALSE? A **tomato** is a **fruit**

Never **cherry-picked** for the fruit bowl, the tomato has spent its **salad days** with the green vegetables. But, by definition, a tomato is a fruit because it contains **the ovary** and **seeds** of a **flowering plant**.

Scientific studies have found that smelling or eating oranges improves people's moods.

Raspberries belong to the rose family.

Blueberries contain more healthy antioxidants than any other fruit or vegetable.

Grapes have been used to make wine since about 5000 BCE.

More than 100 billion bananas are eaten annually worldwide.

FIVE-A-DAY FABLE

In 2011 scientific studies of more than 300,000 Europeans found that eating five portions of fruits and vegetables a day does not guarantee long life. Fruits and vegetables cannot prevent diseases unless combined with a healthy lifestyle and regular exercise.

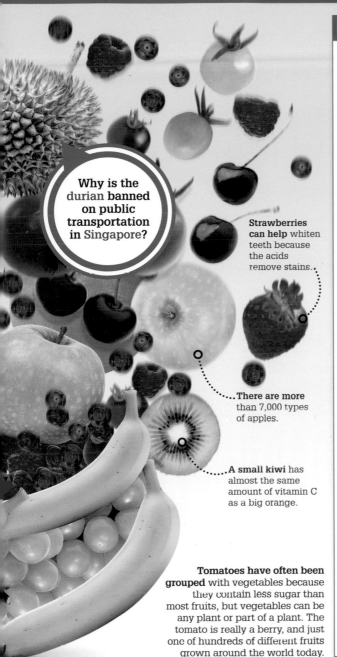

Why is the durian banned on public transportation in Singapore?

Strawberries **can help** whiten teeth because the acids remove stains.

There are more than 7,000 types of apples.

A small kiwi has almost the same amount of vitamin C as a big orange.

Tomatoes have often been grouped with vegetables because they contain less sugar than most fruits, but vegetables can be any plant or part of a plant. The tomato is really a berry, and just one of hundreds of different fruits grown around the world today.

Sand and other minerals are first shoveled into a blazing hot furnace. The intense heat fuses the mixture and melts it into liquid. The resulting molten liquid glass can be blown, molded, poured, and pressed into different shapes, such as windows, ornaments, and lenses.

The addition of lead makes glass sparkle, while limestone strengthens glass, and iron oxide makes glass green.

Glass can be recycled indefinitely and not lose its quality.

TRUE or FALSE? Glass is made of sand

This is not **transparently obvious**. It's strange to imagine grainy **sand** producing **smooth glass**, but sand is the main ingredient in the glass-making process. And it's nothing new. Ancient Egyptians made **glass beads** back in 3500 BCE.

SUPERSTRONG SYNTHETIC

Created in 1966, Kevlar is a flexible synthetic (manufactured) material. Five times stronger than steel but also very lightweight, it is ideal for protective clothing, such as bulletproof vests, as well as canoes, skis, and cell phones.

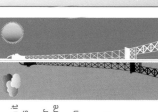

Who first produced transparent glass?

FAST FACTS

AFTER WATER, CONCRETE IS THE MOST WIDELY USED SUBSTANCE ON EARTH

5,000

The crucial ingredient in concrete is cement, which is made by mixing limestone with small amounts of clay and sand, and heating it in a kiln. Four billion tons of cement are produced each year. This is enough to make Egypt's Great Pyramid of Giza 5,000 times!

THE EIFFEL TOWER "GROWS" BY 6 IN (15 CM) IN SUMMER

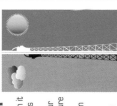

SUNLIGHT

SHADE

Steel expands when it is hot and contracts when it is cold. However, not all four sides of the structure can be in the sun at once. The portion of the structure in direct sunlight expands more than the portion in the shade. This means that the tower can be leaning by up to 7 in (18 cm) at any given time.

TRUE or FALSE? Penicillin was found by accident

Accidents happen, and one took place in Scottish doctor Alexander Fleming's London laboratory on September 28, 1928. Mold that had landed accidentally on Fleming's petri dish was producing a substance that **killed the bacteria** he was culturing. This was **penicillin**, the world's **first antibiotic**.

MICROWAVE MELTDOWN

When American engineer Percy Spencer (1894–1970) brought chocolate to work, it led to a modern-day marvel. As he inspected a magnetron (a device that produces microwave radiation for radar), the heat accidentally melted the chocolate in his pocket. He developed the microwave oven as a result.

Blue-green mold had grown in the petri dish because it was mistakenly left open.

While studying influenza, Fleming saw that a dish being used to grow staphylococcus germs had accidentally developed mold, which had made a bacteria-free ring around itself. Australian scientist Howard Florey and German scientist Ernst Chain worked to produce penicillin as a pharmaceutical drug in the 1940s, and in 1945 Florey and Chain won the Nobel Prize in Medicine.

The discovery of penicillin led to the development of antibiotics—a range of medicines used to treat bacterial infections. Antibiotics have since saved millions of lives.

How did a moldy melon get antibiotics into the mass market?

The mold was releasing a substance that stopped the bacteria's growth and created a bacteria-free barrier around itself.

FAST FACTS

WE CAN THANK A DOG FOR VELCRO

Microscopic view of hooks and loops

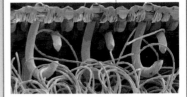

George de Mestral invented Velcro after taking his dog out for a walk. He noticed that the burrs (seeds) of burdock stuck to the dog's fur. Velcro works in the same way—tiny hooks on one strip of material cling to thin loops on another piece.

THE CAN OPENER WAS INVENTED

50 YEARS **AFTER THE TIN CAN WAS FIRST PRODUCED**

Early cans had to be opened using implements such as sharp knives, which was tricky because cans were made of much thicker metal sheets than they are today. The can opener made opening cans a lot less hazardous.

PLAY-DOH WAS INVENTED TO CLEAN WALLS

In the 1930s, coal was often used to heat homes, so Kutol Products invented a substance to remove soot stains from walls. But when schoolchildren began using the cleaner to make models in the 1950s, the product was repackaged and marketed as Play-Doh.

TRUE or FALSE? You can't be in two places at once

Time flies! Imagine making the most of it by being in **two places at once**—snoozing in bed while still being on time for school. Unfortunately it's not possible for you, but modern science has shown that **subatomic particles** can be in **millions of places** at once. At that tiny size, life is in a **permanent state of flux**. Sigh! For now we can only dream.

EINSTEIN'S THEORIES

Modern physics is dominated by two amazing theories that reveal the world as very different from our everyday experience. Quantum theory deals with matter and energy at very small scales, while relativity deals with space and time. Both theories suggest the possibility of time travel and were pioneered by German physicist Albert Einstein (1879–1955) in the early 1900s.

Super small things can be in different places at once because they act as both particles and waves. Light, for example, exists as waves, but also as a stream of particles called photons. Imagine a very dim light source that emits one photon at a time. Each photon exists as a wave spreading out in all directions—until it is detected in one place, as a tiny particle. This "wave-particle duality" is common to all subatomic particles, such as electrons and neutrinos—but not for larger objects like you.

Einstein figured out that if you traveled faster than light, you would go back in time—but his theory of relativity showed that accelerating something beyond that speed is impossible.

According to the theory of relativity, time runs at different rates in different situations. There is no "absolute" rate of time—it is relative. The same is true of distances.

If you travel into space at nearly the speed of light for a few years, and then return to Earth, you will find that much more time has passed back home than it has for you.

The most accurate clock on Earth is a type of atomic clock called strontium lattice. It won't lose a second in five billion years.

Where on Earth do clocks run the fastest?

FAST FACTS

ANSWER TO EVERYTHING

QUANTUM COMPUTERS WILL HAVE THE...

Extremely powerful quantum computers will be able to solve difficult problems very quickly. They will do so by considering all the possible answers simultaneously before coming up with one informed solution.

YOU CREATE A PARALLEL UNIVERSE EVERY TIME YOU MAKE A DECISION

That's true according to one interpretation of quantum theory. For each important decision or action you take, there is another universe in which you do something differently. The parallel versions of you also make decisions, which results in even more universes. Since we can't interact with parallel universes, we may never know for sure whether or not they exist.

GRAVITY IS THE LAST PIECE IN THE COSMIC PUZZLE OF CREATION

According to quantum theory, forces are carried by subatomic particles. Scientists have discovered the particles that carry each of the forces— except gravity. If they exist, the particles that carry gravity, dubbed "gravitons," will be extremely hard to detect.

TRUE or FALSE? The **Internet** and the **World Wide Web** are the same thing

The Internet slows down when other continents wake up and log on.

SOCIAL NETWORKING

The 21st century has seen the rise of social networking. The number of people signed up on Facebook—a website used by friends to keep in touch—reached two billion in 2017. Another hugely popular site, Twitter, has more than 328 million members sharing short messages called "tweets."

Early computers filled up a room, but today's microtechnology has resulted in light, portable smartphones, tablets, and laptop computers. As computers have gotten smaller, so has the world. The Internet has given its users the opportunity to be in constant contact across the continents, with shared access to live news, real-time conversations, and a vast archive of online information.

Don't get your **wires crossed**! It's easy to get **techno-terms** muddled up, but make no mistake here. The Internet is a **network** of computers and cables, while the Web is the **collection of pages** surfed online.

Internet users around the world can choose to log onto any of tens of billions of websites.

Which continent has the most Internet users?

📊 FAST FACTS

MORE THAN 75 PERCENT OF ALL E-MAILS ARE CONSIDERED SPAM AND LEFT UNOPENED

The first commercial spam message was sent in 1978, but the definition of the word *spam* as "unwanted messages" was not added to a major English dictionary until 1998. About 183 billion spam messages are sent every day.

TWITTER USERS SEND OVER 340,000 NEW TWEETS EACH MINUTE

And YouTube users upload 400 hours of new video every minute. There are tens of billions of websites, and this number is growing all the time as new websites are created.

THE SPACE BAR

IS THE MOST POPULAR KEY ON A KEYBOARD

If both keyboards and cell phones are included, the space bar is pressed six million times during any given second. So, in the tenth of a second it takes you to press the space bar, there are 600,000 others around the world doing the same thing. The next most popular key worldwide is the letter "e".

TRUE or FALSE? You are caught on **camera** 300 times a **day**

Can you really be **caught on camera** so many times? This number came from a book called *The Maximum Surveillance Society*, published in 1999. The true number of times **depends on your location**. Off the beaten track, you may **never be seen**, but in the bright lights of the big city, you can't be **camera shy**!

It is estimated there are up to 30 million surveillance cameras in use in the United States. Exact numbers are difficult to gauge as surveillance camera usage is constantly increasing and many cameras are privately owned. Critics complain that this creates a "Big Brother" state in which people have no privacy.

Surveillance cameras are mainly used for crime prevention, travel issues, and crowd control.

ON YOUR STREET

Google Street View and Google Earth are applications that map the world and the streets where people live. Special cars with street-view cameras on top travel around taking 360-degree pictures of neighborhoods.

FAST FACTS

GOOGLE MAPS TECHNOLOGY HAS PINPOINTED DANGEROUS LAND MINES IN POSTWAR KOSOVO

This has allowed mines to be cleared safely. Google Maps is the most used smartphone application in the world. It combines satellite, aerial, and street level imagery.

SOME SATELLITES IN SPACE CAN SEE OBJECTS JUST 5 IN (12 CM) WIDE ON EARTH

5 IN (12 CM)

Observation satellites are like giant telescopes pointed at Earth. They gather information for weather forecasting, mapmaking, and environmental monitoring.

Do surveillance cameras improve people's behavior?

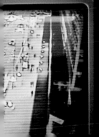

Robots will take over the world

The modern world has been **revolutionized by robots**—automated machines programmed to perform tasks. At least **10 million robots** exist, but world domination is beyond them. Robots cannot show initiative or react spontaneously. They are always ultimately **following human instructions**.

Sony's AIBO is a robot dog, designed to move and behave like a real canine. ......

CHESS CHAMPION

In 2006 Russian Vladimir Kramnik was the chess champion of the world, but he had yet to face his biggest opponent. In a competition held in Bonn, Germany, a computer named Deep Fritz beat Kramnik 4 to 2.

FAST FACTS

THE FIRST ROBOT WAS A
STEAM-POWERED BIRD

It was built from wood in ancient Greece by Archytas of Tarentum about 2,500 years ago. The bird managed to fly 656 ft (200 m) before running out of steam.

THERE ARE ABOUT
5,000 ROBOTS IN THE US MILITARY

These robots carry out dangerous work such as bomb disposal and land mine detection. This means that servicemen and women no longer have to risk their lives doing such tasks themselves.

Robots range from basic, mechanical toys for children to complicated machines, programmed with artificial intelligence skills, such as problem-solving and decision-making. They save employers time and money by working fast at repetitive tasks without the risks of fatigue or human error.

Toyota's robot is a humanoid robot, or android, but most robots don't need to resemble people to be useful.

Most surgical robots carry out procedures remotely on behalf of a surgeon who oversees the operation on screen and takes control of the robot's movements.

This builder robot is a concept idea. Most industry robots are computer-controlled mechanical arms on production lines.

How many car production workers **are** robots?

Honda's ASIMO can climb up and down stairs, and has a camera in its head to detect obstacles.

Cool science

SEEING THE **LIGHT**

Visible light, from red to violet, is part of the electromagnetic spectrum, which also includes other types of **electromagnetic radiation**. It runs from long-wavelength radio waves to short-wavelength gamma rays.

X-ray technology has revealed the **layers of paint** in Leonardo da Vinci's **Mona Lisa**. She once had **eyebrows** but they were painted out.

An incandescent light bulb turns only **three percent of** electrical energy into light.

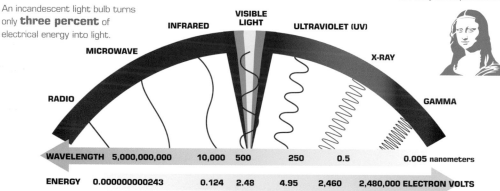

	VISIBLE LIGHT	
MICROWAVE	INFRARED	ULTRAVIOLET (UV)
RADIO		X-RAY
		GAMMA

WAVELENGTH	5,000,000,000	10,000	500	250	0.5	0.005 nanometers
ENERGY	0.000000000243	0.124	2.48	4.95	2,460	2,480,000 ELECTRON VOLTS

On a sunny day about **one quadrillion** photons (light particles) hit an area the size of a pinhead each second.

LIFE **SAVERS** ✚

Vaccination prevents more than **TWO MILLION** deaths every year.

- SMALLPOX **100%**
- DIPTHERIA **86%**
- WHOOPING COUGH **64%**
- MEASLES **60%**
- HEPATITIS B **58%**
- TETANUS (IN BABIES) **33%**
- TUBERCULOSIS **6%**

Estimated percentage of lives saved by vaccination per year

WHAT'S THAT **NOISE?**

AT **115 DECIBELS**, A **BABY'S CRY** IS **LOUDER** THAN A TYPICAL **CAR HORN**.

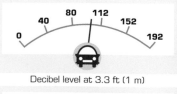

Decibel level at 3.3 ft (1 m)

ON THE MOVE

A sheep, a duck, and a rooster became the first aircraft passengers when they flew in the Montgolfier Brothers' hot-air balloon in 1783.

The **Airbus A380** is the largest passenger aircraft, and can carry *853 people.* The smallest piloted aircraft ever made was the **Bumble Bee II**, which was large enough only for the person flying it.

Bumble Bee II wingspan: **5.6 ft** (1.68 m)

Airbus A380 wingspan: **261.8 ft** (79.8 m)

GREAT **INVENTIONS** OVER THE YEARS

○ **LIGHTHOUSE**
c. 280 BCE

FIREWORKS
c. 1000 CE ○

TELESCOPE
1608 ○

ELECTRONIC COMPUTER
1940s ○

SMARTPHONE
2007 ○

| 500 BCE | 0 | 500 CE | 1000 | 1500 | 2000 |

SCISSORS
c. 100 CE ○

PRINTING PRESS ○
1455

TELEPHONE ○
1876

WORLD WIDE WEB
1990 ○

Earth is the largest rocky planet. Its crust consists of seven large moving plates that rub together, making mountains and volcanoes. The landscape is constantly changing due to the effects of wind, water, ice, and ranging temperatures, as well as the impact of human activity and settlement.

What are the record high and low temperatures on Earth?

The equator receives the most sunlight, while the North and South Poles get the least.

During the last 10,000 years, 25 percent of Earth's forests have been cleared to make room for farms and homes.

WATCHING THE WORLD

Launched in 2013, *Landsat 8* is now orbiting our planet. It is the latest in a series of Landsat craft that together have made the longest continuous record of Earth's land from space. Other craft collect data on our planet's oceans and atmosphere, as well as topical issues such as climate change and car emissions.

More than two-thirds of Earth's surface is water.

TRUE or FALSE? Earth is a perfect sphere

Astronauts dubbed our planet the **"blue marble,"** but the notion that it is spherical falls flat. With its mountains and valleys, it is clear that **Earth's lumps and bumps** can never be whipped into perfect shape. Instead, our planet is an **oblate spheroid**—a sphere squashed at the ends and swollen in the middle.

Earth's circumference is 24,900 miles (40,074 km).

Earth's oceans formed when steam in the young planet's atmosphere condensed into water and fell to the surface.

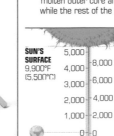

📊 FAST FACTS

EARTH IS THE **DENSEST** OF ALL THE PLANETS

This is because Earth contains a lot of iron. Both its solid inner core and molten outer core are mainly iron, while the rest of the core is nickel.

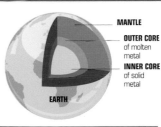

MANTLE

OUTER CORE of molten metal

INNER CORE of solid metal

EARTH

SUN'S SURFACE 9,900°F (5,500°C)	5,000	8,000	EARTH'S CORE 10,112°F (5,600°C)
	4,000	6,000	
	3,000		
	2,000	4,000	
	1,000	2,000	
	0	0	
EARTH'S AVERAGE TEMPERATURE 59°F (15°C)	°C	°F	

THE TEMPERATURE AT **EARTH'S** CORE IS **10,112°F** (5,600°C)

That's as hot as the sun's surface! Thankfully, the earth's surface is much cooler—the average global temperature is 59°F (15°C). The hottest regions of the surface are near the equator, while the coldest are near its two poles.

TRUE or FALSE? There is a **dark side** of the **Moon**

Many moons ago, sky-gazers speculated about a **mysterious dark side** of the Moon that we never get to see because the **same side** of the Moon **always faces Earth**. Thanks to **lunar landings and satellite surveillance**, we're no longer in the dark about the far side.

Photographs of the far side of the Moon have been taken, showing that the far side gets just as much sunlight as the near side.

TIDAL FORCE

The Moon produces the daily tides in Earth's oceans. Gravitational forces on the Moon pull on the water, creating bulges in the sea on either side of the planet. These bulges cause the regular rise and fall of the water level at the sea's edge that we call tides. The world's most extreme tides occur at the Bay of Fundy in Canada (shown above at low and high tide).

Hundreds of millions of years ago, the Moon rotated much more quickly than it does today, taking less time to orbit Earth. As the Moon's gravity slowed Earth's spin, the Moon took longer to orbit Earth and its spin slowed down. Today, the Moon takes 27.3 days to make one rotation on its axis, and to complete one orbit around our planet. Since the rotation and orbit times are equal, the same side of the Moon is permanently visible to us on Earth.

A dusting of rock and soil covers the cratered surface. Most craters formed in the first 750 million years of the Moon's life when asteroids made their mark.

The sun's light sweeps around the Moon as it spins, just as it does on Earth. The Moon's shine is this reflected sunlight.

Why does the Moon turn red during an eclipse?

TRUE or FALSE? The sun is **yellow**

Children's drawings of **bright yellow sunshine** capture its true color. This big ball of glowing gas is a **yellow star**. But there's nothing mellow about this yellow. The sun is seriously **hot stuff**, with a **sizzling surface** of 9,900°F (5,500°C).

> Where on Earth is it sunny during the night?

SOLAR POWER

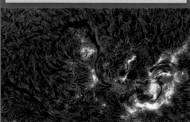

At close range, the sun's surface is a hotbed of activity. Gas jets, called spicules, fire up repeatedly. Great looping clouds and swaths of cooler gas, called prominences, reach into space. The distinctive orange-peel texture of the surface, known as granulation, comes from gas cells rising up constantly.

Clouds, called prominences, extend into space for hundreds of thousands of miles.

The sun's rays take more than eight minutes to reach our skin.

The sun looks yellow from Earth or space, but it looks more yellow on Earth due to the atmosphere. If you viewed the sun from a mountaintop, the yellow intensity would reduce because there is less air. We are so familiar with depictions of the yellow sun that astronomers artificially enhance images to make them more yellow.

Spacecraft SOHO (Solar and Heliospheric Observatory) photographs the sun and studies the surface.

White areas, called faculae, are the hottest regions of the sun.

Darker sunspots are cooler areas of the sun.

The circumference of the sun is 2.7 million miles (4.4 million km).

The sun is three-quarters hydrogen and almost all the rest is helium, held together by gravity.

📷 FAST FACTS

THE SUN CONTAINS 330,000 TIMES MORE MATERIAL THAN EARTH

Everything in our solar system revolves around this massive star. Up until the 16th century, however, it was believed that Earth was at the heart of everything, and that the sun and planets circled around it.

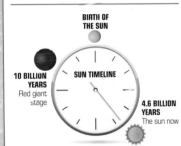

BIRTH OF THE SUN

10 BILLION YEARS
Red giant stage

SUN TIMELINE

4.6 BILLION YEARS
The sun now

THERE WILL BE ANOTHER FIVE BILLION YEARS OF SUNSHINE

The sun is currently middle-aged because its rays have already been shining for at least 4.6 billion years. Toward the end of its life, during the red giant stage, the sun will expand to about 100 times its size, cool, and turn red. The sun will start to die as material is shed from its outer layers. What remains of the dying star will pack together to make a star about the same size as Earth, called a white dwarf. This will fade and cool to become a cold, dark cinder in space.

TRUE or FALSE? Starlight is millions of years old

When you look up at the stars, you're seeing their **original light** created many thousands or even millions of years before. A light-year is the distance light travels in a year—a **mind-boggling** 5.88 trillion miles (9.46 trillion km), so the light of a star **millions of light-years** away has taken **millions of years** to reach us.

The atmosphere surrounding Earth makes stars appear to twinkle in the sky.

The light we see from these stars left before the Great Pyramid was built in Egypt.

JEWEL BOX
Cluster of stars about 10 million years old

TARANTULA NEBULA
Very young stars, between one and two million years old

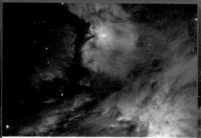

STAR CYCLE

A star is born in a cloud of gas and dust. When nuclear reactions start, the star releases energy and shines steadily. It swells into a red giant or a supergiant. Most stars die slowly, but the massive ones explode as brilliant supernovas.

Stars produce different amounts of light. We find out which stars produce the most light by comparing their luminosity—the energy a star emits in just one second. The brightest stars release more than six million times the light of the sun, while the least luminous stars create less than one ten-thousandth.

Are there more stars in the sky or grains of sand on Earth?

Heat and light are produced when hydrogen turns into helium gas inside the star's core.

Light from these stars takes 16,000 years to reach Earth. This cluster is like a beehive swarm of 10 million stars.

Massive stars can blow up, but we may not know for thousands of years. We see how the star looked when the light left years ago.

FAST FACTS

THE HOTTEST STARS ARE BLUE

You might expect the hottest stars to be red, and the coolest to be blue, but in fact it's the other way around. Blue stars reach a temperature of about 72,000°F (40,000°C), while red stars get no hotter than 7,200°F (4,000°C).

HOW A STAR DIES DEPENDS ON ITS MASS—THE AMOUNT OF MATERIAL IT IS MADE FROM

SUNLIKE STAR → RED GIANT → PLANETARY NEBULA

MASSIVE STAR → RED SUPERGIANT → SUPERNOVA

Sunlike stars shine brightly for billions of years. Late in life, they expand to become a cooler, brighter star called a red giant. It sheds its outer layers, called a planetary nebula. Stars with more than eight times the sun's mass last only a few million years. They become supergiants, which explode as supernovas and leave a neutron star or a black hole behind.

OMEGA CENTAURI
Ancient stars more than 10 billion years old

FAST FACTS

EACH STAR IS CONSTANTLY MOVING IN SPACE

Stars are constantly moving in Earth's sky, but it takes tens of thousands of years before new positions are noticeable and constellations have new shapes. Yet it is possible to see changes since the ancient Greeks first identified constellations more than 2,500 years ago.

THE BIG DIPPER
50,000 years ago

THE BIG DIPPER
Today

ALL THE BRIGHTEST STARS IN THE NIGHT SKY ARE LABELED ALPHA

Stars are named within a constellation in order of brightness using the Greek alphabet, so the brightest stars begin with *alpha*, the next brightest with *beta*, and so on. Many of the stars we can see also have historical names, such as Betelgeuse, named by Arabic astronomers.

SIRIUS
Alpha CMa

BETELGEUSE
Alpha Ori

POLLUX
Beta Gem

ADHARA
Epsilon CMa

YOU CAN SEE MORE STARS IN THE COUNTRY

On a clear, moonless night using just your eyes, about 300 stars are visible from the city, and about 1,000 in a darker small-town sky. In the darkest countryside about 3,000 are visible; use binoculars and you'll see more than 40,000.

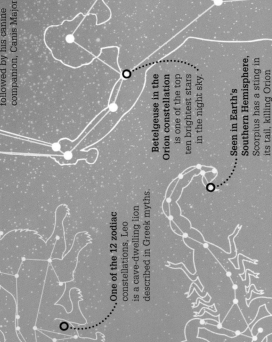

Why do some stars shine brighter than others in the night sky?

Part of Canis Major, Sirius (or the "Dog Star") is the brightest star in the sky, burning 20 times brighter than the sun.

Named after a mythical hunter in ancient Greece, Orion holds a club and a lion's head. He is followed by his canine companion, Canis Major.

Betelgeuse in the Orion constellation is one of the top ten brightest stars in the night sky.

Seen in Earth's Southern Hemisphere, Scorpius has a sting in its tail, killing Orion in Greek mythology.

One of the 12 zodiac constellations, Leo is a cave-dwelling lion described in Greek myths.

TRUE or FALSE?

Stars in a constellation are close together

Although stars appear to shine in glittering groups, it is an **optical illusion**. Astronomers have divided the sky above Earth into **88 imaginary pieces**. Each is a constellation forming its own pattern, but the stars within it are really **spaced out**.

The constellations may appear to contain connected stars, but they are vastly different distances from Earth. A different vantage point would rearrange the stars in a new pattern. However, the constellations are useful for stargazers tracking the night sky. Most of the constellations have been given two names—a Latin name and a common name. More than half are characters from ancient Greek mythology.

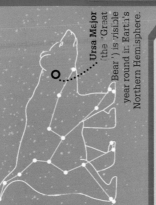

Ursa Major (the "Great Bear") is visible year round in Earth's Northern Hemisphere.

Observatories house telescopes used to look deep into space. The telescopes collect light that forms amazing magnified images of the stars and galaxies.

GALAXY GREATS

Swirling through our skies are galaxies containing masses of stars, dust, and dark matter. Each galaxy has a unique catalog number to identify it. Some galaxies have novelty names to describe their shape, such as the cigar (shown), fried egg sunflower, and sombrero.

TRUE or FALSE? Astronauts would **explode** without **space suits**

This double-layered bodysuit is known as a liquid cooling and ventilation garment (LCVG).

There would be no explosions, but it would still be the **final frontier**. Without space suits, astronauts would die, either from the **freezing cold** or from their **blood boiling** due to the drop in pressure.

SPACE LIFE

The International Space Station (ISS) is about 240 miles (390 km) above Earth. Astronauts spend months there, working in the laboratories or carrying out station maintenance. There is a galley kitchen, exercise equipment, and sleep cabins. Sleeping bags are fixed so they cannot float away in the weightless conditions.

Gloves are thick enough to protect the hands but thin enough to allow ease of movement.

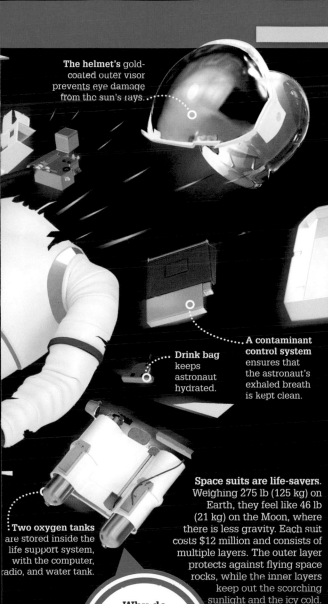

The helmet's gold-coated outer visor prevents eye damage from the sun's rays.

Drink bag keeps astronaut hydrated.

A contaminant control system ensures that the astronaut's exhaled breath is kept clean.

Two oxygen tanks are stored inside the life support system, with the computer, radio, and water tank.

Space suits are life-savers. Weighing 275 lb (125 kg) on Earth, they feel like 46 lb (21 kg) on the Moon, where there is less gravity. Each suit costs $12 million and consists of multiple layers. The outer layer protects against flying space rocks, while the inner layers keep out the scorching sunlight and the icy cold.

Why do astronauts on board the ISS sneeze about 100 times a day?

▣ FAST FACTS

THE FIRST CHIMP TO GO INTO SPACE WAS NAMED HAM

This unusual space traveler went aboard a US Mercury spacecraft in 1961. Other creatures that have reached space include mice, monkeys, rabbits, guinea pigs, insects, cats, dogs, turtles, spiders, and even jellyfish.

A MODERN CAR IS MORE COMPLEX THAN APOLLO 11

In the early days, NASA sent astronauts to the Moon using less computing power than is found in a modern car. Still, the spacecraft was equipped with real-time flight information and an automatic navigation system, and it worked!

PIZZA HUT DELIVERS SPACE PIZZA

In 2001 Pizza Hut "delivered" a vacuum-sealed pizza to hungry astronauts on board the International Space Station. Admittedly, the Russian rocket carrying the pizza took longer than the usual 30 minutes to arrive.

Out of this world

A UNIVERSAL VIEW

75% HYDROGEN

23% HELIUM

2% OTHER ELEMENTS

The elements **hydrogen** and **helium** make up **98 percent** of the matter we can see in the **universe**.

The most distant object that many people can see using just their eyes is the Andromeda Galaxy, **15 trillion miles (25 trillion km)** away.

MOON-GAZING

As the **Moon orbits Earth**, a changing amount of the one face we see is bathed in sunlight. The different shapes are the Moon's **phases.** One cycle of phases lasts **29.5 days.**

NEW MOON

WAXING CRESCENT

FIRST QUARTER

WAXING GIBBOUS

FULL MOON

WANING GIBBOUS

LAST QUARTER

WANING CRESCENT

NEW MOON

The maiden name of **moonwalking** astronaut Buzz Aldrin's mother was **Moon.**

SOLAR SYSTEM

Venus is the hottest planet in our solar system. The surface is hot enough to **melt lead.**

867°F (464°C) — Venus

333°F (167°C) — Mercury

59°F (15°C) — Earth

-81°F (-63°C) — Mars

-162°F (-108°C) — Jupiter

-218°F (-139°C) — Saturn

-323°F (-197°C) — Uranus

-330°F (-201°F) — Neptune

500°

400°

100°

0°C

-100

-200

The solar system's **largest volcano** is **Olympus Mons** on Mars. It is **380 miles (610 km)** wide. That's about the **same width as Spain.**

SEEING STARS

If you counted all the stars in the **Milky Way** at the rate of *one a second*, it would take you about **12,000 years** to count them all.

The **biggest** diamond is in the heart of an old star named **BPM 37093** with a diameter of **2,485 miles** (4,000 km). That's roughly the width of Australia.

BLAST OFF!

Many countries have spaceflight **launch sites.** Sites closer to the equator can launch heavier cargo, because rockets there are given a boost by **the speed of Earth's spin**.

Baikonur, Kazakhstan

Cape Canaveral, Florida

Xjchang, China

Kourou, French Guiana

FIVE ASTRONAUT FIRSTS

1961 — **Yuri Gagarin** first human in space (Russian)

1963 — **Valentina Tereshkova** first woman in space (Russian)

1965 — **Alexei Leonov** first to space walk (Russian)

1969 — **Neil Armstrong** first to walk on the Moon (American)

2001 — **Dennis Tito** first space tourist (American)

Each **toilet** on the **International Space Station** cost **$19 million**.

MAKING AN IMPACT

Large **meteorites** blast out vast craters when they land. **Young Earth** was bombarded with meteorites:

VREDEFORT **(SOUTH AFRICA)**
185 MILES (300 KM) ACROSS
MORE THAN 2 BILLION YEARS OLD

SUDBURY **(CANADA)**
155 MILES (250 KM) ACROSS
1.85 BILLION YEARS OLD

CHICXULUB **(MEXICO)**
105 MILES (170 KM) ACROSS
65 MILLION YEARS OLD

POPIGAI **(RUSSIA)**
60 MILES (100 KM) ACROSS
35.7 MILLION YEARS OLD

LONDON **(ENGLAND)**
35 MILES (50 KM) ACROSS

atmosphere

About **3,000 meteorites** land on Earth every year—most burn up in the **atmosphere**.

TRUE or FALSE? Earthquakes are very rare

Untrue—every year there are **several million earthquakes**. Most are just **gentle wobbles**, while a handful are **earth-shattering**, causing widespread devastation.

Richter scale
6–6.9 = strong, severe, sudden movement, on average 120 a year

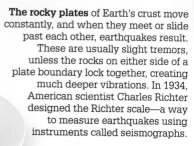

The rocky plates of Earth's crust move constantly, and when they meet or slide past each other, earthquakes result. These are usually slight tremors, unless the rocks on either side of a plate boundary lock together, creating much deeper vibrations. In 1934, American scientist Charles Richter designed the Richter scale—a way to measure earthquakes using instruments called seismographs.

WAVES OF DESTRUCTION

A huge earthquake on the seabed can trigger a series of catastrophic waves, called tsunamis. Traveling at speeds up to 586 mph (943 km/h), they cause mass devastation upon reaching land, bringing down buildings and destroying life.

Richter scale
1–4.9 = light,
minor movement,
more than
64,000 a year

Is there anywhere on Earth where Jell-O does not wobble?

📊 FAST FACTS

THE BIGGEST EARTHQUAKE OF THE 20TH CENTURY MEASURED

9.5 ON THE RICHTER SCALE

The Great Chilean Earthquake in 1960 resulted in landslides, tsunamis, and floods. The earthquake that caused the tsunami in the Indian Ocean on December 26, 2004, measured 9.1–9.3.

MOONQUAKES OCCUR ON THE MOON

The highest a moonquake has reached is 5.5 on the Richter scale. Although earthquakes tend to be stronger, these shallow moonquakes all lasted more than 10 minutes, whereas on Earth vibrations usually last just half a minute.

Richter scale 5–5.9 =
moderate, strong,
sudden movement,
on average
800 a year

Richter scale 8+ =
extreme, destructive
movement, on
average one a year

Richter scale 7–7.9 =
major, very severe
movement, on
average 18 a year

When Earth was young, it was knocked off-kilter by a large object. Instead of rotating with a straight axis, it now spins on an axis tilted at 23.5°. As Earth orbits the sun, it always tilts the same way. When the North Pole is tilted toward the sun, the Northern Hemisphere is heated more and it is summer. At the same time the South Pole tilts away from the sun, making the Southern Hemisphere cool in winter.

In June, Earth's North Pole is tilted toward the sun, giving the land there continual sunshine, with the sun never sinking below the horizon.

TRUE or FALSE? It is warm in **summer** because Earth's orbit is **closest to the sun**

It's time to **see the light** if you believe this! When it is summer one side of our planet, it is winter on the other. Earth is actually **farthest from the sun** during North America's **summer**. The changing seasons are a result of the **tilt in Earth's axis**.

📊 FAST FACTS

EARTH'S DAYS ARE
GETTING LONGER

Due to the tidal effects the Moon has on Earth, a day is 1.7 milliseconds longer than it was a century ago. In the age of the dinosaurs, about 60 million years ago, an Earth day was less than 23 hours long.

AT MIDNIGHT ON JUNE 21 IT IS LIGHT EVERYWHERE NORTH OF THE
ARCTIC CIRCLE

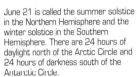

June 21 is called the summer solstice in the Northern Hemisphere and the winter solstice in the Southern Hemisphere. There are 24 hours of daylight north of the Arctic Circle and 24 hours of darkness south of the Antarctic Circle.

Although Earth is closer to the sun at certain times of the year, the difference in distance is so minor that it does not affect the weather.

The North Pole receives no sunlight in January, experiencing 24 hours of darkness.

MONSOON SEASON

A seasonal change in the prevailing wind has dramatic consequences for southern Asia. Warm, moist air blows northeast from ocean to land in summer, bringing the wet monsoon and heavy flooding. Cool, dry air blows from land to ocean in winter. The change in wind direction comes from the differing temperatures of land and water.

Why is it warmer at the end of summer than in the middle?

TRUE or FALSE? A **red** sky at night signals **good weather**

"Red sky at night, shepherds' delight. Red sky in the morning, shepherds' warning." This well-known saying first appeared **in the Bible** to help shepherds get ready for the next day's weather, but it **still holds true** today.

FAST FACTS

BIRDS ON A TELEPHONE WIRE MAY BE A SIGN OF STORMS

Flocks of migrating birds often rest on telephone wires. But if you notice a sudden increase in birds on wires, they could be taking a break to avoid a bad storm in their path.

A **HALO** AROUND THE MOON MAY MEAN A STORM IS COMING

This is caused by ice crystals forming in high clouds, which happens before a heavy rain shower. An old saying goes, "Circle around the moon, rain or snow soon."

WEATHER WATCHING

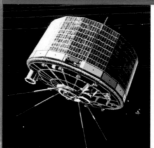

Meteorology, or the study of the atmosphere, can be traced back to India around 3000 BCE. It took off in the 18th and 19th centuries with the invention of accurate instruments to measure weather. By the mid-20th century, satellites were circling in space to track Earth's weather systems from the sky.

The red color comes from dust particles in the air, and increased pollution also plays a part.

Many people believe their bodies can predict the weather. Rheumatic joints or aches from past injuries are said to be a sign of rain on the horizon

Some cultures use the same red sky saying, but change it to "sailors' delight" instead, depending on the people most affected by the weather.

How are seagulls said to predict the weather?

Before scientific forecasting techniques were developed, people relied on their experiences to provide accurate predictions. Red night skies indicate that dust is trapped in the air by high pressure. When this moves in from the west, clear skies and sunshine are coming. Red skies in the morning suggest the good weather has moved east to be replaced by low pressure. This is a red alert, warning of rain to follow.

TRUE or FALSE? Lightning can't **strike** the same place **twice**

This may **strike you as strange**, but lightning often strikes twice. Tall targets, such as skyscrapers and trees, can be struck up to **100 times** a year. American park ranger Roy Sullivan also felt the **full force of nature**, being hit **seven** times. His stroke of luck was surviving!

Each flash of forked lightning can reach up to 6 miles (9 km) from the cloud to the ground.

RETHINKING RAINDROPS

The usual depiction of a raindrop is a classic tear shape. But small raindrops are spherical, while larger ones are more roll-shaped. As raindrops fall, they are flattened from below by air resistance. If this force exceeds the attraction of the water molecules for each other, the raindrop will split into smaller ones.

Intense heat from the electric spark causes the air to expand and vibrate. This is heard as a thunderclap after the lightning flash.

Lightning flashes are immense electric sparks that streak from the bottom to the top of a thundercloud, or from cloud-to-cloud or cloud-to-ground. The electric charges that make the sparks are created by ice crystals and water droplets crashing together in the chaotic up- and downdrafts inside the cloud.

In a split second, a bolt of lightning can heat the surrounding air to temperatures five times hotter than the sun's surface.

Lightning is visible striking the same building in Hong Kong's central business district twice.

How can you tell if lightning is about to strike you?

FAST FACTS

YOU CAN TELL HOW FAR AWAY LIGHTNING IS BY COUNTING

1, 2, 3... RUMBLE

After a lightning bolt, you can count the seconds to find out approximately how far away the lightning struck. Count the seconds between the strike and the thunder, and divide the number of seconds by 5 for the distance in miles, or by 3 for the distance in kilometers.

APOLLO 12 WAS STRUCK BY LIGHTNING DURING ITS LAUNCH

Apollo 12 launched in 1969 into a rainy sky. The Saturn V rocket was struck twice by lightning 30 seconds and 50 seconds after liftoff. But because the rocket was in the air (not grounded), no damage was caused.

LIGHTNING STRIKES ABOUT 8.6 MILLION TIMES A DAY

Each strike carries enough energy to power a city with 200,000 inhabitants for one minute. The average lightning flash would also power a 100-watt light bulb for three months.

TRUE or FALSE? No two snowflakes are the same

The average snowflake has a top speed of 5.6 ft (1.7 m) per second.

This fact can come in **from the cold**. At high altitudes, specks of dust inside clouds develop **ice crystals** that turn them into snowflakes. With at least 275 **water molecules** needed to form a small ice crystal, and at least 50 crystals in a single snowflake, each one falls to Earth in a **unique formation**.

SNOWY SPIKES

In mountain ranges where the air is dry, such as Cerro Mercedario in Argentina, piles of snow can develop into penitentes— tall ice blades. These spiky formations were originally thought to look like the hoods of monks doing penance.

Each snowflake forms its own six-sided pattern, with a change in temperature making the crystal arrangement more complex.

Snow is a form of precipitation, just like rain, hail, and sleet. When flurries of flakes fall, the minimal accumulation can produce dry, new snow called powder snow. Heavy snowfalls for prolonged periods are snowstorms. About 12 percent of our planet is permanently covered in snow and ice.

Snow is not white, but clear and colorless.

As long as the air temperature between the cloud and the ground is below 32°F (0°C), this flake will fall as snow.

The largest snowflake on record, from Montana in 1887, measured 15 in (38 cm) wide and 8 in (20 cm) thick.

Can it ever be too cold to snow on planet Earth?

FAST FACTS

THE WORST SNOWSTORM IN HISTORY KILLED 500 PEOPLE

In 1993 a winter storm wreaked havoc on the East Coast of the United States, causing $5.5 billion worth of damage. One meteorologist called it "a storm with the heart of a blizzard and the soul of a hurricane."

THE WORLD'S LARGEST SNOWMAN WAS A SNOW WOMAN

Built in Maine in 2008, she stood 122 ft (37 m) in height—about the same as a 12-story building. She had trees for arms, and skis for eyelashes.

SNOW MAKES A GOOD INSULATOR

About 90% of snow is trapped air. Since the air can't move, the heat loss is reduced, which makes snow a good insulator. Humans use this property to insulate igloos, and many animals keep warm by burrowing into snow to hibernate in winter.

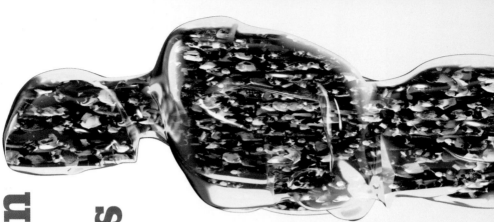

TRUE or FALSE?

The population of the world can fit into Los Angeles

The award for the city that can best squeeze the **global population** inside, standing shoulder to shoulder, is... **Los Angeles**. This American city can carry the **weight of the world**!

ESCAPING THE CROWDS

The least populated parts of the world are usually determined by a remote or challenging landscape, along with limited opportunities for work. This lifestyle does not appeal to everyone. Desert regions, such as the western Sahara, or isolated islands, such as Greenland (shown here), are examples.

Which country makes up one-fifth of the global population?

There are 1.01 men in the world for every woman.

Every year 137 million babies are born and 55 million people die. This means the population grows by 82 million.

Nicknamed Oscar, the gold-plated statue for the Academy Awards was first given in 1929 at a ceremony in Hollywood, California. Thousands of winners have received them since.

Los Angeles, California, the "City of Angels," covers 500 square miles (1,300 sq km). This is just enough to accommodate the seven billion people in the world—but breathe in! Tokyo, Japan, is the world's most populated city, with more than nine million people, while the smallest city by population is Hum in Croatia, with approximately 23 people.

FAST FACTS

THE WORLD'S POPULATION IS GROWING AT A RATE OF 8,760 PEOPLE AN HOUR

This means that almost 150 people are added to the planet every minute. But the world is top-heavy— 90 percent of its total population lives in the Northern Hemisphere.

ABOUT 108 BILLION PEOPLE HAVE LIVED ON EARTH

Seven billion people are alive at present, which means about 6.5 percent of all the people who ever lived are alive now.

ALIVE AT PRESENT
6.5%

8% OF THE WORLD'S POPULATION IS OVER 65

CURRENTLY 8%

2050 25%

This will rise to 25 percent by 2050. Better food, health care, hygiene, and education have all contributed to our rising life expectancy, which has doubled in the last 200 years. It depends where you live, though—illnesses that are treatable in the West can have a devastating impact on poorer populations.

Down to Earth

BLOWN AWAY

The **EYE** (center) of a hurricane can be **20 MILES** (32 KM) across—larger than MANHATTAN, New York.

HURRICANE WINDS CAN REACH SPEEDS OF 186 MPH (300 KMH).

FROGS poured down from the sky in Kansas City in 1873, and **HERRING** fell on a group of golfers in Bournemouth, England, in 1948. These creatures had been *swept into the clouds* by wind and dropped into different locations.

EARTH THROUGH THE AGES

5,000 MYA	4,000 MYA	3,000 MYA

FORMATION OF EARTH
4,540 MYA

FORMATION OF MOON
c. 4,500 MYA

FIRST LIFE
3,800 MYA

HIGH LIFE

Seven highest peaks on the seven continents

MOUNT EVEREST—Asia
29,035 ft (8,850 m)

ACONCAGUA—South America
22,838 ft (6,960 m)

MOUNT MCKINLEY—North America
20,322 ft (6,194 m)

KILIMANJARO—Africa
19,340 ft (5,895 m)

MOUNT ELBRUS—Europe
18,510 ft (5,642 m)

VINSON MASSIF—Antarctica
16,066 ft (4,897 m)

PUNCAK JAYA—Australasia
16,023 ft (4,884 m)

In 2005 Davo Karnicar became the first person to **SKI** down *Mount Everest*.

MAKING A SPLASH

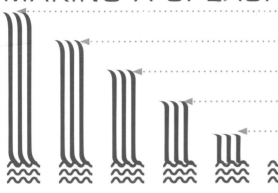

SOUTH AMERICA **ANGEL FALLS— Venezuela**
3,212 ft (979 m)

AFRICA **TUGELA FALLS—South Africa**
3,110 ft (948 m)

AUSTRALASIA **OLO'UPENA FALLS—Hawaii**
2,953 ft (900 m)

EUROPE **VINNUFALLET—Norway**
2,837 ft (865 m)

NORTH AMERICA **JAMES BRUCE FALLS—Canada**
2,755 ft (840 m)

ASIA **HANNOKI-NO-TAKI—Japan**
1,640 ft (500 m)

The tallest waterfall on each continent (except for Antarctica)

In **1901 Annie Taylor** became the first person to go over Niagara Falls in a barrel—she survived!

2,000 MYA

1,000 MYA

IF ALL OF **EARTH'S HISTORY** TOOK PLACE IN A **SINGLE YEAR**, HUMANS WOULDN'T APPEAR UNTIL **25 MINUTES** BEFORE MIDNIGHT ON NEW YEAR'S EVE.

FIRST DINOSAURS
245 MYA

MODERN HUMANS
200,000 YEARS AGO

DEADLY
ERUPTIONS

1902
Mount Pelée,
Martinique
30,000

79 CE
Mount Vesuvius,
Italy
20,000

1985
Nevado del Ruiz,
Columbia
25,000

1815
Mount Tambora,
Indonesia
92,000

1883
Mount Krakatoa,
Indonesia
36,000

Eruptions that
have killed tens of
thousands of people

DELVING
DEEP

Diamonds are Earth's hardest natural materials, and are used for cutting other hard substances. Today's diamond use is:

70%
INDUSTRY

30%
JEWELRY

Emeralds, rubies, and sapphires are all more rare than diamonds.

328

TRUE or FALSE?

Marie Antoinette said, "Let them eat cake!"

Against a background of **revolution (1789–99)**, the **French queen was** said to have mocked **poor peasants** who wanted bread, but there is no supporting evidence. Historians insist Marie Antoinette was **kind and giving**. It is possible that antiroyalists made up stories to give the royal family **bad press** at a turbulent time.

Marie Antoinette was only 14 years old when she was crowned queen, and became well-known for her beauty and flamboyant nature—she came to epitomize all that was wrong with the monarchy.

FAST FACTS

THE FRENCH HELPED TO FUND THE AMERICAN REVOLUTION (1775 – 83)

In 1775, 14 years before the French Revolution began, 13 colonies in America rebelled against British rule, leading to the creation of the United States. The modern US flag has 50 stars for the 50 states and 13 stripes for the original colonies.

Stars represent US states

Stripes represent rebellious colonies

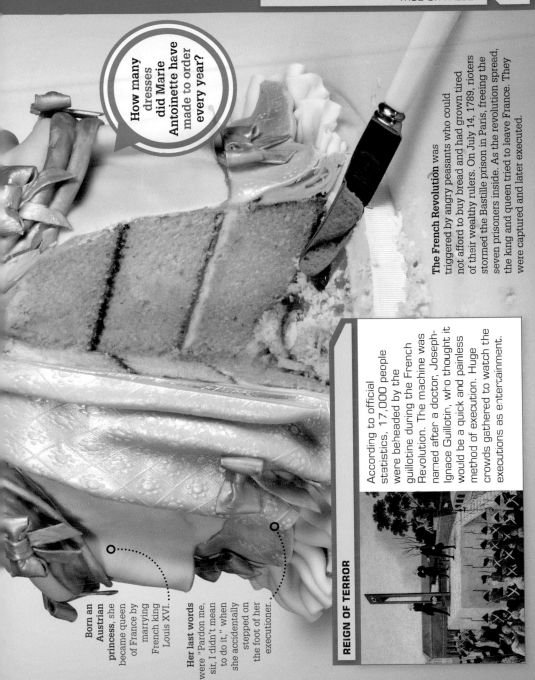

How many dresses did Marie Antoinette have made to order every year?

The French Revolution was triggered by angry peasants who could not afford to buy bread and had grown tired of their wealthy rulers. On July 14, 1789, rioters stormed the Bastille prison in Paris, freeing the seven prisoners inside. As the revolution spread, the king and queen tried to leave France. They were captured and later executed.

Born an Austrian princess, she became queen of France by marrying French king Louis XVI.

Her last words were "Pardon me, sir, I didn't mean to do it," when she accidentally stepped on the foot of her executioner.

REIGN OF TERROR

According to official statistics, 17,000 people were beheaded by the French guillotine during the French Revolution. The machine was named after a doctor, Joseph-Ignace Guillotin, who thought it would be a quick and painless method of execution. Huge crowds gathered to watch the executions as entertainment.

TRUE or FALSE? Napoleon was short

This one is a **tall tale**, with no truth to it. The famous French leader was of **average height** for a European man in the 1800s. His men called him "**le petit caporal**" (the little corporal), but this was not meant to make him feel small. Instead, it was a **term of endearment** toward their emperor.

Which of these leaders has a prehistoric creature named after them?

Left-hander Napoleon made his army march on the right so he could brandish his sword freely at approaching traffic—most European countries still drive on the right.

It is possible that Napoleon appeared shorter than 5'6" (1.7 m) because his guardsmen had to be at least 6'0" (1.8 m). They also wore tall bearskin caps, adding 18 in (46 cm) to their height. Throughout history, leaders have lined up in all different sizes, from towering President Abraham Lincoln to tiny Queen Victoria.

The average height of a French leader today is 5'9" (1.75 m), not much bigger than Napoleon.

MONEY MATTERS

Portraits of leaders have been used to gain influence throughout history. In ancient Roman times, the emperor was depicted as a god on coins to boost his status, from the time of Augustus until the end of the empire. Today the heads of monarchs and influential people are featured on national coins and notes.

FAST FACTS

■ MONGOL EMPIRE

GENGHIS KHAN OWNED 800 FALCONS

But falconry was not his favorite sport. This fierce warrior loved nothing more than crushing his enemies, robbing them of their wealth, riding their horses, and running off with their wives.

IT TAKES 570 GALLONS (2,591 LITERS) OF PAINT TO PAINT THE WHITE HOUSE

Sprucing up the home of the US president is a costly business. George Washington chose the spot for the presidential palace, but he never got to live there. The first president to occupy the White House was John Adams.

6'6" (2 m)
6'0" (1.8 m)
5'6" (1.7 m)
5'0" (1.5 m)
4'6" (1.4 m)
4'0" (1.2 m)
3'6" (1.1 m)
3'0" (0.9 m)

Nationalist leader Mahatma Gandhi refused to use violence in campaigning for India's independence from British rule.

Queen Victoria was one of the world's longest-reigning monarchs, ruling Great Britain for more than 63 years.

The first black president of South Africa, Nelson Mandela was in prison for 27 years for trying to overthrow the previous government.

Before becoming president, Abraham Lincoln was an excellent wrestler who fought in hundreds of matches.

TRUE or FALSE? Enemy soldiers played soccer in the trenches

World War I was one of the most devastating conflicts in history, but from the **horrors of war** emerged an incredible **story of peace**. On Christmas Day 1914, troops from both sides played **soccer in the trenches** near Ypres, Belgium.

Poppies have been the symbol of remembrance since World War I. Canadian surgeon John McCrae wrote his poem "In Flanders Fields" in 1915, describing poppies growing where soldiers died.

WARTIME DIARY

In World War II, a Jewish girl named Anne Frank kept a diary of her time hiding from the Nazis in a concealed Netherlands apartment. The Nazis found the family in 1944 and Anne died in a concentration camp. Her writing captures the hopes and fears of a child caught up in conflict and has since been read by millions.

What was the average life expectancy in the trenches of World War I?

Most of the games were played by soldiers
on the same side, but a few matches involved British
and German soldiers. About 10,000 soldiers took part
in the unofficial Christmas truce, singing songs,
lighting candles, and exchanging presents. As the war
went on, commanders banned the truces. There are
examples of similar camaraderie amid the conflicts
of the Crimean War, the Boer Wars, and the Civil War.

In the trench warfare
of World War I, armies
faced each other from
trenches dug a short
distance apart, protected
by coils of barbed wire.

65 MILLION
MEN FOUGHT IN
WORLD WAR I

This truly was a world war—troops came
from 30 different countries. Germany had
the greatest military strength at the
outset, but also suffered the highest
number of fatalities.

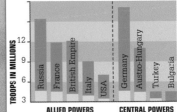

TROOPS IN MILLIONS

12
9
6
3

Russia | France | British Empire | Italy | USA | Germany | Austro-Hungary | Turkey | Bulgaria

ALLIED POWERS   **CENTRAL POWERS**

■ MILITARY STRENGTH   ▫ FATALITIES

PARACHUTING
PIGEONS WERE USED IN
WORLD WAR II

About 250,000 pigeons were
employed in the conflict, many
of which were parachuted behind
enemy lines. The idea was that
resistance fighters opposed
to the Nazis would send
the pigeons back with
secret information.

Only 1,842
pigeons returned.

TRUE or FALSE? Olympic gold medals are solid gold

All that glitters is not gold, and the Olympic medals are no exception. The last time the winners' medals were solid gold was at the Swedish games in 1912. It's been **fool's gold** ever since.

COPPER
7.5%

GOLD
1.34%

COPPER
6.16%

STERLING
SILVER
92.5%

SILVER

GOLD

OLYMPIC FLAME

The ancient Greeks lit a sacred fire during their Olympic Games. In 1936 a burning torch was carried into the arena at the modern Olympics in Berlin, Germany. Ever since, runners bring a torch lit at the ancient site of Olympia to the games to ignite a flame that burns until the closing ceremony.

What was different about the Olympics in ancient Greece?

Silver and bronze did not exist in the ancient Olympics. There was only one winner per event, crowned with an olive wreath from a sacred tree near the temple of Zeus at Olympia.

US swimmer Michael Phelps has won 28 gold medals. The most ever won by a single person, this is 10 more than the number won by the second-highest record holder.

At the ancient Olympics, winners did not receive medals. Instead, they were crowned with the *kotinos*, a wreath of olive leaves taken from a sacred tree. Winners' medals were first introduced at the 1904 Olympics, held in St. Louis. As the price of gold rose after World War I and the Great Depression, the amount used in the winners' medals declined. Today there must be at least 0.2 oz (6 g) of gold in each gold medal.

STERLING SILVER
92.5%

ZINC AND TIN
3%

COPPER
97%

BRONZE

In 1914 Frenchman Pierre de Coubertin designed the Olympic symbol of five linked rings to represent the continents taking part.

📊 **FAST FACTS**

SOCCER IS THE BIGGEST SPECTATOR SPORT

This popular Olympic sport is an energetic business, and players can run up to 6 miles (10 km) in just one game. Perhaps this explains why the world's biggest participant sport is the rather less strenuous fishing.

SOCCER 3.4

CRICKET 2.5

BASKETBALL 2.5
(Billions of fans)

IN *PELOTA* THE BALL CAN MOVE AT UP TO 185 MPH (300 KM/H)

Pelota is Spanish for "ball," and this fiery game from the Basque region of the Pyrenees keeps players on their toes. They use a glove or bat, and a ball with a rubber core. It was played as an Olympic sport at the 1900 games.

GOLF HAS BEEN PLAYED ON THE MOON

On February 6, 1971, Alan Shepard hit a golf ball on the lunar surface, having smuggled the ball and club on board in his space suit. Golf was reinstated as an Olympic sport at the 2016 Rio games.

TRUE or FALSE? Hamburgers were invented in Hamburg

So many people have claimed credit for this **fast food favorite** that it has caused some real **beefs**. It is known, however, that the hamburger was first sold in **the United States**, not Germany. The world soon developed **a taste for them** and hamburgers haven't stopped selling since.

The **"Hamburg steak"** was a 19th-century minced beef dish served in New York to German immigrants.......

STORY OF THE SANDWICH

Another popular snack—the sandwich—also has confused origins. John Montagu, fourth Earl of Sandwich, did not invent sandwiches, but they were named after him. The earl enjoyed sandwiches since he could eat and play cards without getting sticky fingers. But Arabs had already been putting meat inside pita bread for a long time.

The German city of Hamburg became famous for its tasty beef patties in the 19th century, but they were not placed inside buns. It is thought that the first true burger was sold in 1900 by Danish immigrant Louis Lassen in Connecticut. Another rumor has it that sailors from Hamburg named the meat sandwich, while others claim the name comes from the town of Hamburg, New York.

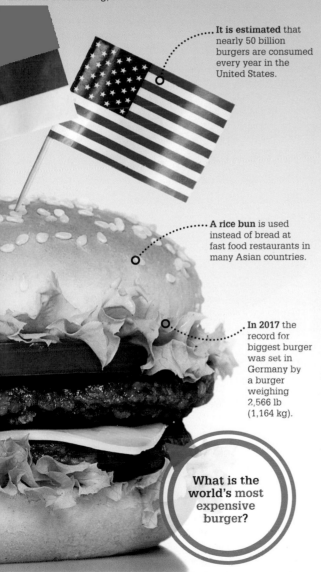

It is estimated that nearly 50 billion burgers are consumed every year in the United States.

A rice bun is used instead of bread at fast food restaurants in many Asian countries.

In 2017 the record for biggest burger was set in Germany by a burger weighing 2,566 lb (1,164 kg).

What is the world's most expensive burger?

FAST FACTS

IN **INDIA** IT IS **RUDE**

TO EAT WITH YOUR **LEFT HAND**

Indians spurn cutlery because they like to feel a spiritual connection to their food. So relish your rice and devour your dal, but don't use your left hand— it is considered "unclean" and should be reserved for less appetizing activities.

NEVER STAND **CHOPSTICKS** UPRIGHT IN A BOWL OF FOOD

In Asia this reminds people of the incense sticks that are burned when someone dies. Instead, you should leave your chopsticks side by side. On the plus side, it's fine to slurp your soup or burp noisily once you've finished.

TERMITES MAKE A NUTRITIOUS **SNACK**

Insects such as termites, crickets, and caterpillars are a popular part of the menu in Africa and parts of Asia. Meanwhile, Sardinians are big fans of *casu marzu*, a local cheese that is infected with live maggots.

| **CRICKETS** 562* | **CATERPILLARS** 370* | **TERMITES** 613* |

*CALORIES PER 3.5 oz (100 g) SERVING

TRUE OR FALSE? Listening to classical music makes you smarter

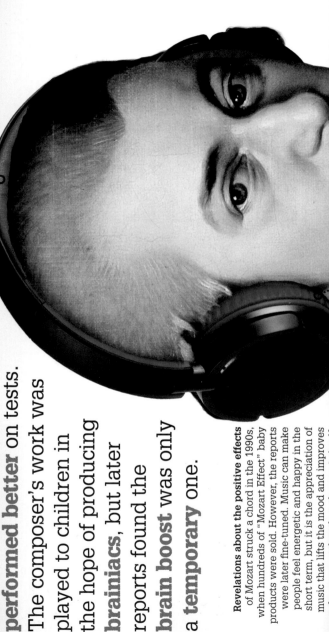

MRI scans of musicians who began playing at a young age show a larger nerve-fiber tract between the hemispheres of the brain. Learning music may increase the connections inside the brain.

Music to the ears of parents everywhere, a study in 1993 claimed that teenagers who listened to Mozart **performed better** on tests. The composer's work was played to children in the hope of producing **brainiacs**, but later reports found the **brain boost** was only **a temporary** one.

Revelations about the positive effects of Mozart struck a chord in the 1990s, when hundreds of "Mozart Effect" baby products were sold. However, the reports were later fine-tuned. Music can make people feel energetic and happy in the short term, but it is the appreciation of music that lifts the mood and improves

Austrian musician Wolfgang Amadeus Mozart (1756–91) could play the harpsichord at age four and compose music at age five.

Up-tempo, **uplifting music** can improve performance, while slower, melancholy pieces may do the opposite.

Which countries have the longest and shortest national anthems?

MUSICAL FIRST

Nearly 40 years before Mozart penned his first opera, English poet John Gay wrote *The Beggar's Opera*, the first musical show to mix song and dialogue. With ordinary people and catchy tunes, it poked fun at the politics and social injustices of the time.

American singer Elvis Presley (1935–77) is the biggest-selling music artist of all time—no wonder 80,000 people make a living imitating the "King of Rock and Roll."

THERE ARE ENOUGH ELVIS IMPERSONATORS TO FILL SHANGHAI STADIUM

FAST FACTS

BEETHOVEN WAS DEAF

Ludwig van Beethoven (1770–1827) was another child prodigy. But this musical marvel began to go deaf at the age of just 25, and wrote some of his best-known works, including the Ninth Symphony, without being able to hear them.

The rest is history

WONDERS OF THE ANCIENT WORLD

1. Great Pyramid of Giza, Egypt, built c. 2500 BCE

2. Hanging Gardens of Babylon, Iraq, built c. 600 BCE

3. Statue of Zeus at Olympia, Greece, carved by the sculptor Phidias c. 435 BCE

4. Temple of Artemis at Ephesus, Turkey, destroyed by Gothic tribes in 262 CE

5. Mausoleum at Halicarnassus, tomb of King Mausolus, Turkey, built c. 350 CE

6. Colossus of Rhodes, a giant statue of the sun god Helios, built in 280 BCE

7. Lighthouse of Alexandria, Egypt, destroyed in 1365 CE

FIVE TYPES OF GOVERNMENT

MONARCHY — The head of state is a monarch (king or queen).

REPUBLIC — The head of state is usually an elected president.

THEOCRACY — A state governed by a religious leader or leaders.

DICTATORSHIP — A state ruled by a single person who may have seized power by force or been elected unopposed.

SINGLE-PARTY STATE — A state governed by one political party where no other parties are allowed to nominate candidates for election.

A JUMBO JOB

The marble and stone used to build the Taj Mahal in Agra, India, in the **17th century** were carried there by **1,000 elephants**.

GREAT CITIES

Many places have held the title of world's biggest city—and their populations keep getting bigger!

Nineveh (Iraq) 120,000 people	**Chang'an** (China) 400,000 people	**Constantinople** (Turkey) 300,000 people	**Ctesiphon** (Iraq) 500,000 people	**Cordoba** (Spain) 450,000 people

Thebes (Egypt) **Xian** (China) 50,000 people	**Babylon** (Iraq) 200,000 people	**Rome** (Italy) 450,000 people	**Constantinople** (Turkey) 400,000 people	**Baghdad** (Iraq) 700,000 people

800 BCE	650 BCE	400 BCE	200 BCE	100 BCE	350 CE	500 CE	625 CE	800 CE	1000

SHRINKING WORLD

Time to cross the Atlantic:

SAILING SHIP, 1600—2 MONTHS

OCEAN LINER, 2014—7 DAYS

PASSENGER AIRPLANE, 2014—8 HOURS

FASTEST PASSENGER AIRPLANE (CONCORDE), 1996—2 HOURS, 53 MINUTES

THE FIRST **TRANSATLANTIC PHONE** CALL WAS MADE FROM LONDON TO NEW YORK ON **MARCH 7, 1926**.

BIG **STADIUMS**

The Circus Maximus used for chariot racing in ancient Rome held **300,000 people**. This is twice the capacity of the largest stadium in the world today, in Pyongyang, North Korea.

MIGHTY AZTECS
IN **1519**, THE AZTEC CAPITAL OF **TENOCHTITLAN** HAD **250,000** INHABITANTS— **FIVE** TIMES LARGER THAN **LONDON** AT THE TIME.

REVOLTING WORLD

History is rife with revolutions. Here are just five of the best (or worst, depending on whose side you're on):

American Revolution (1775—1783): 13 colonies throw off British rule to become the United States of America.

French Revolution (1789—1799): Monarchy is abolished, the king loses his head, and France becomes a republic.

Chinese Revolution (1911): China's last imperial dynasty, the Qing, is overthrown and China forms a republic.

Russian Revolution (1917): Revolutionaries topple the tsar (emperor) and set up a Communist government.

Iranian Revolution (1989): An Islamic republic is set up in Iran after the shah (king) is deposed.

ROMAN STATUES WERE MADE WITH **DETACHABLE HEADS,** SO THAT ONE HEAD COULD BE REMOVED AND **REPLACED** WITH ANOTHER.

Hangchow (China) 250,000 people	Nanjoing (China) 485,000 people		Beijing (China) 705,000 people	Beijing (China) 1,100,000 people			London (UK) 6,480,000 people	New York (USA) 7,774,000 people	New York (USA) 12,463,000 people	Tokyo (Japan) 23,000,000 people	Tokyo (Japan) 33,000,000 people
	Hangchow (China) 430,000 people	Beijing (China) 675,000 people	Constantinople (Turkey) 700,000 people	London (UK) 2,300,000 people							
1200	1300	1400	1500	1600	1700	1800	1850	1900	1925	1950	1975	2005

ANSWERS

256–257 EYES
All blue-eyed people can be traced back to one ancestor who lived 10,000 years ago near the Black Sea.

260–261 TASTE AND SMELL
Both the human tongue and an elephant's trunk are made of a muscle called a muscular hydrostat. This means that they function without help from the skeleton.

262–263 HAIR
Red hair is the least common, owned by only 1–2 percent of the global population. This color is mainly found in Scotland and Ireland.

264–265 ILLNESS
Exposure to bright light. Known as photic sneezing, this condition is inherited from parents.

266–267 EFFECTS OF FOOD
Vitamin D boosts bone density and prevents osteoporosis. Milk and cereals are excellent sources, but sunlight boosts levels of Vitamin D naturally as well.

268–269 GENETICS
People born after 1955 have traces of radioactive carbon in their DNA. This is left over from when the USA and USSR set off nuclear warheads during the Cold War, causing radioactivity to enter the atmosphere.

270–271 GROWTH AND AGING
Long life.

274–275 RODENTS
They never stop growing.

276–277 STINGING INSECTS
They live on every continent except Antarctica.

278–279 FISH
Goldfish prevent the spread of the West Nile virus. They are added to stagnant bodies of water where they eat mosquito larvae, which live in the water. This reduces mosquito populations.

280–281 INSECT FEATS
Cockroaches resist the harmful effects of radiation. They are much more likely to survive a nuclear explosion than humans, though if they were near nuclear ground zero, they would be crisped along with everything else.

282–283 SPIDERS
Up to 20 years.

284–285 FRUITS AND VEGETABLES
It has an awful smell, often compared to rotting meat.

286–287 MATERIALS
The ancient Romans.

288–289 INVENTIONS
Penicillin was in short supply, so a global search for a more productive strain of the mold got underway. In 1943 a laboratory worker found a rotting melon in a market. It became the main source of antibiotics for the next decade.

290–291 MODERN PHYSICS
Clocks run more quickly at higher altitudes because they experience a weaker gravitational force. This is known as gravitational time dilation.

292–293 THE DIGITAL AGE
Asia, with more than one billion users (44 percent of the total).

294–295 TECHNOLOGY
Yes, it has been proven that installing CCTV cameras and reminding people that they are being watched reduces petty crimes, such as dropping litter.

296–297 ROBOTS
One in every 10 car production workers is a robot.

300–301 PLANET EARTH
The high is 136°F (57.8°C) and the low is −135.8°F (−93.2°C). The average surface temperature is 59°F (15°C).

302–303 THE MOON
When Earth is directly between the Sun and the Moon, it keeps sunlight from reaching the Moon. The Moon is in Earth's shadow and is eclipsed. It has a reddish glow due to the scattering of sunlight as this passes through Earth's atmosphere.

304–305 THE SUN
In summer, in northerly latitudes such as northern Scandinavia, northern Canada, and northern Russia.

306–307 STARS
Scientists estimate there are 10 times more stars in the night sky than grains of sand in the world's deserts and beaches.

308–309 ASTRONOMY
Either because the star creates more light, is closer to Earth, or a combination of both.

310–311 SPACE TRAVEL
Due to the weightlessness in Space, dust does not settle down. Because it just floats around, astronauts sneeze a lot.

314–315 EARTHQUAKES
Yes—underwater.

316–317 THE SEASONS
Earth takes time to warm up or cool down. Therefore, the seasons lag behind. The amount of lag is affected by factors such as distance from the poles, amounts of water surrounding the area, and the weather experienced during the year.

318–319 WEATHER PREDICTION
When seagulls stop flying, avoid water, and huddle on the ground together, it is usually a sign of wet weather.

320–321 THUNDERSTORMS
The hairs on your body stand up.

322–323 SNOW
No. Below −22°F (−30°C) there is not usually enough moisture in the cold air for snow, but it is possible. Snow has fallen at −41.8°F (−41°C).

324–325 POPULATION
China.

328–329 THE FRENCH REVOLUTION
About 300.

330–331 LEADERS
Nelson Mandela. In 2013 the prehistoric woodpecker *Australopicus nelsonmandelai* was named after him.

332–333 WORLD WAR
About six weeks, with junior officers and stretcher carriers most vulnerable.

334–335 OLYMPIC SPORTS
They competed naked.

336–337 FOOD
The test-tube burger is the world's most expensive, at $385,000 (£250,000). It was made in a Netherlands laboratory from 20,000 strips of synthetic "cultured beef" taken from cow stem cells.

338–339 MUSIC
Some villages killed off all their cats because they were supposedly associated with witchcraft. Without cats to keep rat numbers down, the population grew and the plague spread even more quickly.

INDEX

ACKNOWLEDGMENTS

Dorling Kindersley would like to thank:
Andrea Mills for authoring text; Helen Abramson, Francesca Baines, Bharti Bedi, Carron Brown, Monica Byles, Steven Carton, Jessica Cawthra, Linda Esposito, Charlie Galbraith, Matilda Gollon, Ciara Heneghan, Wendy Horobin, Rob Houston, Katie John, Gareth Jones, Bahja Norwood, Victoria Pyke, Vicky Richards, Steve Setford, Jenny Sich, Rona Skene, Caroline Stamps, Fleur Star, and Alka Thakur for editorial assistance; David Ball, Romi Chakraborty, Sheila Collins, Paul Drislane, Michael Duffy, Mik Gates, Rachael Grady, Jim Green, Spencer Holbrook, Shipra Jain, Peter Laws, Philip Letsu, Clare Marshall, Isha Nagar, Jeongeun Yule Park, Stefan Podhorodecki, Mary Sandberg, Anis Sayyed, Deep Shikha Walia, Jemma Westing, and Steve Woosnam-Savage for design assistance; Hazel Beynon, Kim Bryan, Jack Challoner, Robert Dinwiddie, Derek Harvey, Chris Hawkes, Simon Holland, Katie John, Susan Kennedy, Ben Morgan, Martyn Page, Carole Stott, Richard Walker, and Chris Woodford for fact checking; Sumedha Chopra, Martin Copeland, Nic Dean, Aditya Katyal, and Sarah Smithies for picture research; Chrissy Barnard, Adam Benton, Stuart Jackson Carter, Anders Kjellberg, Simon Mumford, and Michael Parker, 385Jon@KJA-Artists.com for illustrations; Steve Crozier and Steve Willis for creative retouching; Simon Mumford for maps; Stefan Podhorodecki for photography; Hazel Beynon, Carron Brown, Neha Gupta, and Samira Sood for proofreading; Helen Peters for indexing; John Searcy for Americanization; Jessica Bentall, Laura Brim, Mark Cavanagh, Suhita Dharamjit, Claire Gell, Manisha Majithia, Saloni Singh, Sophia MTT, Surabhi Wadhwa-Gandhi, Jemma Westing, and Maud Whatley for assistance with Jackets; Nityanand Kumar and Pankaj Sharma for assistance with hi-res work; Harish Aggarwal, Neeraj Bhatia, Nikoleta Parasaki, Rebekah Parsons-King, and Jacqueline Street for assistance with pre-production; and Mandy Inness, Ben Marcus, Gemma Sharpe, and Vivienne Yong for assistance with production; and Rosalind Miller for making the Marie Antoinette cake, www.rosalindmillercakes.com.

The publisher would like to thank the following for their kind permission to reproduce their photographs:

(Key: a–above; b–below/bottom; c–center; f–far; l–left; r–right; t–top)

8–9 Alfred-Wegener-Institute for Polar and Marine Research. 9 Corbis: George Steinmetz (br). **10–11 Corbis**: Christophe Boisvieux / Hemis. **11 Corbis**: Christophe Boisvieux (br). **12–13 Corbis**: Martin Harvey. **13 FLPA**: Chien Lee / Minden Pictures (br). **14 Corbis**: Marco Stoppato & Amanda Ronzoni / Visuals Unlimited (bl). **16–17 7ty9 / flickr. 17 Getty Images**: Barcroft Media (br). **18–19 Iurie Belegurschi. 19 Corbis**: Aaron McCoy / Robert Harding World Imagery (b). **20–21 Caters News Agency**: Mikhail Mishainik (b). **21 Getty Images**: Linde Waidehofer / Barcroft Media (cr). **Science Photo Library**: Javier Trueba / MSF (tr). **22 National Geographic Creative**: Stephen Alvarez (bl). **22–23 National Geographic Creative**: Stephen Alvarez. **24–25 FLPA**: Gerry Ellis / Minden Pictures. **25 Corbis**: Anup Shah (b). **26–27 Getty Images**: Juergen Richter / LOOK-foto. **26 Rex Features**: Liam Kidston / Newspix (cl). **28–29 Corbis**: Chaiwat Subprasom / Reuters (b). **29 age fotostock**: Danita Delimont Agency (cr). **Getty Images**: Eye Ubiquitous / Contributor (tl). **30 Alamy Images**: Hemis (bl). **30–31 Corbis**: Steve Kaufman. **32 Getty Images**: Patrick Aventurier / Gamma-Rapho (bl). **32–33 Alamy Images**: Jim Kidd. **34–35 Alamy Images**: Steve Davey Photography. **35 Alamy Images**: Danita Delimont (cr). **36–37 Google. 36 Google**: Street View (bl). **38–39 Getty Images**: Stringer / AFP. **39 Alamy Images**: Robert Harding World Imagery (bl). **40–41 Corbis**: epa (bl). **41 Corbis**: Michael Buholzer / Reuters (tr). **42–43 Alamy Images**: David R. Frazier Photolibrary, Inc. **44–45 Getty Images**: Cultura Travel / Romona Robbins Photography (b). **45 Alamy Images**: Prisma Bildagentur AG (l); Susan Pease making the Marie Antoinette cake, www.rosalindmillercakes.com.

(cr). **46 Alamy Images**: Ecoimage (bl). **46–47 GAP Photos**: Richard Wareham. **48–49 Alamy Images**: epa european pressphoto agency b.v. **49 Getty Images**: Lam Yik Fei (bc). **50–51 Corbis**: Taylor Lockwood / Visuals Unlimited. **51 biology-forums.com**: (bl). **52 Alamy Images**: imageBROKER (bl). **Corbis**: Josef Beck / imageBROKER (cr). **53 Alamy Images**: Arco Images GmbH (cl). **Corbis**: Ch'ien Lee / Minden Pictures (r). **54 Corbis**: Marc Dozier (cl). **54–55 Getty Images**: Blend Images. **56–57 Corbis**: Doug Perrine / Nature Picture Library. **57 Science Photo Library**: Brian Brake (crb) **58–59 Science Photo Library**: Dr George Beccaloni. **59 Richard Seaman**: (tr). **60 Corbis**: Michael Weber / imageBROKER (bl). **60–61 naturepl.com**: Visuals Unlimited. **61 Getty Images**: Visuals Unlimited, Inc. / Thomas Marent. **62–63 Ardea**: Thomas Marent. **63 Alamy Images**: Scott Buckel (tr). **64–65 FLPA**: Matthias Breiter / Minden Pictures (b); Thomas Marent / Minden Pictures (t). **64 Getty Images**: Gallo Images (cl). **65 Dreamstime.com**: Seatraveler (tr). **FLPA**: Gianpiero Ferrari (br). **66–67 Alamy Images**: Paul Strawson. **67 Alamy Images**: AGF Srl (bl). **68 FLPA**: Hugh Lansdown. **Getty Images**: Jim Abernethy (bl). **69 FLPA**: Hugh Lansdown (l, r). **70 Press Association Images**: Peter Morrison / AP (bl). **70–71 Martin Le-May. 72 FLPA**: Kelvin Aitken / Biosphoto (bl). **72–73 ceanwideImages.com**: Rudie Kuiter. **74–75 Science Photo Library**: Christopher Swann. **75 Alamy Images**: WaterFrame (bl). **76–77 Getty Images**: Photographer's Choice. **77 Corbis**: Mark Thiessen / National Geographic Creative (br). **78–79 Science Photo Library**: NASA. **78 NASA**: ESA / J.T. Trauger (Jet Propulsion Laboratory) (bl). **80 NASA**: JPL-Caltech / SETI Institute (bl). **80–81 Stephan Kenzelmann. 82 Getty Images**: blickwinkel (br). **Getty Images**: Thomas Marent (cl). **83 Corbis**: Tatyana Zenkovich / epa (br). **Getty Images**: Photolibrary (t). **84–85 Getty Images**: UniversalImagesGroup / Contributor. **85 Corbis**: CJ Gunther / epa (tr). **86–87 Mick Petroff. 88–89 Corbis**: Gerald & Buff Corsi / Visuals Unlimited.

88 National Geographic Creative: George Steinmetz (bl). **90 Alamy Images**: Triangle Travels (br). **90–91 Barcroft Media Ltd.**: Janae Copelin. **94 Corbis**: TempSport / Jerome Prevost (cl). Dreamstime.com: Alexandr Mitiuc (clb, bc, br). **94–95 Dorling Kindersley**: Zygote Media Group (c). **95 Dreamstime.com**: Alexandr Mitiuc (bl, bc, crb). **96 Getty Images**: Vince Michaels (br). **Science Photo Library**: GJLP / CNRI (clb). **97 Corbis**: 3d4Medical.com (bl). **98-99 Alamy Images**: D. Hurst. **99 Alamy Images**: AlamyCelebrity (tc). **100 Corbis**: Science Photo Library / Steve Gschmeissner (cl) **104 Corbis**: Visuals Unlimited (clb). **105 Corbis**: Minden Pictures / Flip Nicklin (bc). **Dorling Kindersley**: Natural History Museum, London (bl). **106 Dreamstime.com**: Lindsay Douglas (cl). **106-107 National Geographic Stock**: Michael Nichols (b). **109 naturepl.com**: Doc White (tc). **110 Dorling Kindersley**: Bedrock Studios (tc). Dreamstime.com: Ibrahimyogurtcu (bc). **110–111 Dorling Kindersley**: Andrew Kerr (c) **112–113 Dorling Kindersley**: Andrew Kerr (c). **113 Dorling Kindersley**: Jon Hughes and Russell Gooday (cr). **114 Science Photo Library**: Peter Chadwick (clb). **116–117 Science Photo Library**: Christian Darkin. **118 Paul Nylander,http://bugman123.com. 119 Alamy Images**: Michal Cerny (tc). **120 Alamy Images**: Louise Murray (clb). **122–123 Dreamstime.com**: Bruce Crandall (c). **124 Alamy Images**: Kevin Elsby (t). **125 Alamy Images**: Rolf Nussbaumer Photography (bl). **Dreamstime.com**: Pictac (t). **127 Dorling Kindersley**: Natural History Museum, London (tr). **Otorohanga Zoological Society (1980)**: (bl). **130 Dr. Avishai Teicher**: (clb). **132 Alaska Fisheries Science Center, NOAA Fisheries Service**: (c). **Pearson Asset Library**: Lord and Leverett / Pearson Education Ltd (cb). **Dreamstime.com**: John Anderson (cl); Ispace (fbl, bl, bc, br, fbr). **133 Dreamstime.com**: Ispace (bl, bc, br). **Photoshot**: NHPA / Paul Kay (cra). **134 Getty Images**: Jose Luis Pelaez Inc (c); Visuals Unlimited, Inc. / Joe McDonald (clb). **135 Corbis**: Minden Pictures / Suzi Eszterhas (b). **136 Corbis**: imagebroker / Konrad Wothe (cb). **Dreamstime.com**: Juri Bizgajmer (b/ Reproduced four times). **Getty Images**: Joe McDonald (cl). **137 Corbis**: Wally McNamee (fclb); Robert Harding World Imagery / Thorsten Milse (clb). **Dreamstime.com**: Juri Bizgajmer (b/ Reproduced three times). **Getty Images**: Daniel J. Cox (crb). **138 Science Photo Library**: Jim Zipp (bc). **138–139 Alamy Images**: Matthew Clarke. **140–141 Alamy Images**: Transtock Inc. (c). **140 Corbis**: Paul Souders (tr). **Dreamstime.com**: F9photos (tl). Getty Images: Ronald C. Modra (bl). **142 Corbis**: George Hall (t). **142–143 Getty Images**: Marvin E. Newman (c). **143 Alamy Images**: LM (crb). **NASA**: (b). **144 Alamy Images**: DIZ Muenchen GmbH, Sueddeutsche Zeitung Photo (c). **Dreamstime.com**: Brutusman (clb). **145 Dreamstime.com**: Rui Matos (cl). **146–147 Getty Images**: AFP / MARCEL MOCHET. **146 Getty Images**: Bryn Lennon (b). **149 Dreamstime.com**: Richard Koele (b). **Alamy Stock Photo**: Newzulu (tr). **150 123RF.com**: 3ddock (clb). **Dreamstime.com**: Chernetskiy (b/ Reproduced two times). **150–151 A.P. Moller/Maersk**: (c). **151 Dockwise**: (tr). **152 Alamy Images**: Dennis Hallinan (c). **153 Corbis**: Morton Beebe (c/Boeing). **NASA**: (br). **155 NASA**: (cb). **158–159 Corbis**: Science Faction / Louie Psihoyos (finger). **159 University of Michigan**: Martin Vloet (c). **Alamy Images**: David J. Green (tr). **160 Dreamstime.com**: Marekp (cb). **Sebastian Loth, CFEL Hamburg, Germany**: (bl). **165 Getty Images**: Barcroft Media / Imre Solt (br). **167 Corbis**: Ed Kashi (tr). **168–169 Getty Images**: Charles Bowman (c). **169 Getty Images**: Edward L. Zhao (tr). **174 Alamy Images**: Giffard Stock (clb). **178 Corbis**: Jeff Vanuga (clb).**181 Corbis**: Gary Bell (tr). **183 Alamy Images**: ColsTravel (tr). **184 Corbis**:Armin Weigel / Epa (clb). **186 Dreamstime.com**: Joseph Gough (clb); Xi Zhang (cr/Used Twice). **187 123RF.com**: Aaron Amat (tr). **188 Dreamstime.com**: Stnazkul (clb). **190 Corbis**: 68 / Ocean (bc). **Dreamstime.com**: Joggie Botma (br). **191 Alamy Images**: Joggie Botma (bl). Dreamstime.com: Joggie Botma (b). **194 Corbis**: Bettmann (clb/Venus); Walter Myers Stocktrek Images (c). Dreamstime.com: Yiannos1 (clb/Globe). NASA: Johns Hopkins University Applied Physics Laboratory / Arizona State University / Carnegie Institution of Washington (clb/ Mercury). U.S. Geological Survey: USGS Astrogeology Science Center (clb/ Valles Marineris). **195 Dreamstime. com**: Elisanth (ca, fcrb). NASA: JPL (cb); JPL / Space Science Institute (clb); Erich Karkoschka, University of Arizona (crb); Goddard / Lunar Reconnaissance Orbiter (tr). **197 Getty Images**: ESA (cr). Pascal Henry,www.lesud.com: (b/ Planets). **198-199 Dreamstime.com**: Panaceadoll (c). Pascal Henry,www. lesud.com: (All planets). **200–201 Dreamstime.com**: Igor Terekhov (All kitchen scales used on the spread). TurboSquid: atolyee84 (cra/All oranges used on the spread). **200 Dreamstime. com**: Anna1311 (ca); Katerina Kovaleva (Orange quarter pieces on the spread). NASA: (clb); Johns Hopkins University Applied Physics Laboratory / Carnegie Institution ofWashington (cl); JPL (c); NASA Goddard Space Flight Center Image by Reto Stöckli (land surface, shallow water, clouds).Enhancements by Robert Simmon (ocean color, compositing, 3D globes, animation). Data and technical support: MODIS Land Group; MODIS Science Data Support Team; MODIS Atmosphere Group; MODIS Ocean Group Additional data: USGS EROS Data Center (topography); USGS Terrestrial Remote Sensing Flagstaff Field Center (Antarctica); Defense Meteorological Satellite Program (city lights). (bc); JPL-Caltech (cr). **201 Dreamstime.com**: Steven Cukrov (All Clementines in Wood Crate used on the spread). NASA: (bl);SDO (tl). Pascal Henry,www.lesud. com: (c, br). **203 NASA**: Johns Hopkins University Applied Physics Laboratory / Southwest Research Institute (tr). **204– 205 Dreamstime.com**: Yiannos1 (All Earth Globes). **205 NASA**: Science (bc). **206 ESA**: Rosetta / MPS for OSIRIS Team MPS / UPD / LAM / IAA / SSO / INTA / UPM / DASP / IDA (clb, bl). **206–207 Dreamstime.com**: Tomas Griger (b). ESA: Rosetta / MPS for OSIRIS Team MPS / UPD / LAM / IAA / SSO / INTA / UPM / DASP / IDA (Comet). **208–209 ESA. 208 ESA**: (bl). **212–213 Alamy Images**: WENN Ltd. **213 Corbis**: Pete Oxford / Minden Pictures (tr). **215 Getty Images**: Austin Hargrave / Barcroft Media (crb). **217 Corbis**: Hiroya Minakuchi / Minden Pictures (tr). **218– 219 Getty Images**: Jamie Cross (All the stopwatches used on the spread); Vladimir Surkov (Underwater background used on the spread). **218 Dreamstime.com**: Rostislav Ageev (br); Fotosforthought (bl); Michael Price (bc/

Orca); Kotomiti_okuma (bc/ Penguin). Getty Images: Andrey Nekrasov (cl). **219 Corbis:** DLILLC (clb). **Dreamstime. com:** Valentyna Chukhlyebova (cb); Stephanie Starr (tr). Justin Hart: (cr). **221 Corbis:** Ingo Arndt / Minden Pictures (bl). Mary Evans Picture Library: Natural History Museum (crb). **222 Dreamstime.com:** Daniel Cole; Lukas Gojda (Water Splash). **222–223 Dreamstime.com:** Annkozar (Water). **223 Dreamstime.com:** Isselee. **224 Dreamstime.com:** Pti4kafoto (clb). **224–225 Dreamstime. com:** Christian Delbert (t); Thomas Theodore (b). **226–227 Dorling Kindersley:** Thackeray Medical Museum (Bottles used on the spread). **226 Alamy Images:** Rieger Bertrand / Hemis (bl). Photoshot: Tobias Bernhard / NHPA (br). **227 Alamy Images:** Norman Price (bl). Dreamstime. com: Mkojot (c). Getty Images: Auscape (crb). **228 Corbis:** David Scharf (clb). Dreamstime.com: Stephen Sweet (All the drums used on the spread). Science Photo Library: Eye Of Science (cr). **228–229 Dreamstime. com:** Wektorygrafika (b). **229 Dreamstime.com:** Tofuxs (cb). Sean McCann: (cl). **230 Corbis:** Colin Stinson / Demotix (clb). **230–231 Blue whale heart model by Human Dynamo Workshop Ltd - humandynamo.co.nz: (tc). 232 Alamy Images:** Ann and Steve Toon (tl). **232–233 Alamy Images:** NSPRF. **233 Alamy Images:** Ann and Steve Toon (cb); WILDLIFE GmbH (cl). Dreamstime.com: Nigel Spooner (clb); Maximiliane Wagner (tr). **236–237 Alamy Images:** Paul Brown. **236 123RF. com:** marigranula (clb). **238 Corbis:** Thomas Marent / Minden Pictures (cla). **240–241 Alamy Images:** dpa picture alliance archive. **241 Dreamstime.com:** Cathy Keifer (tr); Kmitu (b). **242 Corbis:** Peter Ginter / Science Faction (clb). **244 Photoshot:** Mark Conlin / Oceans-Image (bc). **246–247 Alamy Images:** Don Mason / CORBIS / Flirt (Big Bees). FLPA: Ingo Arndt / Minden Pictures. **247 Alamy Images:** James Williamson (crb). Corbis: Maximilian Stock Ltd / photocuisine (cb). **248 Dreamstime.com:** Michel Bussieres (tl); Darkbird77 (br). Getty Images: Jena Ardell (tr). **249 Alamy Images:** Patrick Lynch (cb). **250 Science Photo Library:** Walter Myers (tl). **252–253 123RF.com:** Glenn Young. **252 naturepl.com:** Visuals Unlimited (bl). **255 Getty Images:** DigitalGlobe / ScapeWare3d (crb).

258 Science Photo Library: Pasieka (bl). **258–259 Dreamstime.com:** Gabriel Blaj (c). **260–261 Alamy Images:** Estiot / BSIP (c). **260 Science Photo Library:** Prof. P. Motta / Dept. Of Anatomy / University "La Sapienza", Rome (clb). **261 Dreamstime.com:** Dimakp (clb). **262 Science Photo Library:** Eye Of Science (clb). **262–263 Dreamstime.com:** Stefan Hermans (bc). **263 Dreamstime.com:** Miramisska (tl). **264 Dreamstime.com:** Alexander Raths (cb). **266 Dreamstime. com:** Antonio De Azevedo Negrão (cl). **268 Dreamstime.com:** Paul Fleet (clb). **269 Corbis:** John Lund / Blend Images (ca/cow); Solvin Zankl / Visuals Unlimited (ca); Allan Stone. **Dreamstime.com:** Ajn (cla). **270–271 Dreamstime.com:** Eldadcarin (c). **270 Corbis:** Pascal Parrot / Sygma (clb). **274–275 Dreamstime.com:** Cynoclub (bc). **274 SuperStock:** Juniors (cl). **275 Dreamstime.com:** Christian Draghici (c). **276–277 Dreamstime.com:** Katrina Brown (c). **276 Corbis:** Erik De Castro / Reuters (bl). Dreamstime.com: Alfio Scisetti (br). **278–279 Dreamstime. com:** Elena Torre (bc); Monika Wisniewska (c). **278 Dreamstime.com:** Sekarb (bl). **280 Manchester X-ray Imaging Facility:** Tristan Lowe (bl). **281 Dreamstime.com:** Tofuxs (bl). SuperStock: imagebroker.ne (c). **282 Getty Images:** Stephen Dalton / Minden Pictures (cb); Steven Taylor / The Image Bank (clb). **SuperStock:** imagebroker.net (bl). **282–283 Alamy Images:** Juniors Bildarchiv / F259 (c). **Getty Images:** Space Images / Blend Images (b). **283 Getty Images:** Aaron Ansarov / Aurora (crb). **Science Photo Library:** Gerry Pearce (ca). **284 Corbis:** 735 / Tom Merton / Ocean (bl). **285 Getty Images:** Creative Crop / Digital Vision (c). **Pearson Asset Library:** Cheuk-king Lo (bl). **286 Alamy Images:** Wayne Simpson / All Canada Photos (br). **290 Corbis:** Bettmann (bc). **292–293 123RF.com:** Anton Balazh (c). **292 Getty Images:** artpartner-images / The Image Bank (clb). **294 Getty Images:** Toussaint Kluiters / AFP (bl). **295 Getty Images:** Daniel Berehulak (Screens). **296 Corbis:** Ina Fassbender / X00970 / Reuters (bl); Photo Japan / Robert Harding World Imagery (r). **Dreamstime.com:** Anankkml (t). **Getty Images:** Peter Macdiarmid (bc). **296–297 Dreamstime.com:** Esviesa (b). **297 123RF.com:** (bc); Viktoriya Sukhanova (bl). **Dreamstime.com:** Ruslan Gilmanshin (cb). **Getty Images:** Spencer

Platt (br). **300 Corbis:** Esa / epa (bl). **Dreamstime.com:** Rtguest. **302 Dreamstime.com:** Fang Jia (bc). **NASA:** Goddard / Arizona State University (crb). **Science Photo Library:** Geoeye (clb). **304 Fotolia:** dundanim (bl). **Science Photo Library:** Greg Piepol (clb). **305 Dreamstime.com:** Rastan (r). **306 ESA / Hubble:** NASA/http://creativecommons. org/licenses/by/3.0 (bl). **309 ESA / Hubble:** NASA/http://creativecommons. org/licenses/by/3.0 (cr). **Science Photo Library:** David Nunuk (br). **310 Corbis:** NASA / Roger Ressmeyer (clb). **311 Dorling Kindersley:** NASA (b). **314 Corbis:** Alison Wright. **317 Corbis:** ibrahim ibrahim / Demotix (cr). **318–319 Corbis:** Image Source. **319 Getty Images:** Science & Society Picture Library (tc). **320 Getty Images:** Michael Siward / Moment. **Science Photo Library:** Dr. John Brackenbury (clb). **321 Getty Images:** Michael Siward / Moment. **322 Alamy Images:** Whit Richardson (clb). **Corbis:** 68 / Cavan Images / Ocean (br). **Dreamstime.com:** James Steidl (cb). **323 Corbis:** 68 / Cavan Images / Ocean (bc). **Dreamstime.com:** Rita Jayaraman (c). **324 Corbis:** Bertrand Rieger / Hemis (br). **328–329 Dorling Kindersley:** Marie Antoinette and Rosalind Miller – cake maker / Stefan Podhorodecki (c). **329 Corbis:** The Gallery Collection (br). **330 Alamy Images:** Lebrecht Music and Arts Photo Library (br). **Getty Images:** De Agostini / A. Dagli Orti (clb). **331 Getty Images:** Media24 / Gallo Images / Hulton Archive (bc); Central Press / Hulton Archive (bl). **SuperStock:** Library of Congress / Science Faction (bc/ Lincoln); Universal Images Group (bl). **332 Corbis:** Reuters Photographer / Reuters (clb). **332–333 bnps.co.uk:** (bc). **Corbis:** Warren Faidley (t); Creativ Studio Heinemann / Westend61 (b). **334 Getty Images:** Milos Bicanski (clb). **336 Alamy Images:** World History Archive / Image Asset Management Ltd. (bl). **336–337 Dreamstime.com:** Nevodka (bc). **337 Dreamstime.com:** Photographerlondon (c); Winai Tepsuttinun (c/America flag toothpick). **338 Getty Images:** Carlos Alvarez / E+ (cb). **338–339 Corbis:** The Gallery Collection. **339 Alamy Images:** Peter Barritt (bl).

All other images © Dorling Kindersley

For further information see:
www.dkimages.com